A Passion for Truth

By
ABRAHAM JOSHUA HESCHEL

A JEWISH LIGHTS
Classic Reprint

JEWISH LIGHTS Publishing
Woodstock, Vermont

Library of Congress Cataloging-in-Publication Data

Heschel, Abraham Joshua, 1907-1972.
A Passion for Truth / Abraham Joshua Heschel.
p.   cm.   — (A Jewish Lights classic reprint)
Previously published: New York : Farrar, Straus and Giroux, 1973.
ISBN 1-879045-41-9 (trade pbk.)
1. Spiritual life—Judaism. 2. Judaism—Essence, genius, nature. 3. Menahem Mendel, of Kotsk, 1787-1859. 4. Kierkegaard, Søren, 1813-1855. 5. Ba'al Shem Tov, ca. 1700-1760. 6. Hasidism.
I. Title. II. Series.

BM723.H47 1995   95-5378
296.7'4—dc20   CIP

Quotations from the following books by Søren Kierkegaard are reprinted by permission of Princeton University Press: *Training in Christianity*, trans. by Walter Lowrie, © 1946 by Princeton University Press; *Stages on Life's Way*, trans. by Walter Lowrie, © 1940 by Princeton University Press, © renewed 1968 by Princeton University Press; *Attack upon "Christendom,"* trans. by Walter Lowrie, new intro. by Howard A. Johnson, © 1944, © 1968 by Princeton University Press; *Either/Or*, Vol. I, trans. by David F. Swenson and Lillian Marvin Swenson, and Vol. II, trans. by Walter Lowrie, © 1944, © 1959 by Princeton University Press; *Philosophical Fragment*, trans. by David F. Swenson, rev. revised by Howard V. Hong, © 1936, © 1962 by Princeton University Press; *Repetition: An Essay in Experimental Psychology*, trans. by Walter Lowrie, © 1941 by Princeton University Press, © renewed 1969 by Princeton University Press; *The Concept of Dread*, trans. by Walter Lowrie, © 1944, © 1957 by Princeton University Press; *The Sickness unto Death* from *Fear and Trembling* and *The Sickness unto Death*, trans. by Walter Lowrie, © 1941, 1954 by Princeton University Press; *Concluding Unscientific Postscript*, trans. by David F. Swenson and Walter Lowrie, © 1941 by Princeton University Press, © renewed 1969 by Princeton University Press.

Quotations from the following books by Søren Kierkegaard are reprinted by permission of HarperCollins Publishers, Inc.: *The Point of View for My Work as an Author: A Report to History*, trans. by Walter Lowrie, © 1962 by Harper & Row, Publishers, Inc.; *Works of Love*, trans. by Howard Hong, English language translation © 1962 by Howard Hong, © renewed; *The Last Years, Journals 1853-1855*, edited and trans. by Ronald Gregor Smith, © 1965 by Ronald Gregor Smith; *The Concept of Irony*, trans. by Lee M. Capel, "Historical Introduction" by Lee M. Capel, Harper & Row, 1965.

Quotations from *Kierkegaard* by Walter Lowrie originally reprinted by permission of Howard A. Johnson.

Quotations from *The Journals of Kierkegaard*, trans. by Alexander Dru, © 1958, 1959 by Alexander Dru, are reprinted by permission of Oxford University Press.

First Paperback Edition
10 9 8 7 6 5 4 3 2 1

Manufactured in the United States of America

Published by Jewish Lights Publishing
A Division of LongHill Partners Inc.
P.O. Box 237 • Sunset Farm Offices, Route 4
Woodstock, VT 05091
Tel: 802 457-4000   Fax: 802 457-4004

To Elemire Zolla

Contents

vii

II   THE KOTZKER AND KIERKEGAARD

III   THE POWER OF THE WILL

X THE KOTZKER TODAY

Introduction

Why I Had to Write This Book

I was born in Warsaw, Poland, but my cradle stood in Mezbizh (a small town in the province of Podolia, Ukraine), where the Baal Shem Tov, founder of the Hasidic movement, lived during the last twenty years of his life. That is where my father came from, and he continued to regard it as his home. He confided in me, "For I was indeed stolen out of the land of the Hebrews" (Genesis 40:15). It was because of the advice of his spiritual mentor, Reb David Moshe, his uncle, the rebbe of Tshortokov, son of Reb Israel of Rizhin, that he took up residence in Poland.

I was named after my grandfather, Reb Abraham Joshua Heschel—"the Apter Rav," and last great rebbe of Mezbizh. He was marvelous in all his ways, and it was as if the Baal Shem Tov had come to life in him. When he died in 1825, he was buried next to the holy Baal Shem. The Apter Rav claimed that his soul had lived in several incarnations, and for his descendants it was as if he had never died.

Enchanted by a wealth of traditions and tales, I felt truly at home in Mezbizh. That little town so distant from Warsaw and yet so near was the place to which my childish imagination went on many journeys. Every step taken on the way was an answer to a prayer, and every stone was a memory of a marvel. For most of the wondrous deeds my father told about either happened in Mezbizh or were inspired by those mysterious men who lived there.

The earliest fascination I can recall is associated with the Baal Shem, whose parables disclosed some of the first insights I gained as a child. He remained a model too sublime to follow yet too overwhelming to ignore.

It was in my ninth year that the presence of Reb Menahem Mendl of Kotzk, known as the Kotzker, entered my life. Since then he has remained a steady companion and a haunting challenge. Although he often stunted me, he also urged me to confront perplexities that I might have preferred to evade.

Years later I realized that, in being guided by both the Baal Shem Tov and the Kotzker, I had allowed two forces to carry on a struggle within me. One was occasionally mightier than the other. But who was to prevail, which was to be my guide? Both spoke convincingly, and each proved right on one level yet questionable on another.

In a very strange way, I found my soul at home with the Baal Shem but driven by the Kotzker. Was it good to live with one's heart torn between the joy of Mezbizh and the anxiety of Kotzk? To live both in awe and consternation, in fervor and horror, with my conscience on mercy and my eyes on Auschwitz, wavering between exaltation and dismay? Was this a life a man would choose to live? I had no choice: my heart was in Mezbizh, my mind in Kotzk.

I was taught about inexhaustible mines of meaning by the Baal Shem; from the Kotzker I learned to detect immense mountains of absurdity standing in the way. The one taught me song, the other—silence. The one reminded me that there could be a Heaven on earth, the other shocked me into discovering Hell in the alleged Heavenly places in our world.

The Baal Shem made dark hours luminous; the Kotzker eased wretchedness and desolation by forewarnings, by premonitions.

The Kotzker restricted me, debunked cherished attitudes. From the Baal Shem I received the gifts of elasticity in adapting to contradictory conditions.

The Baal Shem dwelled in my life like a lamp, while the Kotzker struck like lightning. To be sure, lightning is more authentic. Yet one can trust a lamp, put confidence in it; one can live in peace with a lamp.

The Baal Shem gave me wings; the Kotzker encircled me with chains. I never had the courage to break the chains and entered into joys with my shortcomings in mind. I owe intoxication to the Baal Shem, to the Kotzker the blessings of humiliation.

The Kotzker's presence recalls the nightmare of mendacity. The presence of the Baal Shem is an assurance that falsehood dissolves into compassion through the power of love. The Baal Shem suspends sadness, the Kotzker enhances it. The Baal Shem helped me to refine my sense of immediate mystery; the Kotzker warned me of the constant peril of forfeiting authenticity.

Honesty, authenticity, integrity without love may lead to the ruin of others, of oneself, or both. On the other hand, love, fervor, or exaltation alone may seduce us into living in a fool's Paradise—a wise man's Hell.

PART I

❖❰❖❰❖❰

The Two Teachers

The Baal Shem Tov

IT WAS a time when the Jewish imagination was nearly exhausted. The mind had reached an impasse, thinking about impossible possibilities in Talmudic law. The heart was troubled by oppressive social and economic conditions, as well as the teachings of ascetic preachers. Then a miracle occurred. It was as if Providence had proclaimed, "Let there be light!" And there was light—in the form of an individual: Reb Israel, son of Eliezer, Baal Shem Tov, "Master of the Good Name" (ca. 1690–1760), often known by the acronym of his initials, Besht, or as the holy Baal Shem.

He was born in a small town in the province of Podolia, Okop, to poor and elderly parents. Orphaned as a child, he later eked out a living as an assistant teacher of little children (*belfer*). Tradition has it that at the age of twenty he went into seclusion in the Carpathian Mountains for spiritual training and preparation for his calling. There he lived for several years as a digger of clay, which his wife sold in the town where she kept house. When he was thirty-six, he revealed himself as a spiritual master. Later he settled in Mezbizh or Medzhibozh (Polish: Miedzyborz), another small town in the province of Podolia (which was Polish until 1793, thereafter under Russian rule), where he died in 1760.

3

The Baal Shem Tov was the founder of the Hasidic movement, and Mezbizh was the cradle in which a new understanding of Judaism was nurtured.

When millions of our people were still alive in Eastern Europe and their memory and faith vibrated with thought, image, and emotion, the mere mention of Reb Israel Baal Shem Tov cast a spell upon them. The moment one uttered his name, one felt as if his lips were blessed and his soul grew wings.

The Baal Shem made being Jewish a bliss, a continuous adventure. He gave every Jew a ladder to rise above himself and his wretched condition.

During his lifetime, Reb Israel inspired a large number of disciples to follow him. After his death his influence became even more widespread. Within a generation, the insights he had formulated at Mezbizh had captivated a great many exceptional individuals who, in turn, inspired the Jewish masses with new spiritual ideas and values. And Mezbizh became the symbol of Hasidism.

Rarely in Jewish history has one man succeeded in uplifting so many individuals to a level of greatness. Yet no one in the long chain of charismatic figures that followed him was equal to the Baal Shem. Though he initiated the Hasidic movement, he remained greater than the movement itself. Generations of leaders sought to follow his pattern, and he alone remained the measure and the test of all Hasidic authenticity. Only one Hasidic rebbe dared challenge his teaching: the Kotzker, Reb Menahem Mendl of Kotzk.

The Baal Shem brought about a radical shift in the religious outlook of Jewry. In ancient times the sanctuary in Jerusalem had been the holy center from which expiation and blessing radiated out to the world. But the sanctuary was in ruins, the soul of Israel in mourning. Then the Baal Shem established a new center: the tzaddik, the rebbe—he was to be the sanctuary. For the Baal Shem believed that a man could be the true dwelling place of the Divine.

How is one to explain the rapid spread of the Hasidic movement? What was the secret of the Baal Shem Tov's spiritual power? Why did other great leaders, such as Rabbi Shimon ben Yohai, Maimonides, or Rabbi Isaac Luria, the "Ari," not arouse a similarly swift response?

Rabbi Aryeh Leib Heller,[1] a most brilliant Talmudic scholar who died in 1813, once asked this question, and Reb Zevi Hirsh of Zhydatshov (Polish: Zydaczow) replied with a parable:

The people of a certain land wanted to elect[2] a new king. They had heard a man in a very distant country who had all the desirable attribtues of royalty; he was said to be handsome, good, wealthy, refined—a man of great accomplishments. There could be no one more suited to the royal post than he. But the entire population could not possibly go to see him and verify the truth of the matter because his home was so remote.

At length a person who had traveled afar and had met him personally returned and told the people about him. Although his report made an impression upon some, the majority were not moved.

Finally, a very wise man decided to bring the candidate to the people, so that they could judge for themselves. Vast numbers flocked to see him, fell in love with him, and joyfully invested him with the crown, because they realized that he alone was fit to be king.

Similarly, Rabbi Shimon ben Yohai[3] and his associates were

---

[1] The author of *Ketzot Hahoshen.*
[2] After 1572, following the death of Sigismund Augustus, kings of Poland were elected by vote. No fewer than eighteen candidates competed for the throne on the death of John III.
[3] The first mentor in the Zohar, "The Book of Splendor," the central work in the literature of the Kabbalah.

the first to reveal the deep mysteries concerning God in the Zohar. But what they taught was only designed for, and understood by, the initiated. Then Rabbi Isaac Luria came and disclosed more than Rabbi Shimon ben Yohai. Yet his revelations regarding the lights of the worlds beyond and other spiritual themes were also far above most people's comprehension.

At last, the teacher of all Israel appeared, Reb Israel Baal Shem Tov. He revealed the Divine as present even in our shabby world, in every little thing, and especially in man. He made us realize that there was nothing in man—neither limb nor movement—that did not serve as vessel or vehicle for the Divine force. No place was devoid of the Divine. He taught that the tzaddikim who grasped the bond between Creator and creature were blessed with so great a power that they were able to perform marvelous acts of mystical unification in the sphere of the Divine. Furthermore, every man in this world could work deeds that might affect the worlds above. Most important, attachment to God was possible, even while carrying out mundane tasks or making small talk. Thus, unlike the sages of the past, who delivered discourses *about* God, the Baal Shem, like the wise man in the parable, brought God to every man.

Why was Reb Israel called the Baal Shem Tov, master of the good name? A poetic answer illustrates what subsequent generations felt about him.

When the Baal Shem appeared in Eastern Europe, the community of Israel was on its sickbed, full of sorrow and, following the weird end of the Sabbatian excitement, consumed with anguish. Oppressed and persecuted, the people were fainting, gasping, trembling. They nearly expired. When a person is having a fainting fit and is in danger of wasting away, it is advisable to whisper his name into his ear, because his name has the power to call a person back to life. The Baal Shem saw that the Jewish heart was faint, torpid, in danger of laying down its life. So he called it by its name: Jewish heart. And the Jews of Eastern Europe rallied, seeing the light of the Messiah shining overhead.

Other great teachers bore the message of God, sang His praises, lectured about His attributes and wondrous deeds. The Baal Shem brought not only the message; he brought God Himself to the people. His contribution, therefore, consisted of more than illumination, insights, and ideas; he helped mold into being new types of personality: the Hasid and the tzaddik.

The charisma of many tzaddikim defies description. Their sheer presence was a source of exaltation. It was impossible to see a tzaddik and remain a non-believer. The tzaddik's words thrilled the hearts of those who heard him and worked like a catharsis, helping them to cast out falsehood from truth and releasing disillusioned hearts from darkness and despair. His very being was an illumination.

The Kotzker was a rebbe, and at first glance he would seem to be a descendant, a leader in the founder's line of succession. Yet he was not a follower by nature or temperament; nor was he able to conform to a model or transmit a message from the past. His existence was a continual self-renewal; he could live only in the present.

Certainly, several principles stressed by the Baal Shem have remained part of the Kotzker's teaching. Even some of the customs and forms of conduct developed and observed by other rebbes were included in the Kotzker's style of living. He held the founder in high esteem, hailed the movement initiated by him, and once declared:

The Baal Shem Tov has come to redress the Prophet's complaint: "And their fear of Me is a commandment of men learned by rote" (Isaiah 29:13). His doctrine has spread from Podolia to Volhynia [4] then to Galicia,[5] and from there to Poland. It is desirable to introduce the teachings of Hasidism to the Jews of Lithuania [6] as well.

The Kotzker did not, however, feel bound by the norms and forms of the movement. Kotzk brought a revolution into the history of Hasidism, and was in many ways diametrically opposed to Mezbizh.

The period of the Baal Shem was one in which poetic imagination was suppressed by Talmudic speculation. Blinders seemed to have been placed upon the eyes of the soul. The Besht removed them, hearts opened, and fantasy began to sing. Fountains of joy bubbled forth, followed by passionate insights, intoxicating tunes, exquisite tales. It was as if the world had regained its chastity, and holiness was gazing at itself in the mirror of all things. Faith was at home with beauty.

The Kotzker, on the other hand, was troubled that truth was in distress. Dormant imagination did not concern him. Somber and plaintful, he had no patience with the playful or the rhapsodic.

[4] Where the Mezeritcher Maggid held sway.
[5] Under the leadership of Rebbe Elimelekh of Lishensk.
[6] At that time the fortress of opposition to Hasidism.

The Antithesis

Jewish teachers insisted that everything must be regulated, codified; for every moment there must be an established form, a recognizable pattern. Dedicated to such an order of living, the practice of Judaism was in danger of becoming a series of acts performed by rote. Then came the Baal Shem, who reminded the people that spontaneity was as important as pattern, faith as essential as obedience, and that obedience without fervor led to stultification of the spirit.

The Baal Shem Tov's intention was to prevent Jewish piety from hardening into mere routine. Yet his path also became a habit, a routine. When first conceived, an idea is a breakthrough; once adopted and repeated, it tends to become a cul-de-sac.

About the year 1810, a small party of men gathered around Reb Yaakov Yitzhak of Pshyskhe (1766–1814), known as the "Holy Jew." They were stirred by what they regarded as the trivialization of the Hasidic movement. They recognized that stultification was due to the tendency to imitate, to duplicate. They "conspired" to bring about a spiritual renewal.

Fervor, too, had become habitual. Spontaneity had become distorted by those whose ardor was an excuse for self-indulgence and self-love. Faith had become a way of life immune to challenge and doubt.

The movement that began with the great master Reb Yaakov Yitzhak and reached its climax in the Kotzker is one of the most important chapters in the spiritual history of the Jews. Here one may observe the Jewish soul on its most precipitous pilgrimage; it dared hazardous leaps, braved conceits, and shattered pleasant convictions as it advanced slowly toward peaks of purity.

Who was the Kotzker? Born in 1787 in Bilgoraj near Lublin, Poland, into a non-Hasidic family, Reb Menahem Mendl was attracted to the movement in his youth. First he became a disciple of Reb Yaakov Yitzhak of Lublin, the "Seer," then of Reb Yaakov Yitzhak of Pshyskhe, and finally of Reb Simha Bunam. He was named Bunam's successor and lived first in Tomashov and then in Kotzk. He died in 1859, at the age of seventy-two.

Hasidism was a great drama enacted on the stage of East European Jewish life, and the Kotzker played a crucial role in it. It is my view that the movement called into being by Reb Israel Baal Shem Tov, the Besht, reached both its climax and its antithesis in Reb Menahem Mendl of Kotzk. The Kotzker brought about a revolution within Hasidism. While Mezbizh emphasized love, joy, and compassion for this world, Kotzk demanded constant tension and unmitigated militancy in combating this-worldliness. The Baal Shem was kind to everyone, the Kotzker harsh. The passionate indignation of the Prophets came back to life in the Kotzker.

Classical Hasidism tried to reach all Jews. The Kotzker was interested only in the select, the few. He inscribed one word on his banner: *Emeth*, Truth. To achieve Truth he was ready to sacrifice everything else. Worst of all were the imitations of Truth—the closer to the original, the worse. The way to Truth was a tortuous one. For its sake one must do away with habit, with emotional bias, and with all kinds of outward appearances, even those hallowed over the generations. If a man offered prayers today because he did so yesterday, he was worse than a scoundrel, said the Kotzker. Every day prayer had to have a fresh approach. One ought to search out the Truth daily, as if it had not been known before.

Truth, taught the Kotzker, could be reached only by way of the utmost freedom. Such freedom meant not to give in to any outside pressures, not to conform, not to please oneself or anyone else.

The passion of freedom within the Kotzker was not stifled or tranquilized by comfort or easy belief. He knew that he was nothing but a man, weak in every respect yet great in the possession of freedom. He rejected the notion that the purpose of man is to restore the purity of his soul and insisted that "man was created to exalt the heavens." He did not preach asceticism or negate this world; he insisted, however, that to get to the truth a man had to go against himself and society.

This approach was actually practiced by the disciples of Reb Mendl. Scholarly young men left their homes, wives, and children, their studies, and flocked to Kotzk in search of living Truth, of honesty. The true worship of God, Reb Mendl seemed to say, was not in finding the Truth but, rather, in an honest search for it.

This quest required total abandonment of self. It was best conducted by studying Torah, the Talmud. But the Kotzker also pointed out that while Torah study might be the safest way, it was also the most dangerous. The hazard lurked that a man might be filled with himself, with conceit, with self-satisfaction. Such feelings were nothing less than idol worship and kept him far from the Truth he sought.

Hasidism had instilled and nurtured noble qualities in many people: justice, compassion, humility, awe; spirituality of rare splendor. It was a blessing that called for appreciation and gratitude. Yet the Kotzker demurred. Of what avail were virtues in a world from which Truth was absent? Since it lacked integrity, compassion was not real, humility was not genuine; nor could there be authentic justice. Truth was the beginning, the end, and the heart. Without it, all labor was in vain. Yet was it at all possible for Truth to prevail?

The habit of lying is tantamount to lynching the soul. Yet people generally consider the utterance of a lie to be a triviality. The first sin of man came about as a result of deception—Adam and Eve were told not to eat the forbidden fruit, but Eve reported that they were not to touch it—and throughout history mendacity has been the mother of cruelty, canards, and deception, the prelude to murder and war. Cruelty, the disposition to inflict suffering, indifference to or pleasure taken in another's pain or distress—these proceed from a deceptive view of oneself.

Truth Is in the Grave

A parable. Rabbi Shimon said:

When God was about to create Adam, the ministering angels split into contending groups. Some said, "Let him be created!" while others cried, "Let him not be created!" That is why it is written: "Mercy and truth collided, righteousness and peace engaged in a clash" (Psalms 85:11).

Mercy said, "Let him be created, for he will do merciful deeds."

Truth said, "Let him not be created, for he will be false." Righteousness said, "Let him be created, for he will do righteous deeds." Peace said, "Let him not be created, for he will never cease quarreling."

What did the Holy One, blessed be He, do? He took Truth and cast it into the ground.[1]

It seems that this parable haunted the Kotzker. Indeed, after all the heady discourses are over, the intoxication gone, one begins to wonder: is Truth really buried in a grave? The parable openly declares once and for all that man's very existence is founded upon the tomb in which Truth is imprisoned. Man prevails only because Truth lies buried . . . But who is truly concerned?

According to the parable, man owes his existence to mercy. In Mezbizh it was held that in this world love and compassion took precedence over Truth. One must be ready to forgo veracity for the sake of mercy. There was only one reality: the good. What was good existed; what was evil was merely an illusion, a shadow of the good. In Kotzk it was believed that as long as man was false, his mercy, his goodness were illusions, a mockery, mere shadows.

The Kotzker knew that Truth lies buried, stifled in the grave, yet it remains alive. Truth wants to emerge, but man does not permit its appearance. Man's structures stand like a mausoleum

---

[1] *Genesis Rabba* 8, 5.

While the image of truth being out of man's reach was known to the skeptics of antiquity, the thought stressed in this parable goes further in maintaining that truth is not congruous with man; it disagrees with his very being.

"Of truth we know nothing, for truth is in a well" is a saying ascribed to Democritus, Diogenes Laertius, *Pyrrho*, Book IX, Section 12. Similarly, "Nature has buried truth at the bottom of the sea," Cicero, *Academicarum Questionum*, Book II, Section 10. "Truth lies wrapped up and hidden in the depths," Seneca, *De Beniticiis*, Book VII, Section 1.

on the grave of Truth, preventing it from raising its head. Actually, deep in every soul there is a longing to embrace Truth, but it has ceased to be felt. Nor do many people seem to care.

The Kotzker cared. He lived in consternation, always aware of the chasm separating man from Truth. A resounding cry went forth from Kotzk, and Jews were stirred.

A tragedy had occurred: the soul had been perverted; it had become a piece of flesh. People were more concerned with their empty pockets than their empty souls. They were obsessed by their material wants. Even in the synagogue they were moved to tears only while reciting the prayers for a livelihood. Yet they dared to dream of the luxuries to be enjoyed in the life to come. Their conceptions of Heaven were a travesty, a distortion. They devoured large portions of *afikomen* [2] and took pleasure in their own righteousness! They talked about the Messiah—but their lips were not worthy of even uttering His name. When they performed good deeds, they thought they were doing the Almighty a favor.

The criticism applied not only to simple folk. It was directed at those who claimed to rise above the level of basic faith and observance—namely the Hasidim, the followers of the Baal Shem's teachings.

What were the major principles introduced by this great master, and how did the Kotzker differ from him?

[2] The Law requires that a tiny piece of matzah be eaten at the end of the Seder meal. Foolish piety motivates some people to eat a large portion of the matzah.

The Baal Shem and the Kotzker

A harp was hanging above David's bed. As soon as midnight arrived, a north wind came and blew upon it, and it played of itself.[1]

When we listen to the Baal Shem, we hear words issuing without premeditation from an overflowing heart, like the strains from the harp hanging over David's bed. He inspired joy, the Kotzker contrition. The former began with grace, the latter with indignation. A light glowed in Mezbizh; a fire raged in Kotzk.

The ancient fury of the Prophets, the wrath of the moralist chastisers of earlier ages, fell down again upon Jewry. The Kotzker cried out in the manner of Rehabeam, son of Solomon: "And now, whereas my father laid upon you a heavy yoke, I will add to your yoke. My father chastised you with whips, and I will chastise you with scorpions" (I Kings 12:11).

The Kotzker was the Ecclesiastes of his age. He too saw that "under the sun that in the place of justice, even there was wickedness, and in the place of righteousness, even there was wickedness" (Ecclesiastes 3:16). "Vanity of vanities," says Ecclesiastes, "vanity of vanities! All is vanity!" (1:2).

The Baal Shem Tov was the Song of Songs of his time, intoxicated with a love of God, which "many waters cannot quench, neither can floods drown it. If a man offered for love all the wealth of his house, it would be utterly scorned" (Song of Songs 8:7). The Baal Shem's teaching turned the exclamation of Ecclesiastes's "Vanity of vanities!" on its head.

[1] *Berachoth* 3b.

The Kotzker's distrust of the world stood in contrast to the popular Jewish stance of trust and respect, as reflected in many Yiddish idioms: "He is as good as the world," "as beautiful as the world," "as wise as the world."

The Kotzker did not consider himself an heir to the tradition of the Baal Shem Tov. Reb Mendl of Vitebsk (1730–88), a revered disciple of the great Maggid of Mezeritch, expressed the view of nearly all Hasidic rebbes when he wrote that no one like the Baal Shem had ever lived or would ever appear again.

It is related about the Kotzker that, while he was still a young man and a disciple in Pshyskhe, he was admonished, "Are you striving to become as great as the Baal Shem Tov?" Unabashed, he answered, "Really! Did the Baal Shem vow that no one would ever surpass him in greatness?" Once, while speaking of his Hasidic forebears, he did not even mention the Baal Shem Tov's name: "Do you know who I am? There was Rebbe Reb Dov Baer, Reb Shmelke, Rebbe Elimelekh, the Rebbe of Lublin, the 'Holy Jew,' Rebbe Reb Bunam—and I am the seventh—the quintessence of them all. I am the Sabbath."

The Kotzker's disciple, known as "the Gerer," Reb Yitzhak Meir of Ger, held him to be as great as the Baal Shem. Until the time of the Great Master, the "Holy Jew" of Pshyskhe, all tzaddikim had sought to interpret the Baal Shem's doctrines. But since Pshyskhe, said the Gerer, all Hasidic teaching had been a commentary on Pshyskhe. In Kotzk, he added, there were three hundred young men, each of whom could have attained the level of the Baal Shem, had not envy and public attention prevented it.

When the news of Reb Mendl's serious illness reached Warsaw, where Reb Yitzhak Meir lived, the latter began to heap inordinate praise upon the Kotzker: "There is no other truthful Jew like him. I think he is as great as the Baal Shem Tov."

Hasidim have always extolled their rebbe, but the Kotzker is the only one who has been compared to the Baal Shem Tov.

Hasidim studied the classical works written by the disciples of the Baal Shem and the great Maggid of Mezeritch. The Kotzker Hasidim, however, did not—not even *Kedushat Levi*.[2] There was one exception: the writings of Reb Nahman of Bratzlav.

Significantly, the writings of the Seer of Lublin were in a class by themselves. In spite of the dissent that propelled the movement away from Lublin to Pshyskhe, Reb Yitzhak Meir said:

I have never looked into any Hasidic work, because the authors wrote them only for their generation. The works of the Rebbe of Lublin are an exception, however, and I study them very closely. Each word is a book in itself. His work is permeated with humility and joy. He was like that, his works are like that . . . I can grasp the meaning of the Five Books of Moses from the first word to the last, just as the Rebbe of Lublin understood them.

The Baal Shem believed that the gates of sanctity were open. It was easy to be righteous, simple to keep the commandments. The Kotzker proclaimed that a gaping chasm separated man from God; that it was audacious to mention God's name with our profane lips; that one must purify himself thoroughly before undertaking the fulfillment of a commandment. It is written, "You shall therefore lay up these words of Mine *upon* your heart" (Deuteronomy 11:18). Why not *"in* your heart"? The Kotzker explained that it would be preposterous to demand that Truth lie in the heart. Was anyone's heart capable of containing Truth within itself? Moreover, how could Truth penetrate hearts that were blocked and ossified?

Therefore, the verse means that Truth should lie like a stone upon one's heart. There were moments when the heart did open

2 A volume by Reb Levi Yitzhak of Berditshev.

up. If the words lay upon it, they might seep in. It was then that Truth could enter it. One could become a different person, one realized what to do, what to correct . . . and the words were absorbed into one's very being.

We pray daily, "Open my heart to Your Torah . . . He shall open our hearts." When one prays with one's whole heart and soul, God will surely help.

The Kotzker sought to go beyond the Baal Shem. He succeeded in disclosing the antithesis, the counterpole. Yet he has neither refuted nor eclipsed him.

A World of Veils

God is a father full of love and mercy. But why is He hidden, why is He evading us?

He is not hidden, said the Baal Shem; He is hiding. He is very near, hiding behind veils and screens. He is playing "hide and go seek" with His children, waiting to be found, but we forget to look for Him—explained the grandson of the Baal Shem.

God's absence is an illusion. The senses deceive us into believing that God is nowhere to be found. The world lives by revealment and concealment . . . the Glory is everywhere, but with the palm of one hand upon our eyes, we obstruct our own view. To a large degree, the darkness is due to a failure of experience. Our mind is obscured by the eclipse, not the sun.

The soul is "a part of God from above," but man thinks he is all from below, all made of dust. Every man must think of himself as a stairway set on the ground, its top reaching heaven. It is within his power to affect what should happen in the upper worlds.

The greatest sin of man is to forget that he is a prince—that he has royal power. All worlds are in need of exaltation, and everyone is charged to lift what is low, to unite what lies apart, to advance what is left behind. It is as if all worlds, above and below, are full of expectancy, of sacred goals to be reached, so that consummation can come to pass. And man is called upon to bring about the climax slowly but decisively.

Nothing, therefore, is accidental. Even an intruding thought does not come at random. A thought is like a person. It arrives because it needs to be restored. A thought severed, abused, seeks to be reunited with its root. Furthermore, it may be a message sent to remind a man of a task, a task he was born to carry out.

All facts are parables; their object is God. All things are tales the Teacher relates in order to render intelligible issues too difficult to comprehend literally, directly. Through things seen, God accommodates Himself to our level of understanding. What a shame it is that people do not comprehend the greatness of things on earth. They act as if life were trivial, not realizing that every trifle is filled with Divinity. No one makes a move that does not stir the highest Heaven.

The Baal Shem's vision of the world, richly nourished by the doctrine of Jewish mysticism, stands in sharp contrast to the Kotzker's conception of it.

A World of Phantoms

For most of us, life is a series of evasions, pretensions, substitutes, and rationalizations. We do not see the world as it is but as a projection of ourselves, and so we are prisoners of delusions that hold us in their spell even after we become aware of their deceptiveness. Gradually pretensions are converted into certainties, rationalizations become entangled, and madness sets in.

So many people become salesmen of their delusions. So few people are fully conscious of the non-finality of our here-and-now world.

In analyzing and discussing problems of Jewish Law, possible solutions are often advanced in the Talmud with the introductory words, "I might have thought," "I might have been led to believe." After proving that these arguments are mere suppositions or hypotheses, a conclusion is usually reached.

One must learn to understand thoroughly the precise meaning of these phrases, Reb Bunam said. For the world in which we live is a mere supposition or hypothesis. The conclusion is still to come. "At that time I will change the speech of the peoples to a pure speech, that all of them may call on the name of the Lord and serve Him with one accord" (Zephaniah 3:9).

How did the Kotzker, who was consumed with a passion for veracity, for eternity, look at people whose whole life was spent serving spurious goals?

Falsehood is not merely a discrepancy between what is said and what is meant. It twists and distorts the basis of a man's life, deceiving him into believing he lives in a reality that does not exist. A person living a lie and taking it to be the Truth moves in a world of self-delusion.

Falsehood is not just a stigma that sullies man's thinking. A healthy life consists in knowing what one wants, seeing an ultimate goal ahead, and hoping to reach it by means of clearly understood actions. And mendacity is a disease that binds a man's entire existence. As a result of it, our perceptions are false. We regard as real what can be measured and controlled; what defies measurement and control we reject as irrational and unreal.

In Jewish mystical literature the world here and now is called "the world of falsehood"; each grain of truth may be surrounded by shells of falsehood. Our truths are often half-truths, acquired piecemeal and preserved precariously, their only refuge being the lips of a few dying men. For so many people die for the sake of a lie. So many who profess truth really shun it. Their solemn proclamations are often veiled deceptions.

This is what Abraham did. He forsook community and deception to live with Truth in solitude.

Genuine solitude is the prelude to a new community. However, if you do not withdraw but remain part of "the world," your supreme effort must be not to deceive yourself. Clearly one of man's strongest inclinations is to deceive himself.

People do not know whether they are alive and where they are. The world abounds in misrepresentation—lives without design, movement without aim, roofs without walls. They think they dance, yet they are paralyzed. Delusion holds them enraptured. They feel so comfortable in the clutches of their self-deception that when Satan himself embraces them, they think he is in love with them.

Mendacity is the enemy of man, and yet more and more love

is lavished on guile and lies. Truth is homeless in our world. We suffocate for lack of honesty. As a result, man dies while yet alive. Who can speak of resurrection when life itself has become death?

Coarse and swaggering, men make insolent speeches and engage in presumptuous dealings. But they are dead, while Truth, though buried in the grave, is alive. Sometimes a voice cries out from underground, and a few isolated individuals sigh and weep.

When a man does not delude himself, he does, at the least, recognize the world's falsehood. As long as he believes that his delusion is ultimately coherent, that his conceits have final meaning, he lives in a realm of phantoms. Though idle, he is convinced of his achievements. Even as he lies dying, he persuades himself that he is alive.

Each person should wrestle with this question: am I living in a world of phantoms? Is my life, are all my concerns mere delusions?

Many of the people who populate the so-called world do not really live. What you see, said the Kotzker, are phantoms, apparitions, specters, ghosts moving around in the realm of the lost, a large and broad limbo. They are too restless to settle down in either Heaven or Hell and be quiet forever with the mortal world.

Wherever there is turmoil, a crowd, you find them. They talk and are counted among the living. They have the attributes of bodies but are fleshless ghosts. They do business and go to conferences. They take sea voyages, trade, make and lose money, never realizing that they are living in a world of phantoms. They do not understand that their buying and selling means nothing, that they neither make profits nor sustain losses, for there is no substance to all their comings and goings.

For thousands of years these homeless souls hover about in the whirligig of their lives, until just one human being recognizes and stops them, sending them to their final rest. Merely being forced to stop and think activates their release. They realize that they don't belong on earth and make off.

Reb Bunam and Reb Mendl have told of their frequent meetings with the dead who did not know they had died, people who lived in an imaginary world, homeless spirits whom even Hell would not admit . . . They lived in neither this world nor the next. Driven and confused, they roamed about without goal or reason.

One day Reb Bunam said to the Kotzker, "Let's go out into the fields."

When the horses were hitched to the cart, they left town and arrived in the open.

"Well, what do you see?" asked Reb Bunam.

"I see peasants mowing wheat."

"Call one of them over."

When he stood before them, Reb Bunam continued, "You think he is wearing clothes, don't you? Well, he's not. He is enveloped in a shroud. He belongs to the world of phantoms. Let him go to his eternal rest . . ."

Some years later, when the Kotzker had become Rebbe, he drove out of town with Reb Hirsh of Tomashov. They came to a bridge where several women began to throw stones at them.

"Have no fear," said the Kotzker. "They are not real women, nor are their stones real. They are mere phantoms."

Reb Hirsh was silent for a moment, then asked, "Might we not be phantoms too?"

"No," came the Kotzker's answer, "as long as we have at some time had a genuine urge to repent."

Vanity of Vanities?

It is an assumption in many religions that, in order to reach the Divine, you must first abandon the mundane. Saintliness and worldliness are mutually exclusive. The world of the Spirit is eternity, the world of here and now vanity.

Rationally, such a dualism seems plausible. Yet those who adore the Creator may feel challenged by the question: how can we love Him whose Being is holy and hiding without adoring the world He created?

The Baal Shem exhorted us to prize highly everything that exists. How else can we come close to the Creator, if not through the things He has made? It is hardly possible to revere Him and at the same time despise His creation. This, then, determines the outcome of our groping: either to love or to hate, to revere or resent, the world, people, things.

Man must cherish the world, said the Baal Shem. To deprecate, to deride it was presumption. Creation, all of creation, was pervaded with dignity and purpose and embodied God's meaning.

"Vanity of vanities," said Ecclesiastes, "vanity of vanities, *all is vanity.*" The Baal Shem's interpretation of these words was as follows: the verse needed to be divided into two parts, the assertion of Ecclesiastes that all was vanity and its sharp refutation. "You contend that all is vanity, Ecclesiastes? What you say is vanity." Whoever dares to assert that the world God has created is vanity, all his good deeds, his piety and worship are vanity! It was the Baal Shem's genius to drive out sullenness with adoration. Man's melancholy was an affront to God.

Even in the densest darkness one could see the flicker of a spark, for a ray of the Holy was at the core of all that was. It was a man's task to redeem the hidden radiance, the divine kernels sealed in their husks. Since the Divine was everywhere, one might easily experience the radiance of the Holy in any place at any moment. "There is nothing that does not contain a glint of holiness, for without it nothing could possibly exist."

This view is not to be equated with pantheistic notions. According to the Baal Shem, world and God, matter and Spirit, were totally separate entities. There was no equation, no identification, as pantheism claims. Although the essence or the soul that sustained the material world was spiritual, the world in its concreteness remained material; it was qualitatively distinct from God.

What distinguishes the righteous from the wicked? The wicked are trapped by material things that bring them pleasure; the righteous are enchanted by the mystery of the Divine inherent in things. Their wonder sustains their lives.

Before the Baal Shem's time, pious Jews felt that to be close to God, the body must be chastised, one must fast and scourge oneself. Bodily enjoyment was considered despicable; sexual pleasures filled them with revulsion. But the Baal Shem and his followers held that all delights come from Eden. "A longing for things material is an instrument by which one may approach the love of God; even through coarse desires one may come to love the Creator." Lust, desire, evil inclination, all should be elevated, not uprooted.

This view was entirely alien to the Kotzker. He felt the crassness of the world, its falseness, its corruption. In the spirit of the text "Vanity of vanities, all is vanity," he preferred to alienate himself from the world.

Reb Mendl was neither a mystic nor a poet. His outlook was somber, his manner austere. His moral rigor suppressed his aesthetic sensibilities. Even though he agreed with the Baal Shem in repudiating fasting and self-affliction, he could not acclaim or extol the pleasures of this world. He was suspicious of man's inclinations; rather than elevate the evil inclination, as the Baal Shem suggested, he wanted it plucked out.

Classical Hasidism stressed the idea that man's soul was "a part of God come from above." Reb Shlomo of Karlin said, "The greatest sin a Jew can commit is to forget that he is a prince."

While the Kotzker did not question the divine origin of the soul, he found on looking at man that he contradicted his origin. To him man was "smelly semen."

Did the Kotzker lack a sense of human worth? He had many more harsh things to say about self-centeredness and the nature of man. Yet they did not stem from disparagement but, rather, from an overestimation of man's capacities if he but exercised his powers of will. The Kotzker set exalted goals for his disciples because he believed in their ability to make the prodigious efforts required to reach them.

The Kotzker seems to have held that the truthful man is one who has a will toward Truth. Yet man's will power is often confused in the turmoil of his inner life, in the roar of cataracts and the gloom of subterranean caverns.

A major cause of Reb Mendl's bitter disappointment was the realization that man let his aptitude for good be perverted and dissipated. Those who love man often serve him to their own detriment. It would have repelled the Kotzker to grow rich and popular. The true lover of man will deceive neither his neighbors nor his own self.

The Baal Shem rejected the traditional proposition that body and soul were engaged in bitter rivalry. The body, he held, should cooperate with the soul in the service of God; therefore, its basic needs required satisfaction.

When word reached him that his disciple Reb Yaakov Yosef engaged in ascetic acts, mortifying his body, he admonished him by letter to abstain from such practices. In this context, the Prophet Isaiah's appeal, "Do not hide yourself from your flesh" (58:7)—which literally means, Do not remain indifferent when another of your own stock is miserable—was interpreted by the Baal Shem Tov as, Do not remain indifferent to your own flesh, your own body's needs.

In contrast, the Kotzker regarded sexual desire as the great antagonist. Even though he agreed that one could not prevail over the body by self-affliction, he was convinced that indulgence, even gratification, must stultify the soul.

In the thought of the Baal Shem, love was the beginning of all experience. Whoever came to him felt how his reverence for God blended with his affection for all men. He was warmhearted, easily approachable. He sought people out, traveling from town to town, from village to village in order to befriend simple folk. In those days of complete segregation between men and women, when a pious Jew was careful not to enter into conversation with a strange woman, the Baal Shem's behavior was bold indeed. He received women who requested his counsel and blessing. The Kotzker, however, drove people away. Women were certainly never allowed to enter his study.

To be accepted as a disciple of the Kotzker, one had to possess a marked amount of Talmudic learning.

One day a simple man without learning came to the Kotzker. Said Reb Mendl to him, "A Jew like you need not travel to see me, but should rather sit at home by his stove reciting the Psalms."

The Baal Shem started out in solitude and self-concealment and ended by revealing himself to the world. The Kotzker began his career with open doors, teaching in public, and ended in solitude, in self-isolation.

In his famous epistle to Reb Gershon of Kitev (Polish: Kuty), the Baal Shem related how his soul ascended to Heaven:

> It went up stage by stage until I entered the palace of the Messiah . . . And I asked him, "When will you come?" He answered, "Not until your teaching is known throughout the world, and the wellsprings of your spirit burst forth."

The Baal Shem strove to spread his message among the Jewish masses, so that they might recognize God as the root of everything. In contrast, the Kotzker was interested only in teaching select individuals, in instructing an intellectual elite.

The itinerant preachers, the maggidim of the eighteenth century, traveled from town to town, telling the people how sinful they were. Their printed books described how vile spirits and demons lay in wait everywhere, threatening man with terrifying punishments for the slightest deviation from the prescribed codes. One of the most popular works in the field of ethics and homiletics, *Shevet Musar (The Rod of Correction)*, was written by Elijah of Smyrna, who died in 1729. There he depicted in detail the tortures the wicked go through in Hell.

Then came the Baal Shem, who told the people how precious every man was to the heart of God. He explained by means of parables how God Himself, the Divine Presence, was to be found in everything and everybody. The preachers flayed; the Baal Shem Tov extolled.

The Baal Shem's power of love, his feeling for the divine worth of each individual, his concern for the ordinary cares of common folk, as if all were his equals—these qualities were missing in the Kotzker's attitude toward people.

Not only did the Baal Shem deal with the tangled problems of existence; he also uncovered the rich potentials, the natural treasures that were to be found in life—joy, love, song, fervor. He opened wells that had long been sealed. Entire areas of Jewish life that were parched like a wasteland were transformed into gardens full of intoxicating fragrance. He believed that Jewishness must be felt, must be loved; one should find delight in it.

But the Kotzker held that feeling without learning, love without self-reflection, ardor without self-control might wreck all boundaries. Emotions led astray; the heart alone had no eyes.

The Baal Shem was guided by the rabbinic maxim "God asks for the heart"; the Kotzker harbored the prophetic view: "The heart is deceitful above all things, and desperately corrupt; who can understand it?" (Jeremiah 17:9).

The Baal Shem held to the principles that one must serve God with zeal, with joy. The Kotzker said the opposite: one must serve despite oneself, not because one wanted to but precisely because one did not want to. Biblical laws for which no reasons were apparent stood higher than laws that had rational explanations. God commanded Moses to count the daughters of Midian (Numbers 31:35). "Is Moses, our master, ordered to count pagan girls?! Nevertheless, if it is so ordered, so be it! One puts one's own opinions aside."

Immanence and Transcendence

To say that God is somewhere comes close to saying that He is nowhere. It is inconceivable that a majesty that overwhelms the infinite Heavens should withhold its glory from the finite corners of the earth.

Throughout the ages, Judaism has celebrated God's lordship and transcendence as well as His nearness and presence. Poets have sung of it and mystics have alluded to it, while theologians have mostly been too restrained to articulate it. Eager to deepen their understanding of God's unity and uniqueness, medieval Jewish philosophers entirely disregarded the *Shekhinah,* God's Presence and Indwelling in the world, which was so passionately taught by the great Rabbi Akiba and his disciples. Even in later Jewish mysticism, the doctrine of the Shekhinah was upheld mostly in terms of theosophic transcendence, rather than intimacy and involvement in the experience of man.

More than anyone else, the Baal Shem instilled the thought of the Shekhinah in men's hearts and souls; God's nearness became the most important aspect of Him that a human being could attain. Keeping His distance was seen as a game that God played with man, His perennial child, like any father with his child.

To the Kotzker this thought was irritating. How could the consuming force of God be so near without consuming a world bristling with malice? As we shall see in subsequent chapters, he shared some important concerns with the great Danish theologian Søren Kierkegaard. Just as the Kotzker reacted to the emphasis of God's immanence in Hasidic thought, Kierkegaard took issue with a similar aspect of Protestant thought.

The whole trend of post-Renaissance thinking has been toward a concept of God immanent in life, in history, in man's experience. One of Kierkegaard's major attacks on Hegel was directed against his view that Infinite Being was not distinct from the finite and was necessarily manifested in it, incorporated into the world. To Kierkegaard God was all transcendence. He was, as it were, on the far side of the abyss.

To the Baal Shem, God was both transcendent and immanent, and his thought, in its total intoxication with God's nearness, occasionally favored a view of immanentism that overshadowed God's transcendence. On this fundamental issue the Kotzker parted ways with the Baal Shem Tov.

But though the Kotzker emphasized the chasm that separated man from God, he also pointed to the bridges that might lead across it, from the heart to God.

God and Man

The world was filled with vicious, harmful spirits, warned the preachers of the eighteenth century. The Baal Shem saw the world filled with light, glory, divinity.

Between God and man stands a wall of iron, says the Talmud. But the Baal Shem saw no barrier when a man studied or prayed. Even in wayward thoughts or the pleasure of a sin God was present, though concealed or suppressed.

All of man's sorrow is the sorrow of the Shekhinah as well. ("When man is in pain, what does the Shekhinah say? 'Woe unto my head! Woe unto my limbs!'") This thought, as expressed by the sages of the Mishnah, became a vast spiritual reality, opening a new dimension to all experience: my grief is God's grief. If there is some consolation in the anguish that is shared by many, the anguish shared by the Divine Presence is far more than a consolation.

For the Baal Shem, the awareness of the Shekhinah's exile among men was a source of constant anxiety, of deep woe. By contrast, the thought of God in exile was not to be found in the sayings of the Kotzker. Passivity and Divinity were contradictory ideas. For him God could never be suppressed, least of all by human stupidity. Words that sounded like a song when the Baal Shem spoke turned into a bitter groan in the Kotzker's throat.

The Baal Shem constantly reminds us how close God is to man and to all things. Reb Mendl perennially recalls how alienated, how estranged man is from Truth, from God. The Baal Shem discloses the presence of God, the Creator of the Universe, within the world; he brings Heaven nearer to man. But for what purpose, says Reb Mendl, since man's corruption spurns the Divine?

The Baal Shem interprets "Know what is above you, yourself" [1] in this fashion: You will know God, who is above, from within, out of yourself.[2] Man has a soul which is itself a divine

[1] *Sayings of the Fathers*, II, 1.
[2] The Hebrew word *mimkha* can also mean "out of yourself."

portion of Divinity and through it he can intuit something of the Divinity of God who is above.

The Baal Shem taught that God was everywhere; only when one sinned was He suppressed or blocked. An intimation of this lay in the Hebrew word *het*, which means "sin." The letter *alef* in the Hebrew spelling of the word *het*, signifies God, Lord (*aluf*) of the Universe. He thus was present in the Hebrew word for sin but remained mute, not articulated.

Reb Mendl, however, felt that there was an essential disparity between the Divine and the mundane, that the human often operated in defiance of the Divine. He was profoundly opposed to the Baal Shem Tov's conception that the world was infused with the Divine. When asked where God dwelt, the Baal Shem answered, everywhere; the Kotzker, where He is allowed to enter . . .

The Kotzker believed that the self was a cavern of misery and woe. When man looked into himself, he saw darkness and turmoil. The self was too wayward to reach an understanding of God. The groundwork had to be laid by striving to subdue the self.

The Baal Shem gave every Jew the benefit of the doubt. He perceived the presence of holiness even in those who went astray. Did not the Talmud say, "Even sinners in Israel are replete with good deeds as a pomegranate is filled with seeds?" The Kotzker inverted its meaning: one can be replete with good deeds as a pomegranate with seeds yet still be a sinner . . .

Isaiah and Job

One may look upon the world with enthusiasm and absorb its wonder and radiant glory; one may also see and be shocked by its ugliness and evil. The Prophet Isaiah heard the seraphim proclaim, "The whole earth is full of His glory" (Isaiah 6:3); Job, however, maintained that "the earth is given over to the power of the wicked" (9:24). Reb Mendl drew closer to Job than to the seraphim.

The Baal Shem adopted the perspective of the seraphim; the world was filled with glory, evil being but an instrument of the good, capable of conversion to good. The Kotzker did not want to listen to angels; what he heard and saw was a world dominated by falsehood.

The Baal Shem implored the moralizing preachers to stop chastising the people and hurling caustic words at them. Whoever wanted to censure others had to understand that he himself shared responsibility for their sins. One ought not to scorn people toiling to make a living for their failure to spend their time studying Torah. In general, no one should rail against his fellow man.

The Babylonian Talmud relates a story about Rabbi Shimon ben Yohai and his son Eleazar.

The two hid in a cave to escape persecution by the Romans. When they emerged after twelve months and saw people plowing fields and sowing seed, they exclaimed, "These people are concerned with temporal life, and not studying Torah. They are forsaking eternal life." Whatever they looked upon was immediately consumed by the fire in their eyes.

Thereupon a voice from Heaven exclaimed, "Have you emerged to destroy my world? Return to the cave!"

So they returned and spent another twelve months there; for, they said, the punishment of the wicked in Hell lasts only twelve months.

When this period had come to an end, the voice from Heaven called, "Go forth from your cave!"

And so they came out. Wherever Rabbi Eleazar harmed, Rabbi Shimon healed. Said Rabbi Shimon, "My son, even if only we two remain to study the Torah, it will be sufficient for the world."

So ends the tale.[1]

Do not denounce sinners, said the Baal Shem. Do not offend them; do not generate pain. Let him who cannot refrain from fault-finding remedy his own faults. Let him who seeks to censure criticize himself.

Reb Mendl denied the pedagogical value of leniency. He was unable to witness deception and remain calm. The falseness of the world hurt him—and when in pain, we cry out. Can a man whose house is on fire be concerned with remaining gentle and not hurting other people's sensibilities? His chief purpose is to quench the fire, to save whatever can be saved. To Reb Mendl it appeared that the world was on fire, in deadly peril. When he became rebbe, he gave notice that he would make demands on his disciples along the lines taught by Rabbi Shimon ben Yohai. Presumably he referred to the severe way of life called for by Rabbi Shimon when he first emerged from the cave.

The way and the message of the Kotzker were meant for an elite; the way and the message of the Baal Shem were intended for all. In Mezbizh, love of Israel prevailed; it was stressed that

[1] *Shabbat* 33b. See A. J. Heschel, *The Sabbath: Its Meaning for Modern Man* (New York, Farrar, Straus and Giroux, 1951), pp. 35ff.

even an ignorant person had dignity, for he was cast in the image of God. An ordinary Jew was often dearer in God's eyes than a scholar of repute. The Baal Shem prayed for "every mother's son." In Kotzk the untutored were kept at arm's length, even snubbed. There was only scorn for the masses; "a mixed multitude," the rebbe called them, "a rabble." "In my youthful years, such followers could never have attached themselves to me," he complained after he had grown famous.

Humanity wallowed in mire. Man had indeed fallen. To extricate the whole world, or even all of Israel, from the swamp was to attempt the impossible. It would be like trying to make pastry out of snow. One could attempt to raise only a few individuals out of the morass. "All I want is that ten Jews stand on the rooftops and cry out 'The Lord is God!' " the Kotzker said.

Once a Jew came to the Kotzker and said, "Rebbe, pray for me."
"Are you too ill to take your prayer shawl and pray yourself?" he responded.

Reb Bunam of Pshyskhe, Reb Mendl's master, sought to elevate every one of his followers spiritually. But the Kotzker wanted everyone to raise himself. He shouted, "If you obey me, well and good. If not, I will clothe myself in a garment of awe, and you will flee into the mouse-holes!"

In Kotzk they did not pat themselves on the back; they belittled and derided one another. In this they took their cue from their rebbe, who never comforted, never lightened the heart. He dispensed no favors; no benefits were conferred upon his followers. Instead, his words were like salt on wounds. His rebukes were daggers thrust between the ribs, piercing the heart.

A scene from the Kotzker's later years.

Some of his most eminent disciples are seated in the House of Study. Suddenly the door bursts open, and the Kotzker appears, quoting God's fearsome invective from Hosea: "I will fall upon them like a bear robbed of her cubs . . ." (13:8). The disciples take fright and hasten off.

Exaltation or Self-examination

Wonder and exaltation infused the words of the Baal Shem Tov. His teaching called for fervor, joy, and ecstasy. Suffering and torment suffused the maxims of the Kotzker. His teaching called for earnest reflection and self-inquiry, for sobriety and severity.

In Kotzk they quoted a saying by Reb Moshe Leib of Sosov: living in this world was like walking along the edge of a knife; hell yawned on either side.

Reb Bunam said, "You must imagine the evil spirit as a thug hovering over you with a raised hatchet, ready to chop off your head."

"What if I can't imagine it?" asked a Hasid.

"That's a sure sign that he has already chopped it off."

If a man spent one instant of his life without awe, Reb Bunam maintained, Hell was too good for him. One of his disciples testified to the fact that Reb Bunam never laughed, although he liked to make others smile with his amusing tales.

We live permanently on the brink of a precipice. A false move and we are flung into the abyss. Even a Hasid or a tzaddik could readily commit idolatry. Yet how could we suppose that a pious Jew, a tzaddik, could pay homage to an idol? To this Reb Bunam replied:

If, for example, he denies himself food for an ulterior motive, that is, he wants to eat but wishes to make an impression of self-discipline upon the people about him, this would be an instance of idolatrous behavior.

And the Kotzker added:

Ecclesiastes says, "Let your garments be always white; let not oil be lacking on your head!" (9:8). A man should always be aware that he is dressed in precious, white, silken clothing, and that he carries a pitcher of oil on his head. If he forgets for one moment, the pitcher will overturn. The oil will pour out and his clothes will be stained.

The world is full of disguises and delusions. It is therefore difficult to arrive at the nature of reality. To win the battle against falseness, one has to rise above one's experience and self-interest. A disciple of the Kotzker once said that a man may work hard and long to improve himself and may indeed reach a high level, but if he is motivated by self-regard, he will not be saved from Hell. Reb Bunam said the distance between paradise and Hell was no more than the width of a hair.

One day the Kotzker asked his Hasidim, "What does praying in earnest mean?"

They did not understand him. He continued, "Is there anything that should *not* be done in earnest?"

How does a diligent person differ from a lazybones? The former always acts upon reflection; the latter is too sluggish to think and thus acts without deliberation. That is why the Book of Deuteronomy asserts: "When you go forth [1] to war against your enemies" [2] (21:10), not simply "When you go to war . . ." The verse refers to the war against the enemy within. It can be waged only if you "go forth" from the self—that is, if you leave yourself behind.

Good and Evil

Classical Hasidism maintained that the right way to depart from evil was to be involved in the Holy, to do good. Do not fight evil directly; bypass it. The Psalmist's injunction, "Depart from evil and do good" (34:15) really means: by doing good you will depart from evil. Be involved in what is good; turning away from evil will follow. As Reb Shlomo of Karlin said, this is the way of *teshuvah,* of returning to God: turn away from evil by doing good.

The Kotzker did not believe that evil could be subdued so easily, so indirectly, by skirting it. Evil was a fierce enemy, stubborn and mighty. One must fight it boldly, head on. He said to his Hasidim: "First you must learn to hate evil and begin by turning away from it. When you are ready to do good, I shall help you along."

[1] Meaning "leave behind you."
[2] "Enemies" refers to "delusions."

In Mezbizh the road to virtue was wide and open. The good could come to pass anywhere at any time. In Kotzk they believed that carrying out a good deed required deliberation and preparation. The elimination of ulterior motives came hard, and to perform a good act with ulterior motives was equivalent to idolatry.

The Baal Shem was enraptured by his intuition that evil concealed a seed of the good; yet the good and the Holy might at times be pregnant with unpremeditated evil. Maimonides's view was that evil had no positive existence and was merely the absence of good, a privative *modus* of the good. Reminiscent of this, the Baal Shem taught that evil was a temporary manifestation of the as-yet-hidden good; it had a subsidiary function, acting as a kind of footstool to the good. His concern was to liberate the good within the evil, whereas the Kotzker's concern was to eliminate the evil found in the good. "This is the law of the guilt offering: it is most holy" (Leviticus 7:1)—said the Kotzker, "Where is the guilt to be found? In the most holy . . ."

The Baal Shem Tov stressed the necessity for transforming "evil" into "good," the unholy into the Holy. To him, then, "Depart from evil and do good," meant, *convert* evil into good. The Kotzker apparently questioned the very possibility of such a transformation. Evil was too stubborn to be capable of conversion.

Reb Henokh of Alexander, a disciple of the Kotzker, expressed this in a metaphor.

If two sheets of metal are to be smelted together, they must first be cleansed of all impurities. As long as rust adheres to them, they will not fuse. So long as a heart is impure, it cannot attach itself to God.

Above all, it was reasoned in Kotzk, you had to make every effort to rid yourself of impurities. Not until then could you attain the Hasidic way of life. It was exceedingly difficult to do the Holy perfectly, for all our acts are tainted by self-interest. In the battle with our evil impulses, we had to take the initiative. Nor could we indulge in self-congratulation. The Kotzker was averse to "a tongue that makes great boasts."

Kotzk was not the first stop for Jews who longed to walk the Hasidic road. Before going to Kotzk, one had to make basic changes in oneself. The Kotzker was no kindergarten teacher. At times he would chide:

What do you come to me for? To wash the mud off you? To help you discipline your passions? "From Kibroth-hattaavah the people journeyed to Hazeroth"[1] (Numbers 11:35). You have to do it yourselves first. Bury your passions first. Not until then should you go to the rebbe's court.

Reb Henokh once said about a great Hasid who traveled to Pshyskhe, then to Kotzk, and finally to Ger, "In Pshyskhe he was cleansed of his vileness, in Kotzk he was straightened out, and in Ger he was put on a high plane."

The Kotzker's successor, Reb Yitzhak Meir of Ger, in many ways softened his master's razor-edged doctrine. Although turning from evil had to precede doing good, he thought it hard to wait until one could rid oneself entirely of sin. To disengage oneself from all evil without the aid of doing good required too hard a struggle. That was why performing good deeds had to come first; departing from evil would follow in due course, as the Baal Shem had taught.

[1] The place name "Kibroth-hattaavah" means "the graves of passion"; "Hazeroth" means "courts."

The Solution Is the Problem

Scholars of Jewish Law have been concerned with the problem of what a man should or should not do. At the center is the deed, they have said. Philosophers and Kabbalists have debated what a man should or should not think. Hasidim have chiefly been absorbed by the problem of how a man should think while acting. Their first premise has been that what one thinks while acting determines the quality of religious life.

This assertion—that what goes on in one's inner life is of decisive importance—came as a shock to the stalwart guardians of tradition. Had they not always taught that the essence of Jewish living was in the doing? That inwardness, good intentions were desirable but not indispensable? Was it not an established principle that the value of good deeds remained unimpaired, even when devoid of good intentions? Many authorities had even questioned whether good deeds needed to be accompanied by good intentions.

In defiance of this long-accepted view, the Hasidim proclaimed that intention was of the essence. What a person thought and felt was not simply an adjunct to good deeds, a decorative jewel that lent luster and beauty, but constituted the very core of living. One had to develop a variety of sensibilities, a capacity to rise to higher levels of awareness. At times an inner experience had to take place so that the deed could follow.

The Kotzker went to extremes. He claimed that a virtuous act performed routinely, without the participation of heart and mind, did not pay homage to God. It was a gift to Esau instead, to the power of darkness that draws its vital energy from good deeds performed with ulterior motives. Not only evil deeds, but even those that seemed to be holy and religious in the eyes of men might, in fact, be sacrilegious if the intention behind them was not pure.

This stern voice insisted upon the absolute primacy of intention. In his daily life a man could be expected to serve his own interests. But when he devoted himself to the service of God, he ought not to be motivated by his ego. "A transgression for God's sake is better than a *mitzvah* without such a motive." [1] The meaning of this astonishing statement was echoed in Reb Henokh's reflection on the Biblical verse, "You shall be holy unto your God" (Numbers 15:40). All of the Holy belonged to God, which meant that every religious action had to be pure in intention. If a Holy deed was tinged with self-interest, the evil impulse would gain dominion over it and claim its holiness for itself . . . For evil could not exist without the Holy; it fed on the holiness of a *mitzvah* tinged with self-centeredness. Any act of worship that was not exercised for the sake of Heaven was idolatry. "For is there any difference between worshipping an idol and worshipping Him not for His sake?" [2]

Jews have always believed that the Torah glows with Divinity. Yet the Baal Shem thought that there were other sources of the Divine. Human souls, for instance, radiated spirituality. The merit of a drunken Jew, who had at least once resisted temptation and then, for instance, rescued others from jail, surpassed that of a haughty scholar. This preference was not stressed by the Kotzker.

[1] *Nazir* 23b.
[2] *Hashava Letovah*, p. 72.

The Baal Shem sensed that there were many problems that would not lend themselves to a solution by means of the halakah, the Law; there were situations that were not, and could not be, tackled in terms of permission or prohibition, the method of Rabbi Joseph Caro's *Shulhan Arukh,* the Code of Law.[3] The tzaddikim did not devote themselves to making decisions regarding ritual problems but to kindling lights in troubled souls. In this, as in some other instances, the Kotzker followed the example of the Baal Shem.

The compelling originality of the Baal Shem was apparent in his perspective on Jewishness and Jews. While others judged a person in terms of his actions, the Baal Shem saw him in relation to the whole personality. Nobility of character was as important to him as piety. Without intending to downgrade acts of goodness, he reaffirmed that their purpose was to enhance the quality of a man's being.

There were rabbis who saw human beings in terms of rules and regulations. The Baal Shem saw rules and regulations in terms of what men did and how they did it. The Kotzker also realized that a slackening in the observance of certain laws was not the main issue. Man was sick, sick with deceitfulness. Moreover, he held on to the unclean, even in the act of cleansing himself. The total person needed healing.

Some people think that religion automatically offers solutions to all problems. Jews, too, have believed that the study of Torah combined with the performance of good deeds can solve all dilemmas. Yet the Baal Shem saw that the study of Torah and the performance of good deeds engendered new predicaments. The solution turned out to be another problem.

The Kotzker's intuition led him to the same realization.

[3] First published in 1565.

Love or Truth

Love and Truth are the two ways that lead the soul out of the inner jungle. Love offers an answer to the question of how to live. In Truth we find an answer to the question of how to think.

This division, however, is dangerous and arbitrary. There is love at the heart of Truth. But is there Truth in our heart, in our love? Significantly, "love" is both a noun and a verb. Yet "truth" is never a verb . . .

It is impossible to find Truth without being in love, and it is impossible to experience love without being truthful, without living Truth.

According to the teaching of the Baal Shem, the essential goal is living in attachment to God. To the mind of the Kotzker such striving was an affront. Since man's heart was deceitful, his piety often a sham, his inner life a slum, how dared he consider himself worthy of attachment to Him Who was the source of Truth!

The shift of emphasis from striving after mystical experience to reflective self-critical discipline was part of the revolution in Hasidism initiated by the Holy Jew. The meaning of living was found in commitment to Truth as the infallible standard for all decisions. The central issue is not Truth in terms of a doctrine, but veracity, honesty, or sincerity in terms of personal existence. The Kotzker taught that everything should be sacrificed for the Truth—oneself, one's home, even one's portion in the world to come.

A man might take extreme care to commit no sins, to be

thoroughly observant, but if there was a lack of honesty in him, all his observances were mere sport. Knowing that a man could attain only a sliver, a hair, of Truth, Reb Yitzhak Meir of Ger declared that once the evil spirit had stolen this hair of Truth, a Hasid could continue to study and pray, for those activities had simply lost their power.

The parable mentioned earlier says that man exists by virtue of his goodness and love. The Baal Shem taught that love ranked higher than Truth. What really counted was a little compassion. There was only one kind of reality—love. Whatever was good was real; whatever was not good simply did not exist. Evil was an illusion, a mirage. In Kotzk they maintained the reverse: as long as a man was false, his love and his goodness were sham.

The Baal Shem quoted the Psalm, "Truth shall spring out of the earth" (85:12) and asked, "Surely it must be easy to find Truth?"

"Indeed it is easy," he continued, "but no one wants to bend down. No one is willing to stoop to pick up a little Truth."

By contrast, the Kotzker believed that it was exceedingly hard to come by a bit of Truth. It was like pulling teeth or sailing against the wind. He was dismayed to realize that lies lurked within Truth.

The Baal Shem, persuaded that there was some good in every evil, thought that even a lie contained a modicum of Truth. Yet he also sensed the misfortune of mendacity. A popular saying states that one can walk the length and breadth of the whole world with the Truth. The Baal Shem accepted this, since the Truth is knocked about everywhere on earth.

Being Aflame or Having Fire Within

There are activities that man performs with delight, passion, and fire. In contrast, acts of ritual and worship can sometimes be carried out without zest, without relish. There are people who pray absentmindedly and often act as if the service of God consisted of manual labor. Obedience is holy. But does God ask for only automatic conformity?

The Baal Shem was one of those souls who thought that to love God was the natural state of man. He believed that man was prone to love God as the seed was to grow. It was the most delightful act, and without it man was stifled, a burden to himself.

The Baal Shem thought of the Jew's relationship to God as a romance, and it disturbed him to see how many rituals had become routine rather than rapturous acts, exercises in repetition rather than gestures of surprise—a hand without a heart. Faith was fire, not sediment. Did not a pillar of fire serve as a guide when the people Israel roamed in the wilderness? And fire was the beginning of light.

The Baal Shem stirred the fervor that slumbered in the ashes, and as a result of his inspiration, a new feeling of potency flowed into communities and drew people along in a stream of enthusiasm.

One of his contributions was to awaken a zest for spiritual living, expressed in *hitlahavut,* which literally means "being aflame"—the experience of moments during which the soul is ablaze with an insatiate craving for God, when the memory of all other interests and the fear of misery and persecution are forgotten. In such instances a man seeks to give himself to God and delights in his being a gift of God.

Exaltation may last an hour, but its flower, joy, the jewel that wins the hearts of all men, lasts forever. The garnered fervors of great moments can flare forth again and again. In the new light that came from the Baal Shem's fire, the pressures of daily life no longer encumbered. People made of sighs and tears were re-made into people of awe and joy.

Obedience to God in carrying out His commandments is fundamental to existence. The Baal Shem, however, thought that obedience without passion, conformity without spontaneity was but a skeleton, dry, meager, lifeless. A Jew should serve God with ardor. It was necessary, vital, to have fire in the soul. Far from resembling an iceberg or a glacier, one's inner life is a hotbed of sinful desires, occasionally mixed with cruelty and self-destructive passion—a hotbed that can be purged only with Holy fire.

When we face temptations, our power of will grows weak and all reasonable restraints break down. It is then that the ability to be aflame with the thought of God and His love may burn out lowly desires and give our will new strength.

The result of Hasidic teaching was a new style of living. A Hasid prays, studies, and lives in exaltation. One can see and feel the fire in his every feature, his speech, his bearing. When he hears an inspiring word, he gives himself up to ecstasy. His emotions are not hidden in some compartment of his mind. His soul shines. It is suffused with light.

The new movement of dissenters from classical Hasidism, which developed around the Holy Jew of Pshyskhe, accepted the demand of the Baal Shem for fire and spontaneity but were wary of giving way to religious extroversion. Fire is by nature indiscreet; it tends to show off. But nothing is as obnoxious as demonstrative piety. This is why the Hasidic norm underwent modification. No worship without concealment. A flame there must be, but it should burn chastely and privately, deeply hidden within the individual. Let there be no outward show of ardor. When you are carried away by enthusiasm, veil it.

Reb Bunam, the Kotzker's teacher, warned that ecstasy could lead to self-deception. When it enveloped a man, he soon assumed that he had become an accomplished Hasid; his heart was on fire for God, the whole world seemed like a void, and he deemed himself uplifted. But in reality, exaltation was a temptation sent by Heaven. The flame burned for a while. What remained? Mere ashes and smoke.

The Kotzker scorned Hasidim who experienced moments of ecstatic fire and then returned to their former selves, sober and gray. He perennially demanded firmness, consistency.

The greatness of the patriarch Abraham did not consist in his readiness to sacrifice his son at the call of the Lord. Anyone would have been aroused to ecstasy and done God's bidding. But Abraham's exaltation had not subsided even on the third day after God's command. He had had time to reflect by then.

It is not enough to do a good deed. One must be involved in it wholeheartedly. Each action should be performed with life and soul, with every limb, with all one's vitality.

When the children of Israel sinned, and God commanded, *Each shall pay the Lord a ransom for his soul . . . This they shall give: half a shekel* (Exodus 30:12–13), Moses asked, "Master of the universe, who can give a ransom for his soul?"

The Holy One, blessed be He, replied, "It is not as you think!

But: *This they shall give . . ."* He brought forth from under the Throne of His Glory something like a coin of fire and showed it to Moses, saying: *"This they shall give."* [1]

Thus, when the levy is offered with fire, with passion, then and only then does it constitute a ransom for the soul, because a particle of it has been proffered, not just a coin.

In his youth a man is capable of serving God with passion. But as he ages, his ardor lags. Reb Henokh of Alexander therefore cautioned, "None of them shall defile himself" (Leviticus 21:1). Let no man defile his soul by growing dim or lukewarm. Let him constantly rekindle and fan the flame in his soul.

Other tzaddikim also called for a fire within. But the Kotzker demanded in addition that the flame be steady and burn at full force, though deeply concealed.

The Lord said to Moses: Command Aaron and his sons, saying: This is the law of the burnt offering. The burnt offering shall be on the hearth upon the altar all night until the morning, and the fire of the altar shall be kept burning on it (Leviticus 6:1–2).

The fire was to burn steadily *inside* the altar. The word "hearth" is written with a lowercase "h" (*mem* in Hebrew).

By contrast, a verse in Deuteronomy proclaims, "You must be Wholehearted with the Lord your God" (18:13). Here the word "wholehearted" is spelled with a capital "W" (*vav* in Hebrew). Wholeheartedness affects all of a man, whereas ecstasy must be concealed in his depths. The fire should not be displayed.

What do we mean by "fire"? Its nature is restlessness, constant motion. What is the good of nurturing an internal fire? "Why," said Reb Yitzhak Meir, "ecstasy burns up all meanness." He felt that open fervor could also be considered an achievement of the soul.

[1] *Pesikta Rabbati* 16, 7.

Reb Yitzhak Meir quoted the Psalm: "Fire goes before Him, and burns up His adversaries round about" (97:3). When a man carried his enthusiasm with him, extinguishing all his meanness, then "lightnings light up the world" (97:4). The radiance of the Sabbath would then shine through him. And if he approached the day in humility, saying, "Am I worthy of being related to the Sabbath?" the Sabbath itself would relieve his embarrassment.

Unconditional Joy

The Baal Shem Tov, like the Christian quietists, reached a holy indifference in which the individual accepted prosperity and adversity with equanimity. Yet he was far from demanding the suppression of all desire for joy, pleasure, or happiness. Unlike the quietists, he did not insist only upon passivity or a mortification of all desires; on the contrary, he revived the ancient Biblical spirit of joy.

Joy is wisdom, preparation for prophecy, said Reb Bunam, voicing an intrinsic, unique quality of Jewish spirituality frequently stressed in Biblical and post-Biblical literature. This is indeed a peculiar, unheard-of fact. Normally the attitudes in accord with religious existence all over the world are humility, contrition, obedience, sorrow, remorse.

Joy is not a theological category in the teachings of most religions and is never discussed in handbooks of theology. Those who are overwhelmed by spiritual solemnity and are unable to forget that faith lives in a constant state of tension between ignominious death and eternal life find it difficult to comprehend the Jewish conception. Even within Judaism the teaching that joy lies at the very heart of worship, that it is a prerequisite for piety, is a scandal to the dullards and a stumbling block to the bigots.

And yet a sense of humor is also a necessary ingredient of Jewish faith. Under the impact of exile and persecutions throughout the generations, the Jewish experience of gladness and delight was reduced to sorrow and grief. A spirit of moroseness hung over the people. The constant admonitions of Hasidic pioneers against the people's gloom and melancholy prove how sullen and depressed the prevailing mood must have been.

The Baal Shem proclaimed joy to be the very heart of religious living, the essence of faith, greater than all other religious virtues. He and his disciples banished melancholy from the soul "and uncovered the ineffable delight of being a Jew." God is not only the creator of earth and heaven. He is also the One "who created delight and joy."

When we talk about the need for joy, says one of the great Hasidic masters, we do not mean the joy that comes from fulfilling the commandments; for the ability to feel such spontaneous joy is the privilege of illustrious souls, and one cannot expect it of every Jew. What we mean then is the banishment of sadness. A Jew who does not rejoice in his Jewishness is ungrateful toward Heaven; it is a sign that he has failed to grasp the meaning of being born a Jew. Even lowly merriment originates in holiness. The fire of evil can better be fought with flames of ecstasy than through fasting and mortification.[1]

[1] See A. J. Heschel, *The Earth Is the Lord's* (New York, 1950), pp. 75f.

The following story in the Talmud was particularly cherished by the Baal Shem.

Rabbi Beroka used to visit the marketplace where the Prophet Elijah often appeared to him. It was believed that he appeared to some saintly men to offer them spiritual guidance.

Once Beroka asked the Prophet, "Is there anyone here who has a share in the world to come?"

He replied, "No . . ."

While they were conversing two men passed by, and Elijah remarked, "These two men have a share in the world to come."

Rabbi Beroka then approached and asked them, "What is your occupation?"

They replied, "We are jesters. When we see men depressed, we cheer them up . . ."

Joy in Spite of Anguish

For four generations the message of the Baal Shem had stirred and captured the hearts and minds of a major part of the Jewish people, and the time was ripe for a renewal of the Hasidic movement. Whether the Kotzker consciously strove for the renewal or for the termination of the movement in its original form, it is certain, as I have said, that he was aware of his deviation. Indeed, the inner dialectic of the movement called for something more than the benign rapturous joys preached by many Hasidic rebbes. New challenges had to be faced. He regarded as irresponsible joys that disregarded the dark abyss even as men stood at its brink.

What the Kotzker taught was joy not in disregard of but in spite of anguish. To experience absurdity was a prerequisite for renewal. It was out of the caldron of boiling absurdities that the striving to proceed beyond them was born and sustained.

In contrast to the Baal Shem, the Kotzker had a cloud in his face and gloom in his heart. When, as a young man, he went to seek spiritual guidance from the Seer of Lublin, the latter said to him, "I am not pleased with you. The way you have chosen leads to melancholy . . ."

The venerable master's disapproval made little impression upon the determined young rebel. Was melancholy the worst defeat that a soul might court? Did not an uglier, a viler danger lurk in the unconditional fervor and joy so widely preached? Was a man not likely to slip from joy to complacency and sink into a quagmire of indifference and decay?

When a person experiences the shipwreck of his noblest expectations, he becomes aware of a disinclination to allow any ferment in his mind. The Kotzker, who lived in a state of spiritual agitation, thought that melancholy was a spiritual necessity. Surely it was a way for a restless soul to come to terms with the human condition.

Kierkegaard—who, as we shall see, shared many insights with the Kotzker—once wrote:

My melancholy searches in every direction for the dreadful. Then it grips me with its terror. I cannot and will not flee from it, I must endure the thought; then I find a religious composure, and only then am I free and happy, as spirit. Although I have the most enthusiastic apprehension of God's love, I have also an apprehension that

He is not a dear old grandpa who sits in heaven and indulges people, but that in time and in temporal existence one must be prepared to suffer everything. It is my conviction that it is . . . [an] habitual cowardice or indolence, to think that one enjoys a special relationship to God . . . Bustling spiritual and worldly expedients for keeping the terror away are a disgust to me, because these expedients have no understanding of what the terrible is . . . He who wills in a religious sense must have a receptive attitude to the terrible, he must open himself to it, and he has only to take care that it does not stop halfway, but that it leads him into the security of the infinite.[1]

Faith Cannot Come of Itself

Hasidism is falsely reproached for having disparaged the value of Torah study. It merely belittled the view that studying Torah was enough. The Baal Shem Tov restored and strengthened an old Jewish precept whereby learning without awe was of questionable value.

One of the celebrated sages proclaimed, "Woe to him who has no courtyard yet makes a gate for the same." Learning is a gate whereby one enters the courtyard, the life of piety and awe. Woe to him who builds the entry without concern for the court itself. Study, learning must coincide with a striving for intimate attachment to the Lord. It must be raised to the level of prayer, become a kind of praying, not merely understanding.

It is easier to study than to pray. It is harder to become a God-fearing person than a scholar. The evil spirit permits learning Talmudic dialectics because such mastery satisfies a man's vanity and adds to his prestige; but when one sits down to the books dealing with moral conduct or to the *Shulhan Arukh,* the evil spirit interferes because such study might arouse awe in him.

Moreover, the Baal Shem Tov believed with many Kabbalists that the study of Talmudic dialectics was of a lower order than that of mysticism. When years are spent studying Gemara,[1] we forget the vital issue: to find out who God is. While many people were inclined to be impressed with any pious busybody or erudite bookworm, the Baal Shem was drawn to those who craved for God in secrecy, who lived by prayer, immersed in faith.

Faith cannot come of itself; one must work at it. Hasidism contended that Mitnagdim [2] devoted all their energies to accepting the responsibility of the commandments, an easier task, but did little toward assuming the burden of the Kingdom of Heaven. Reb Bunam claimed that one had to strain in all directions to learn how to take on this burden.

The first section of the *Shema* [3] speaks of our duty to love God with all our heart, all our soul, and all our strength. The second section speaks of our duty to observe His precepts carefully. The first section says, "And these words . . . you shall

[1] That part of the Talmud containing arguments and discussions, usually studied in conjunction with the Mishnah, which is the collection of laws composed by Rabbi Judah ha-Nasi in the third century, constituting the basis of the Talmud.

[2] "Opponents", i.e., the avowed opponents of Hasidism.

[3] The twice-daily recitation of the declaration of God's unity.

impress them upon your children." The second states, "You shall teach them unto your children." The first calls for awe, the second for obedience. The latter can be learned, but awe and fear of Heaven, the burden of the Kingdom, must be carved into the heart.

The first Hasidim made the painful discovery that zealous study alone did not purify man. It was possible to devote oneself to the Torah and remain sinful. One could be a scholar and a scoundrel at the same time.

Reb Yitzhak Meir, the renowned Gaon, once said, "During the period of the Baal Shem Jews studied day and night. But they were smug, and he could not endure it."

Reb Mendl of Primishlan and Reb Pinhas of Koretz, outstanding pioneers of the Hasidic movement, sharply criticized scholars who concentrated exclusively on Talmudic dialectics, neglecting the cultivation of awe. According to them, the greater the scholarship, the less fear of Heaven there was.

Reb Yaakov Yosef of Polonnoye, a disciple of the Baal Shem, berated scholars who devoted themselves to studying Gemara and its commentaries in order to boast of their learning and acumen. The "Great Maggid," Reb Dov Baer of Mezeritch, himself a distinguished scholar, looked upon such men with contempt.

Torah and God

Jews have often loved the Torah with homage due to God Himself, acting as if God and Torah were one and the same. Although such identification is hardly ever expressed, few have had the audacity to say that this was not the case.[1]

Such devotion, while greatly extolled, carries danger within it, according to Rabbi Judah Loew of Prague, known as "the Maharal" (1525–1609). Since one cannot be in love with two realities at once, a great love of Torah excludes a *simultaneous* love of God. The Maharal was the first to discuss this point of tension in the introduction to his book *Tiferet Israel (The Splendor of Israel)*.

The Maharal's books were greatly loved, both in Pshyskhe and in Kotzk. The Kotzker accepted his thesis that a distinction had to be made between God and Torah. A Hasid lived in fear of the Lord, he said, a Mitnagid in fear of the Code of Law (*Shulhan Arukh*).

Stressing the inequality or disparity of Torah and God, the Baal Shem insisted that a man could devote himself to Torah yet remain distant from God. It was beautiful to be submerged in Torah study, but the most urgent goal was to be close to God.

According to a legend, the Baal Shem commented one day upon a scholar immersed in study, "He is so deeply absorbed that he

[1] See, e.g., *Zohar*, III, 73a. See also A. J. Heschel, "God, Torah, and Israel," in *Theology and Church in Times of Change* (Philadelphia, 1970), pp. 71–90.

has forgotten there is a God in the world." Awe of Heaven was above learning, he taught. Though it was necessary to render particular aspects of life holy by carrying out commandments and doing good deeds, the primary aim was to hallow the whole man.

It is often tacitly assumed that Torah is the highest source of wisdom and that all divine mysteries are revealed in it. Yet some Jewish mystics insisted that the Torah as we know it is but a reflection of the hidden wisdom and that only some of its mysteries have been revealed.

Reb Bunam cited an early source that only three men—Abraham, Job, and Hezekiah—grasped the nature of God by their own efforts, without studying Torah. He explained how: "Their souls sprang from *a source higher than the Torah,* and thus they were able to comprehend the nature of God without its help."

In contrast to the Maharal's thesis that involvement with Talmudic dialectics interfered, for moments at least, with a man's wholehearted attachment to God, Reb Bunam believed that the study of the Talmud "restored the soul" (Psalms 19:8). Without the Gemara, he felt, life in exile would have been unbearable even for one single hour.

This view about the relative importance of God and Torah was more sharply defined by Reb Mordecai Yosef of Izbica, a disciple of the Kotzker in his formative years. He did not question the sanctity and exaltedness of the Torah but accentuated that God's majesty was more sublime. It stood above Law, above halakhah. He maintained that there was a distinction between the Torah and the Lord, that one could not really comprehend the Torah unless the thought of God was present. That was why at times the Torah had to be laid aside for the sake of God, as indicated in the Psalms: "There is a time to act for God; set aside the Torah" (119:126).

Many a problem could not be unraveled through study of the Law. Intuition was needed to decide upon them. If a man was [in spirit] descended from Abraham, Isaac, and Jacob, whose lives were dedicated to Heaven, he might rely upon his intuition where the traditional laws did not offer adequate guidance. When the Torah's wording was ambiguous and the course of conduct therefore uncertain, Reb Mordecai Yosef counseled that we should put ourselves in God's hands, for He would open our eyes.

There is a famous saying by Rabbi Shimon ben Yohai: "A time will come when the Torah will be forgotten." [2] This generally filled a Jew with nightmarish dread. What would become of us without the Torah! But Reb Mordecai Yosef interprets the saying thus:

There is no need to fear that the Torah will be forgotten. A time will come when it will no longer be possible to learn God's will by studying Torah. But that will be a time of illumination, when all things shall have regained their pristine quality, when men's hearts shall be so firmly attached to the Lord that they will not be capable of straying from His will.

When might this be? Surely after the Messiah's coming?

2 *Shabbat* 138b.

Study Is a Means to an End

The published works of the Baal Shem Tov's period give the impression that the Jewish community was almost addicted to the fancy needlework of Talmudic dialecticians. Ransacking the mind for fantastic logical possibilities was a favorite parlor game. In numerous books, anthologies, and sermons, authors wrestled with farfetched inconsistencies in, for example, the Code of Maimonides or other authoritative sources that contradicted each other. The dramatic or poetic tales of the Bible were transposed into sophisticated logical yarns. Stories of human passion were read as subtle debates and deliberations concerning Jewish Law.

The scholars pondered self-created problems—for instance, how to reconcile a legal opinion held by an authority of sixteenth-century Poland with a view implied in an argument of Laban the Aramite in his dialogue with his son-in-law, the Biblical patriarch Jacob. Both problems and solutions were ingenious, incisive, but empty, barren. Sermons were as dull as ditch water, without a tinge of emotion. While Jews were in trouble and suffering all manner of pain, the rabbis were busily treading water. Their arguments could no more help a worried man than an *afikomen* could cure the ague.

To used modern terminology, the Baal Shem repudiated an approach that took knowledge as an end in itself. He believed the aim of Torah study was to acquire nobility of character, integrity, and good habits. He could not endure well-fed, self-satisfied intellectuals who cared little about the poor. Arrogance and snobbery disgusted him. He therefore brought about a transformation in the history of Torah study. His words enchanted the listener. They illumined and inspired. He offered insight, warmth, radiance in place of mental fireworks.

For centuries it was a certainty in every mind that study was the most rewarding occupation. Through the most popular lullaby, children learned in their cradles that Torah was the most precious property, the best possible commodity. To be a learned man placed you ahead of others.

Yet the Baal Shem Tov and his disciples set awe above learning. What good was a head crammed with knowledge if the heart was haughty? Could wine be any good if fermented in a contaminated vat? In this connection Reb Pinhas of Koretz once boldly remarked:

Today's generation doesn't learn as much Torah as earlier ones, because it lives in great awe of the Lord. Previously there was less awe, and therefore people devoted themselves more to Torah study. There are still places now where they study a great deal—no awe there!

The Baal Shem Tov believed that hard work was needed to attain awe. Dutiful study was not enough.

It was important for rabbis and scholars to dedicate themselves to people and to exert their influence upon them, rather than to remain apart and study with zeal. "Great is the study of Torah because it leads to action," says the Talmud. Study should be a means, not an end in itself.

Rabbi Hanina ben Dosa used to say, "Anyone whose deeds exceed his wisdom, his wisdom shall endure; anyone whose wisdom exceeds his deeds, his wisdom shall not endure."[1]

1 Sayings of the Fathers, III, 12.

According to a tradition preserved in manuscripts, the early disciples of the Baal Shem, and perhaps he himself, were concerned lest their wisdom exceed their deed. As soon as one of them acquired a new insight, he was eager to follow it up with a new good deed.

He Wanted to See Alfasi

Torah study is a way of coming upon the presence of God, the Baal Shem taught. A man learning Torah should feel like a son who receives a letter from his father and is most anxious to know what he has to say to him. The letter is precious to him upon every rereading, as if his father stood there beside him.

"I" (*anokhi*), the first word of the Ten Commandments, consists of four letters in Hebrew and forms an acrostic for the words "I give Myself in written form," it is said in the Talmud. God has given Himself in the words, and man must learn how to encounter Him. He is concealed in the letters, and through their mystical contemplation one can discover His light. The purpose of immersing oneself in the Torah is not only to understand its rational meaning but also to become united with the divine presence therein.

Persuaded that one should be capable of learning more from people than from books, the Baal Shem sought to add a personality dimension to the study of the Talmud, a great part of whose contents consists of views of sages cited by name. He urged students to seek communion with the sages as well as comprehension of their ideas. Thus, it was maintained that, while learning "Abbaye said" or "Rava said," one should see Abbaye and Rava [1] (as well as understand their utterances). One had to live with them, to enter their minds and souls, not just grasp their thoughts.

Reb Mendl of Rymanov, born in Neustadt on the Vistula in 1745, as a young man studied at the House of Learning established by Daniel Yafe in Berlin. He gathered knowledge with burning eagerness, but after a while a yearning for something more began to glow in him. He was no longer satisfied to master a Talmudic discourse intellectually, to comprehend a pointed hypothesis, or to make a fine distinction between two opinions. He refused to believe that his soul could reach no higher than an understanding of the Gemara's arguments, that there were no deeper perceptions to be gleaned from the Torah. He wanted both head and heart to be involved in his studies but did not know how to achieve this.

According to the Jerusalem Talmud, "He who quotes a tradition in the name of a sage should at the same time be able to sense his presence."

When Reb Mendl of Rymanov pored over Alfasi,[2] he wanted to be able to see him, to experience the Rabbi himself. Having striven in vain, he wept with anguish and fell asleep; whereupon Alfasi appeared to him.

"Mendl, you are to go to Elimelekh," he said.

[1] Abbaye and Rava developed Talmudic dialectic to its peak in the first half of the fourth century.
[2] Rabbi Isaac Alfasi (1013–1103), known as "Rif," the author of the most important Code of Jewish Law prior to the work of Maimonides.

Reb Mendl left the House of Learning to search for this unknown Elimelekh. He journeyed from one city to another, from one village to the next. When he arrived in Galicia (a province in Poland), he heard that a great tzaddik called Reb Elimelekh lived in Lishensk, a great distance away. He hired himself out to a coachman who was driving to Lishensk. Weary and in tatters on his arrival, hungry and freezing, he barely managed to reach the Rebbe's house. The secretary refused to admit this person who looked liked one of the beggars that had lately pestered the Rebbe. But Reb Mendl tore past him into the house.

"Who sent you?" asked Reb Elimelekh.

"Alfasi did."

Reb Elimelekh raised his bushy eyebrows, looked at the stranger for a long moment, then said, "You can stay with me."

That is how Reb Mendl became a disciple of Reb Elimelekh. When his master died, Reb Mendl became the Hasidic leader of Galicia.

Love of Israel Precedes Love of Torah

The Baal Shem had the genius of discovering ways to live in accord with the world, with people. He thought of the holiness and beauty every man's soul contained, and whenever he met the plainest man, he would offer love first and only then ask him to divest himself of the shackles that prevented him from being in love with God.

He related to people as if everybody were his equal. The glory in being human, in being a Jew, enchanted him. He could discover jewels in every soul, and wherever he went he sought to foster conciliation.

The most important prerequisite of love is appreciation. The Baal Shem, who treasured the excellence of Israel, fostered a new appreciation of the people, opening up fresh wells of love.

Love of Israel is an old concept, mentioned in the Talmud as a quality possessed by Moses, the greatest of all Prophets. The Baal Shem's decisive contribution was that he raised it to a higher rank in the hierarchy of religious qualities. Judaism, as implied in the Zohar,[1] has three essentials: God, Torah, Israel. According to a tradition, the Baal Shem said, "I came to teach love of God, love of Israel, and love of Torah."

The change in order is important. In contrast to the view of many scholars that love of Torah should precede love for Israel, the people, the Baal Shem gives primacy to Israel: the Torah was created for the sake of Israel, not the other way around.

The test of love is in how one relates not to saints and scholars but to rascals. The Baal Shem was able to sense an admirable quality in every human being. In fact, he recommended a conciliatory attitude toward sinners and evildoers, true to his conviction that God loved all men. This concept was later expressed by Reb Aaron of Karlin in this way: "I should like to love the greatest tzaddik as God loves the lowliest villain."

The Baal Shem's influence on Hasidism was reflected in the eagerness of tzaddikim to befriend, even to feel love for people who had become estranged from faith and observance. They were

[1] "The Book of Splendor," the central work in the literature of the Kabbalah.

convinced that Jews who sinned also had a place of honor in God's world.

The Baal Shem related lovingly to sinners who were not arrogant and kept his distance from scholars who were. He explained his attitude:

Sinners who know that they sin are humble. Therefore the Lord remains close to them—who "abides with them in the midst of their uncleanness" (Leviticus 16:16). But he who is arrogant, though no evildoer, alienates God, for He says of him: "He and I cannot live together in the same world." [2]

The Seer of Lublin also preferred the sinner who knows that he does evil to the tzaddik who knows that he is a tzaddik. For the sinner who knows what he is faces the Truth, and God is Truth and is called Truth. But the tzaddik who is certain of his own virtue is mistaken, since "surely there is not a righteous man on earth who does good and never sins" (Ecclesiastes 7:20). Indeed, he is far removed from the Truth.

Reb Borukh [3] interpreted the Baal Shem's tenet thus: is a man who leaves the righteous path ever a total villain? Part of him remains honest and pure. "When I look at such a person," he said, "I sense what is good in him without seeing the evil."

The Baal Shem Tov established an important maxim: when we detect a mean quality in a man, we do so because we possess it ourselves. Heaven wants us to become aware of it, thereby hinting at the need for our repentance.

Jews had for generations firmly assumed that scholars and tzaddikim should be treated with deference, while the lowly, the untutored, could be readily ignored. The Baal Shem challenged this assumption. He knew that one could be a scholar and

[2] *Arakhin* 15b.
[3] Grandson of the Baal Shem Tov.

a scoundrel, and that the lowly man could perform an action that justified the existence of the whole world. An evildoer ought not to be abused, since his prayer or his mite of Torah was often more welcome to God than those of the tzaddik.

This thought, expressed by Reb Pinhas of Koretz and the Maggid of Kozhenitz (Polish: Kozienice), stems in essence from the Baal Shem Tov. There are two kinds of people: those who are wholly bad and those who are convinced that they are wholly good, who study diligently and mortify their flesh. But the latter experience no ecstasy; they do not really know how to study, to pray, or to carry out a commandment for the sake of Heaven. The difference between the two kinds of men is that the bad one may undergo a spiritual awakening and do penance, whereas there is no hope for the self-styled tzaddik. It will never occur to him to be contrite.

One day a man complained to the Baal Shem about his son. He had discarded the path of piety. His conduct had become un-Jewish.

"What shall I do, Rebbe?" he asked.

"Do you love your son?"

"Of course I do."

"Then love him even more."

"Even the most impious of men is as dear to me as your only son is to you," the Baal Shem Tov once said to a disciple.

When Reb Zusya of Hanipoli was in Mezeritch, he saw a man who had committed a serious transgression entering the Maggid's house. Reb Zusya was extremely upset that this man should have the impudence to stand in the Rebbe's presence without shame. The Maggid sensed what Reb Zusya was thinking and blessed him, so that from that day on he would see no evil even when a man acted dishonorably. He would only perceive that good might come of it.

The finer qualities of simple people were often valued and praised by the Baal Shem Tov and other tzaddikim, but only rarely in Kotzk. The Baal Shem's change of order, placing love of Israel before love of Torah, was not compatible with the Kotzker's scale of values. Reb Mendl would have followed the original order: God, Torah, Israel, as mentioned in the Zohar.

The Tzaddik Decrees, God Fulfills

An ancient belief maintains that events on earth are preordained in heaven, and that, despite their harshness, God's decrees are wise, just, and holy. Are such decrees irreversible? Is it within the power of man to contest them and to pray that they be revoked, as Abraham did when he pleaded for Sodom and Gomorrah? . . . Opinion is divided.

The Talmud recounts:

The people once turned to Honi ha-Me'aggel [1] and asked him to pray for rain. He prayed, but no rain fell. What did he do then?

He drew a circle and, standing within it, exclaimed, "Master, they believe me to be a member of Thy household. I swear by Thy great name that I will not move from here until Thou hast shown mercy unto Thy children."

[1] Renowned miracle worker in the period of the Second Temple (first century B.C.E.).

A light rain began to fall. Honi said, "It is not for this that I have prayed but for rain to fill cisterns, ditches, and pools."

The rain then began to come down with great force. Again he spoke: "It is not for this gentle rain that I have prayed but for the rain of benevolence, blessing and bounty."

Then rain fell in the normal way. Thereupon the renowned scholar Shimon ben Shetah sent this message to him: "Were it not that you are Honi, I would have placed you under the ban, but what can I do unto you who importune God and He accedes to your request as a son importunes his father and he accedes to his request?"

Rabbi Shimon ben Shetah, one of the most prominent scholars of the Second Temple period, known for the vigorous action he took to eradicate witchcraft, looked askance at miracle working. He considered Honi's action impudent. Scholars who followed the teachings of Rabbi Yishmael did not accept the audacious belief that tzaddikim had a say in Heaven, and later generations made rare mention of it.[2]

However, during the period of the Amoraim [3] in Palestine, the belief that the tzaddikim could influence God's decisions was apparently widely accepted. "Tzaddikim govern the actions of the Holy One, blessed be He." "The tzaddik decrees, the Holy One fulfills." "The Holy One decrees, the tzaddik annuls."

Hasidism revived and emphasized the idea. The Seer of Lublin, for instance, believed that for a man in distress the tzaddik had to stand up to Heaven. Even if a decree had already been ordained, he had to nullify it then, according to the saying, "The Holy One decrees, the tzaddik annuls." The Seer inter-

[2] See A. J. Heschel, *Theology of Ancient Judaism* (Hebrew) (London and New York, 1965), Vol. II, pp. 360ff.

[3] Scholars who were active from the period of the completion of the Mishnah (ca. 200) until the conclusion of the Babylonian and Jerusalem Talmuds (end of the fourth and fifth centuries, respectively). During this period the Gemara originated.

preted the admonition "You shall not do *so* to the Lord your
God" (Deuteronomy 12:4) as follows:

The word "so" is an expression of consent in Hebrew.[4] Therefore,
"You shall not do so" also means "do not consent," which is to say, do
not accept evil dictates against Jewry.

In the books written during the first two generations of Hasidism, there is frequent reference to the tzaddik's power to nullify
a Heavenly decree. Faith in such power is a central theme in the
thought of tzaddikim and Hasidim.

Hasidim of Pshyskhe and Kotzk, however, regarded the matter
in a very different light. Although they did not deny the principle, they seldom mentioned it. This may also account for their
tendency to diminish the importance of miracles. To work a
miracle meant commanding Heaven to do something against the
laws of nature, and there was no inclination at these courts to
compel Heaven to intervene in worldly affairs at the expense of
natural laws.

All the statements minimizing or even derogating the significance of miracles indicate certainty that tzaddikim were capable
of performing them. The crux of the objection was this: if miracles could not engender faith, what was their use?

The Kotzker did not want to avail himself of the power "to
annul God's decrees."

One day Reb Mendl's personal attendant Reb Feivl tried to persuade him to bless an impoverished Hasid. The Kotzker replied, "If
such a blessing were to be given, it would surely bear fruit."

When Reb Feivl heard this, he said, "In that case, give the order
and let it come about."

But the Kotzker asked in a loud voice, "How can I go against
Heaven?"

4 See Numbers 27:7.

It is indeed true that the tzaddik decrees and God fulfills. "But where, for Heaven's sake," the Kotzker said at another time, "would reverence be?"

At the conclusion of the Day of Atonement we humbly acknowledge, "Who would dare to challenge Thy decisions?"

The Ideas of Mezbizh Live On in Kotzk

As a young man the Kotzker embraced Hasidism, joining its fellowship in defiance of his father, who opposed the movement. The message was new; its spiritual militancy, its uncommon freshness held great promise.

But as time passed, the Kotzker began to feel its decline. To his mind it was slipping from the right path. "They have made an abomination of Hasidic teaching," he said.

Many practices instituted by the Baal Shem Tov were upheld in Kotzk, such as receiving and counseling Hasidim, accepting petitions, and giving attention to individuals. This was done to spread love and awe. The Hasidism of Kotzk was also based on the importance of the disciple's attachment to his tzaddik. Yet there was a difference in the conception of the tzaddik's obligations toward his disciples.

One of the Baal Shem Tov's influential innovations was the Third Meal on the Sabbath. The two other Sabbath meals were for the good of both body and soul. The Third Meal was intended for the soul alone. A little food was eaten as a symbolic gesture, but the real aim was deep and prolonged meditation. The first two Sabbath meals were celebrated at home; family became a melody, peace a certainty. The Third Meal was observed in the synagogue in the fellowship of yearning, dreaming, worship, and contemplation, communal prayer. During certain visible rituals—the withdrawal of the Torah Scrolls from the Holy Ark, candles burning in the Menorah, the cantor chanting at his lectern—all members of the congregation could watch what was going on. During the Third Meal, however, there was nothing to watch. Worshippers sat in the gathering twilight, in near-darkness. The blessing was said, they savored a piece of bread and herring, sang soul-expiring melodies, and their capacity to absorb the inner light expanded.

The Sabbath was all precious, but the Third Meal yielded the most marvelous minutes of the day.

An ancient maxim states, "One hour of returning to God (or 'walking with God on earth') . . . is worth more than all of life in the world to come."

"Which hour is that?" the Kotzker asked and then answered his own question: "It is the hour of the Third Meal. The Sabbath is like the life to come, and the Third Meal is better than all of life to come."

A particular aspect of the Baal Shem Tov's teaching, later to be reinforced by the Kotzker, was the concept that Jewishness was not fulfilled by following the crowd. Everyone had his individual goal, his special service. Though each person was an integral member of the group, he should never forget his individual destiny. The Baal Shem Tov even taught the spiritual redemption of the individual—a most daring idea, since Jewish thought had always seen redemption in terms of the people and the world as a whole.

The Baal Shem stressed inwardness, the workings of the heart, thought, which lent importance to the personal situation of an individual. Not only did he emphasize the importance of praying that the Messiah come to redeem the entire people, the entire world, but he insisted that each man should strive for his own redemption as well.

The Hasidism of Kotzk was dominated by intense individualism. Little attention was paid to the people as a whole; the focus was upon the individual.

One requirement has always been central to Judaism: if an individual is to live like a Jew, he must be bound to the community. The Baal Shem Tov added a new and vital element: to live like a Jew, one had to be bound to a rebbe, a tzaddik. He repudiated the practice of mortification of the flesh, substituting in its place the Hasid's attachment to the rebbe. The term "Hasid" no longer meant a man who possessed only certain qualities, and adhered to a certain type of conduct. It came to denote a relationship—that of the Hasid to his rebbe. One never said he was a Hasid without adding whose Hasid he was. And this has remained a keystone of Hasidism.

There were certain noteworthy resemblances between the Kotzker's teaching and that of a disciple of the Baal Shem Tov, Reb Pinhas of Koretz. It is said that he strove for a life illumined and dominated by Truth for twenty-one years: for seven years he sought out the Truth, during the next seven he drove out all falsehood, and seven more he spent absorbing the Truth.

The Kotzker also agreed with Reb Pinhas that it was hard to resist the corruptions of wealth. "Now Abram was very rich [1]

---

[1] The Hebrew word, *kaved,* also means "heavy" or "irksome."

in cattle, silver and gold" (Genesis 13:2). Reb Pinhas commented that it was irksome for Abram to be rich.

Hasidism and Kabbalah

The Baal Shem—as well as many of his disciples—was immersed in Kabbalah. Indeed, it is difficult to comprehend his teaching without an adequate appreciation of Lurianic mysticism. Though he laid greater stress upon its existential appropriations than upon mastering its theology, he incorporated many of its elements into his preaching. Yet under his guidance the emphasis changed. It was important to live mysticism, not simply to know it.

Under the impact of the Hasidic movement, Kabbalah, which had for centuries been studied in conventicles and been understood only by the initiated, now reached and affected the minds and lives of a vast multitude.

The Baal Shem, according to several traditions, lived the life of a Kabbalist. His prayers and rituals were pervaded with mysterious acts. His own prayer book was filled with Kabbalistic meditations. He often carried out acts of *yihudim*, spiritual concentration, "mystical unification" within the sphere of the Divine, or meditations on the combination of sacred names. He often interlaced his discourses with Kabbalistic doctrines and recommended habits and modes of conduct which had until then been restricted to Kabbalists.

The great Maggid Reb Dov Baer of Mezeritch (died 1772), successor of the Baal Shem, wove the strands of Lurianic doctrine still further into the teachings of the Baal Shem. He studied the mysteries of the Kabbalah with his disciples and guided them in the meditations and *yihudim*. The doctrines of his disciple Reb Shneur Zalman, known as Habad, were almost entirely dominated by Lurianic Kabbalah.

The Seer of Lublin reminds us that there were differences of opinion between Rabbi Yitzhak Luria (1534–72), "the sacred Lion," who was a renowned Kabbalist, and the Baal Shem, and also between Rabbi Hayyim Vital (1542–1620), the principal disciple of Luria, and Reb Dov Baer. The Seer wrote, "We cannot decide between two masters, nor do we want to choose between two disciples."

In contrast to classical Hasidism, the teachings of the dissenters, the rebbes of Pshyskhe and Kotzk, contain no vestige of Lurianic theology. Though there are no explicit declarations, there are many indications of a clear intent to remove Kabbalistic speculation from Hasidic concern.

A Hasid was once appointed to blow the *shofar* or ram's horn on New Year's day. He began to make elaborate inner preparations in order to experience the intimate mystical contemplations prescribed for this moment by the Kabbalah. Whereupon Reb Bunam turned to him and said, "The prayer book says, 'S.B.' This abbreviation means, 'Simpleton, blow!' You need not indulge in contemplations. Just think 'blow' to carry out God's will."

Reb Bunam's opposition to Kabbalah was also expressed in a remark made to a disciple:

Ask a Kabbalist for the secret contained in the verse of the *Shema* in which two capital letters occur, making up the word "witness." According to the Law, the *Shema* may be recited in any language. But the letters would be different then, wouldn't they, and there would be no secret!

The Holy Jew displayed an ironical attitude toward the mystical contemplations relating to eating. The only thought you should have while eating, he said, was not to be a glutton. Reb Bunam's attitude was similar. According to him, the main point was to chew food properly . . .

Clearly, Reb Bunam had little respect for those who were preoccupied with the practice of Kabbalah. He once asserted about a renowned Kabbalist, "He knows no Kabbalah." When one of the Kabbalist's disciples showed surprise, Reb Bunam explained: "What I mean is that he doesn't know any Kabbalah the way a person doesn't know a certain town unless he's been there. Knowing Kabbalah means being there and seeing for oneself."

However, Reb Bunam accepted the principle that the chief task of a tzaddik was to carry out *yihudim* in everything he undertook, whether it was voluntary or mandatory. Each of our acts was so mysterious and of such grave significance that, though carried out by mortal man in this world, it would affect the worlds on high.

This particular pathway was adopted by the Seer's disciple, Reb Zevi Hirsh of Zhydatshov, and later by Rebbes Zevi Elimelekh of Dinev and Ayzik of Zhydatshov.

The Kotzker and Kabbalah

The Kotzker and Reb Pinhas were both thinkers with keen insight. They were also in accord that Kabbalah should not be studied with Hasidim.

There was no talk at all in Kotzk of "mystical unification" or of the upper heavens. The Kotzker's discourse was influenced by neither the Zohar nor the so-called writings of Rabbi Yitzhak Luria. No Kabbalists emerged from among the Hasidim of Pshyskhe and Kotzk. Many of them studied the works of the Maharal (Prague, ca. 1525–1609), but there was rare mention of any disciple's concern with the Lurianic writings.

Moses had performed the first act of unification, and it had resulted in the giving of the Torah at Sinai. The second would take place when the Messiah came. And no genuine unification was possible, the Kotzker believed, between these two points in time. If there were, the Messiah would have come by now.

One day a distinguished Hasid arrived in Kotzk on the Sabbath eve. It was too late for him to take the customary ritual bath, so he decided to practice spiritual ablutions by immersing himself in the appropriate Kabbalistic meditations. He did indeed feel cleansed.

At that very moment the door burst open and Reb Mendl stormed into the synagogue: "Who dares to meddle around with meditations and mysteries here? What impudence! Let him never do it again!"

There was absolutely no mention in Kotzk in the teaching of the Baal Shem of such important themes as "Nothingness and

Being," "the Mystery of the Divine," "the Presence of the Creator within His Creature," "the Redemption of the Sparks," "the Sublimation of Alien Thoughts," and "the Sweetening of Severity in its Root."

The Kotzk method was to intellectualize Hasidism. Reflection took precedence over emotion, analysis over imagination. Apocalyptic thoughts were kept at a distance. Rather than devote time to the mysteries of the worlds on high, one was to learn what to do about the confusion in his own soul.

In Kotzk fantastical or mystical realities were transmuted into human experience. A disciple of the Kotzker once said, "There are mysteries still to be disclosed. The Torah's secrets are so well concealed that even those who know them cannot articulate them. And even when they are revealed, they remain hidden."

That was why Reb Mendl wondered that the Mishnah forbade the teaching of the mystery of the Divine Chariot except to those who were "wise and who possessed an intuitive grasp." No matter how diligently they studied, the unqualified would not understand. If a man had not first been cleansed of his "crude corporeality," would it do him any good to acquaint himself with the Torah's secrets? No. He should not even be taught the rudiments, since he might become frustrated and weaken in his devotions. They were evidently not meant for his dull brain. If a person who has not been cleansed of his crudeness is taught something of the Torah's mysteries, he will not grasp their meaning and may conclude that there is no meaning to Judaism. He might even become an unbeliever. It is preferable, therefore, to tell him nothing.

The implication here was that the Kotzker opposed the study of Kabbalah unless a man was purified and ennobled. But did anyone ever reach this state?

Reb Mendl's attitude to Habad [1] further reflected his view of Kabbalah:

The adherents of Habad work their way down from above. They start with doctrines and reflections about the upper spheres, seeking to apply them to the human situation. We work in reverse.

The Kotzker and the Gaon of Vilna

Rabbi Elijah, "the Gaon" of Vilna (1720–97), leader of the harsh and passionate opposition to the Hasidic movement known as Mitnagdim, did not enjoy particular respect among most rebbes and Hasidim in spite of his enormous learning.

The Kotzker, however, felt and demonstrated tremendous veneration for him. He once described how at the Gaon's death some Polish rebbes lined up to prevent his entry into Paradise until eventually a few Tannaim [1] and Amoraim came along and begged them: "Let him in! He studied our words." Then they took him by the hand and led him into Paradise.

Rebbes Yitzhak Meir and Moshe Mihael of Byale (Polish: Biala) once sat in the synagogue arguing about a complicated Talmudic

---

[1] A school in the Hasidic movement founded by Reb Shneur Zalman of Lyady (1745–1831), which taught theosophical doctrine on the concepts of God, the world, and man.
[1] Masters of the Mishnah before 200.

commentary. Suddenly the Kotzker entered and said bluntly, "According to a correction by the Gaon of Vilna, the whole problem raised in the commentary is irrelevant."

He promptly went back to his private room. The two rebbes began to look up the Gaon's comment. Just as suddenly the Kotzker returned, saying, "And according to the explanation of the pilferer of Vilna, the problem of this commentary has already been solved."

Everyone was astonished. Whereupon the Kotzker explained, "When God gave Moses the Torah, He revealed all the possible interpretations that future generations would come upon. Several souls hid behind Moses and eavesdropped, hearing everything. One of these pilferers was the Gaon of Vilna."

In contrast to Hasidim in Volhynia, who talked with bitterness about the Gaon of Vilna, Reb Bunam of Pshyskhe spoke of him without rancor and occasionally with irony.

One Sabbath, during the Third Meal, the soul of Reb Bunam ascended to the Seventh Heaven. There he heard the Gaon of Vilna being asked why he had been so unfair in his feuds with the Hasidim.

"My intentions were honorable," he answered naïvely. Whereupon the Heavenly household shook with laughter.

Reb Abraham of Sokhatshev (Polish: Sochaczew), the Kotzker's son-in-law, highly praised the Gaon and ended the story about his extensive scholarship in the following way: "His erudition was immense. Imagine how much greater he would have been if he had accepted the authority of the Maggid of Mezeritch!"

Hasidim have said that the Kotzker was a chip off the Gaon himself, and that his soul came into the world to make amends for the Gaon's animosity toward the Hasidic movement. Yet the Kotzker was one of the few major Hasidic figures to express great esteem for the Gaon of Vilna. Indeed, they were somewhat alike. Both lived in solitude, cut off from the world.

The Gaon would not receive people in order to save all his time for his studies. When his sister came to see him after an absence of twelve years, he said to his attendant, "Tell her we'll see each other in the next world. I have no time for such meetings here."

The Kotzker's attitude was somewhat similar.

Yet the two men differed in their essence. The Gaon waged war on Hasidism. The Kotzker carried on a battle against ulterior motives and vested interests, against falsehood and hypocrisy. The Gaon engaged in corrections of classical texts, while the Kotzker devoted himself to the improvement of souls, the elevation of worlds beyond. The Gaon attained tranquillity through Torah study; the Kotzker delved into spheres where spiritual volcanoes erupt. His reward was restlessness and agitation.

PART II

❖❖❖❖❖❖

The Kotzker and Kierkegaard

The Affinity of Strangers

W H E N, long ago, I began to read the works of Kierkegaard, the father of modern existentialism, I was surprised to find that many of his thoughts were familiar to me. I realized that a number of his perspectives and basic concerns had reached me from the teachings of the Kotzker. Two of his adherents had profoundly influenced me in my youth.

Kierkegaard is world-famous. The Kotzker is hardly known; his remarkable insights have been disregarded.

The Kotzker was born in Goray, Poland, in 1787 and died in 1859. Kierkegaard was born in 1813 in Copenhagen, Denmark, and died in 1855. By the time Kierkegaard published his first book, *Either/Or,* in 1843, the Kotzker had withdrawn from the world, and he lived in isolation until his death.

Neither man knew the other. Had they met, they would hardly have understood each other. In their upbringing, religious needs, and commitments, their scholarly interests, their ways of living, they were totally dissimilar. The Kotzker immersed himself in the study of Talmud and its dialectics; Kierkegaard was steeped in Western philosophy.

The similarity of their concerns is all the more striking because of their profound heterogeneity, rooted in the differences between Judaism and Christianity. Their affinity is so impressive that it must have been elicited by requisites inherent in their respective traditions.

The parallels to be discussed here are all in the realm of theology. For the problems of philosophy to which Kierkegaard richly contributed lay entirely outside the scope of the Kotzker's world.

This book is a study in depth-theology. It discusses moments, battles, situations rather than doctrines or beliefs; confrontations of the conscience with God rather than summaries of theology; involvements and appropriations rather than rituals or recollections. In short, this study will deal with self-reflection rather than speculation.

Theologically—in dogma and ritual—the Kotzker and Kierkegaard were worlds apart. Particularly, the central belief in the Founder of Christianity was objectionable to the Kotzker. Yet, though their points of departure and their contexts were basically different, the problems they confronted on the level of living their commitment, on the level of *depth-theology*, were often the same. The two resemble each other in many of their inner situations—in depth-experiences, in modes of concern, in earnest intensity. Creed and commitment are final; but how does one live one's creed? How does one exercise one's ultimate commitment? Neither was satisfied to accept a definite, final commitment, once and for all. The issue was: how does one renew his commitment day after day? Man lives in time, and there is no finality, no standstill in existence.

Human personality, the Kotzker and Kierkegaard insisted, was never to be interpreted as a simple, static entity. The self was always in motion. Because it lacked permanence, because it was in conflict with itself and passionately concerned with itself, the existence of the self was fraught with danger. The great task was to perpetuate one's condition to challenge it.

To many people the inner life is a no-man's-land. To Kierkegaard and the Kotzker it was of the deepest concern.

Being a Jew, thought the Kotzker, was an infinite process. All conclusions were but a premise. "He who thinks that he has finished *is* finished," he said. Self-contentment was a sign of defeat. Life was the battleground of ongoing effort and tension.

A major phase of the struggle was to disentangle oneself from enslavement to the self. The inexhaustible intransigence of self-interest bore the poison that destroyed individuality and freedom. For the Kotzker, one became an authentic Jew only when he moved out of the prison of self-interest, responding with abandon to Heaven's call. He who remained deaf to it was devoid of faith and lived a farce, for to have faith meant to forget the self, to be exclusively intent on God.

Whereas Kierkegaard left behind a vast number of writings affording insights into an exceedingly rich inner life, the Kotzker is known only by his brief sayings. Kierkegaard dealt with a host of problems, while the epigrams preserved in the name of the Kotzker reflect a limited scope.

Scrutinizing the life of faith with fierce earnestness, neither man was eager to produce fixed doctrines. Rather, they sought to engender new attitudes and sensibilities. Their legacy is not a set of final tenets but a limitless challenge.

Endemic to all traditional religion is the peril of stagnation. What becomes settled and established may easily turn sour. Faith is replaced by creed, spontaneity by hackneyed repetition. Assaults like those launched by Kierkegaard and the Kotzker are acts of liberation.

Both preached alienation from the world as a basic require-

ment. In his contempt for the self-centeredness of man, the Kotzker exacted the abandonment of all self-interest. Such a demand
may seem disturbing and absurd. Yet in our age, which threatens
to destroy the world and man with it, these demands could serve
as important warnings.

Both men leaped toward an extravagant level of spiritual being, where most people could not follow. Kierkegaard ascended
to a Christianity conceived as absurd paradox. The Kotzker rose
to perpetual self-transcendence combined with utter abnegation.

What is their pertinence today? Their common impact is to
challenge our delusions, our certitude and complacency, to overwhelm us and leave us disturbed. As gadflies, not models for imitation, they deprive us of contentment and peace of mind.

Who Was Kierkegaard?

Søren Kierkegaard, Danish philosopher and theologian, was born
in Copenhagen in 1813, the youngest child of a wealthy, devout
Lutheran. The Danish word "kierkegaard" means "cemetery," a
fitting surname for his father, a man of gloom. Because of a secret sin committed in his youth, the old man believed that a curse
lay on his family. When his wife and seven of his children died
in quick succession, he felt sure that the curse was being fulfilled.

Søren himself believed that he was doomed to die young. After an unhappy childhood, he began his studies at the Copenhagen University at the age of eighteen. He lived the epicurean life of a student of means, dressing expensively and gaining the reputation of a wit. On his twenty-second birthday he was shocked by a sudden disillusionment about his father. As a result, he let his studies slide and gave himself up to a life of riotous dissipation. Three years later he underwent a deep religious experience, became reconciled with his father, and completed his degree.

At twenty-seven Kierkegaard became engaged to a seventeen-year-old girl, Regina Olsen. Though he loved her deeply, he felt that marriage was irreconcilable with his melancholy temperament and his inner calling to be a religious writer. So thirteen months later he broke off the engagement. This decision shook him intensely and affected his whole life. He found himself facing the alternative, "Plunge either into wild debauchery or into absolute religiousness." He chose the latter.

In the twelve years after 1843, the year of the publication of *Either/Or,* until his death, Kierkegaard produced the series of works which were to place him in the front rank of modern philosophical writers (though his influence was long postponed because he wrote in Danish). In 1844 he was subjected to a long and cruel attack by the comic Copenhagen paper *Corsair,* and in 1854 he launched his assault on the Established Church, for its accommodation of the Christian Gospel to human desires.

Kierkegaard died in 1855, a bachelor, at the age of forty-two. His writings comprise thirty books, plus the long, detailed journal that he began when he was twenty and which, in the Danish edition, runs over three thousand large-format pages.

Kierkegaard's Way

Modern man's greatest fault, Kierkegaard maintains, is his total self-reliance. It is his nineteenth-century delusion that he has progressed far beyond his ancestors. This conceit derives from egoism. There is but one remedy for him: despair. It is only when he finds himself in the deepest extremity that he understands his true condition; then, and only then, does he realize that his self-reliance is a delusion.

In such a crisis hopelessness forces man to contrition. Kierkegaard called this the "existential moment," for at that point man recognizes his helplessness, his dependency. At his existential moment, man is alone. Afraid to examine his ego, he escapes into society. Kierkegaard totally rejects this "solution," a "social religion," and stresses individual search and commitment instead.

Kierkegaard also opposes rational religion, for the reasoning faculty is incapable of a direct apprehension of God. God is always perceived by man as a paradox: the intellect is completely confounded by contradictions. All religious themes—conscience, sin, repentance, faith—are mystifying, beyond reason. Faith is not a sustained, comfortable state of consciousness but a painful, hard-won, and impermanent conviction—a breathing spell in the midst of an ongoing conflict.

God transcends the grasp of the intellect; rational evidence can never provide religious proof. An ethic that seeks to adapt itself to societal interests is not a religious ethic. Modern man is responsible to society; he thinks truth is established by majority opinion. For religious man, responsible to God, God alone determines Truth, and one should forgo judgments based on false, human criteria. God stands diametrically opposed to world.

Men were false—God was Truth: an unbounded abyss separated them. Both Kierkegaard and Reb Mendl the Kotzker understood the tragic void in the inner life of every individual, the tension between the ideal and the real—between what is expected and what can be accomplished.

The vast majority of people are satisfied with compromises, or they remain unaware that they are worshipping a multitude of gods, that their actions constitute a maze of contradictions. Kierkegaard, who despised compromise, declared that a person must maintain either one position or the other. For both the Lutheran and the Jew, the essential problem was the individual, his attitudes, his aspirations, his inner life. Both strove to re-create man whole.

Kierkegaard attacked the Hegelian system. For Hegel the Divine was immanent in nature. God was a process, working itself out in human history. God was present in the intellect and manifested Himself in the history of human thought. Religion and philosophy were closely related, for both aspired to a comprehension of the Absolute. Religious life, Hegel thought, fits neatly into the rational structures of intellect and intelligence.

Kierkegaard completely rejected the notion that God could be found in nature, in history, by the human intellect. He maintained that there was a limitless gap between God and world. He denied that true religion required social justice before all else.

There was only one solution to the human dilemma: man must abandon society. He must cease being social man and become superior, able to live in constant tension with himself, resisting his own inclinations so that he might eventually attain the highest excellence—that is, a comprehension of God. Thus, Kierkegaard's pessimism did not end in despair but, rather, in militant individualism and a radical theology.

Against Trivialization

The Kotzker apparently felt that overemphasis on strict adherence to patterns of religious behavior tended to obscure the individual's relationship to God. He never questioned the validity of the traditional pattern and regarded living by the Law as essential. Observance as a matter of routine, however, he considered odious.

What appalled the Kotzker was the spiritual stagnation of religious existence, the trivialization of Judaism. He scorned praying by rote. In opposition to the traditional preference for verbose recitation, he pleaded for brevity, even taciturnity. He dared to teach that the preparation for prayer surpassed prayer itself in spiritual value and found a basis for this reformative principle in an ancient tradition: "One should not stand up to say a prayer save in a reverent frame of mind. The pious men of old used to wait an hour *before praying* in order to concentrate their thoughts upon their Father in Heaven." [1] One would expect the phrase "*while* praying" to appear at the end of the sentence, since the goal is concentration in prayer. The intention, however,

---

[1] *Mishnah Berachoth* V. 1.

is to teach us that concentration should precede the act of prayer. Preparation for prayer is valuable in itself, perhaps more so than prayer itself.

In the Kotzker's synagogue one could see the disciples with prayer shawls over their shoulders walking up and down the room, their lips hardly moving. They gave the impression that they had not begun to pray yet and were still immersed in preparation. They prayed quietly. Suddenly they would stop, take off phylacteries and shawls, join one another at the table, and consume a little vodka together . . .

Even piety will not sustain the tedium of unlimited repetition. To preserve one's commitment with the intensity of its first ardor requires more than obedience. Surprise, spiritual adventure, the search for new appreciation—all these are necessary ingredients for religious renewal.

Judaism lived because it was both a religion of finality, conclusive and irrevocable, and a faith of commencement, of inauguration. To act as a Jew, thought the Kotzker, meant to make a new start upon the old road.

Self-inspection

Unlike medieval Jewish philosophers or the teachers of Habad Hasidism, who were concerned with metaphysical problems, such as the nature of the soul and ultimate reality; unlike the Kabbalists, who sought to explore the divine design of the spiritual cosmos, or the theologians, who speculated about the final purpose of history, Kierkegaard and the Kotzker turned their attention to their own lives. They pondered the design and the direction of their own existence: how was one to disentangle its confusions and establish a framework for it?

Other Hasidic masters counseled their disciples not to meditate excessively, not to brood on the meaning of matters of faith. They spoke in praise of simplicity: too much speculation led into dark chambers of doubt.

The Kotzker encouraged questioning, reflection; he was not afraid of doubts, of deliberations that might lead astray. To him simplicity could be dishonesty in disguise, naïveté—a camouflage for self-deception.

The problem was not whether to trust God but whether to trust one's acceptance of God. "For in much wisdom there is much pain, and he who increases knowledge increases pain" (Ecclesiastes 1:18). Said the Kotzker, "Though it pains you, increase your knowledge." [1]

To Kierkegaard and the Kotzker self-examination was a necessary prerequisite for religious integrity. One had to scrutinize one's motivations, purify one's intentions, always be on guard against the intrusions of the ego. The first step to self-knowledge was self-doubt.

Reb Mendl was not original in stressing the need for self-examination. But he felt that it had become a lost art. So he made training in self-examination an essential part of Hasidic instruction in Kotzk.

Both Kierkegaard and the Kotzker were concerned with the problem of truth as it pertains to self-knowledge. The problem is

[1] Yiddish lit. *Krenkn zollstu, ober vissn zollstu.*

acute because nothing is easier than to deceive oneself. As the mind grows sophisticated, self-deception advances. The inner life becomes a wild, inextricable maze. Who can trust his own motivations? his honesty? Who can be sure whether he is worshipping his own ego or an idol while ostensibly adoring God? There is a credibility gap within the soul, and it can be bridged only by the Spirit of Truth.

Certain issues brook no compromise. There is no greater discord than that between faith and hypocrisy. Religious commitment can never yield to mendacity. God as a pretext, piety as pretension are blasphemies. God is either of supreme importance or of none.

Kierkegaard and the Kotzker, each in his own way, illumined what was at stake in existence, what was decisive in an earnest attitude to God. They offered an answer to the question, what does God demand of me? Integrity first of all.

A disciple of the Kotzker complained to his master that he was unable to worship God without becoming aware of his pride. "Is there a way of praying that prevents the self from intruding?" he asked.

"Have you ever met a wolf while walking alone in the forest?"

"I have," he answered.

"What was on your mind at that moment?"

"Fear. Nothing but fear, and the need to escape."

"You see," replied the Kotzker, "at that moment you were afraid without being self-conscious or aware of your fear. It is in this way that we must worship God."

Of his disciples the Kotzker required that they shun self-deception assiduously and be at one with every word they uttered, with every deed they carried out. At the instant when God's will was done, the fulfillment and the person had to be one and the same. Just as one could not separate word or deed from the person, the person must in no way be disassociated from them. No one could eliminate whole periods of perplexity and ugliness, or even all occasions of vanity and egocentricity, from his life. But neither should the moments of honest sentiment, simple conviction, be ignored or downgraded.

In the Kotzker's thought the aim of reflection was to overcome the dualisms within a person. Self-knowledge implies honesty, wholeheartedness. Self-inspection is a necessary technique for the purpose of attaining Truth because we know that a person may sincerely believe something about himself that is not true.

The Kotzker did not seek to convert his disciples into quietists, who might exalt the motionless inner state of the soul. His ideal was *not* to dwell in tranquillity. His goal was to persuade people to cultivate repugnance for the material life, so that they could engage in elucidating the self. Undeceive yourself!

Pitfalls in the Soul

Most religious thinkers have assumed that the predicament of man is due to his failure to obey the Law or to adhere to orthodox beliefs. Kierkegaard and the Kotzker saw its source in the ubiquitous pitfalls within the soul, in men's amazing disregard of their presence. Therefore, they demanded alertness to the camouflage concealing these pits, as well as continuous awareness of the precariousness and hazards of the religious challenge. Beware, they said, of too much faith, of blind belief in dogmas, of a willingness to weed out doubts rather than face them, for these bespeak an unhealthy self-assurance precluding a reaching out for God.

With incisive radicalism, the Kotzker set out to knock down the façades that thinkers had spent centuries constructing to protect man from the shattering recognition of the disparity between his desire for reward and contentment and religious demands for holiness and contrition. The Kotzker refused to let men, shorn of their illusions, seek solace through study, good deeds, or the hope of deserving forgiveness through shallow repentance.

The "I" becomes the central problem in the Kotzker's thinking; it is the primary counterpart to God in the world. The sin of presumptuous selfhood is the challenge and defiance that God faces in the world.

The clamor for purity of heart, which has been heard throughout the history of Jewish reflection, often sounds like a signal of distress. "Create in me a clean heart, O God, and put a new and right spirit within me," says the Psalmist (51:12). This cry reverberates throughout the Bible and Jewish liturgy. But modern Judaism has not concerned itself sufficiently with the uncleanness of the heart.

Self-love or Inner Anonymity

Narcissus, a beautiful youth, loved no one till he saw his reflection in water and fell in love with himself. Finally he pined away and was turned into the flower that bears his name.

This intriguing tale describes a condition that affects most of us, touching upon the very nerve of our inner life. It is not self-love as such that is inherently wrong but, rather, its consequences: the lack of concern for others so easily fostered by self-love, the increasing isolation of the self. Self-love in its extreme form brings about man's destruction; it is its own enemy.

In its depths, egocentricity amounts to a demonic attempt to depose God and to remake the world in the image of man. Reb Mehel of Zlothshov interpreted the words in Deuteronomy, "I stand between God and you" (5:5) to mean that the "I" stands between God and man.

According to rabbinic understanding, the commandment "Love your neighbor as yourself" in no way excludes self-love. Self-love even takes precedence over love of his fellow when a man is in personal danger, maintained Rabbi Akiba.

The Son of Patura taught that if two men are traveling far from civilization and both will die if they share their remaining water, but one will survive if he drinks it all, it is better that both drink and die rather than that one should watch his companion die. Then Rabbi Akiba came and said: " 'that your brother may live with you' (Leviticus 25:36)—your life takes precedence over his life." [1]

[1] *Baba Mezia* 62d.

The words "with you" imply that your life comes first, but that he, too, has a right to life after yours is assured.

Augustine, too, interprets the commandment "Love your neighbor" to mean that love of neighbor is bound up with and, in some sense, conditioned by, love of self.[2]

However, the commandment to love God—"You shall love the Lord your God with all your heart, and with all your soul, and with all your might" (Deuteronomy 6:5)—is interpreted as demanding unlimited and unqualified love, even martyrdom, if a choice has to be made between loyalty to Him or denial of Him.[3]

Love of God as an absolute requirement asserts itself not only in moments of crisis but as a criterion of the ongoing impetus behind religious motivation. Is the ultimate incentive love of God, or is it hope for reward and fear of punishment that make a person do what is holy? This question, a concern in Judaism for more than two thousand years, agitated the Kotzker with special intensity. It was for him the test of integrity, of authenticity, of purity of heart.[4]

Single-minded seriousness is the mark of an honest man. The inner man, however, is not accessible to public scrutiny. Does not conformity to the rules of society necessitate a certain amount of insincerity? Any individual knows that, since private motives do not always correspond to external actions, he will tend to a degree of cynicism or, if endowed with moral sensitivity, to a split personality.

La Rochefoucauld (1613–80) maintained that Hell was ourselves, not others. Man's fundamental aberration was, in his view,

2 See H. Thielicke, *Theological Ethics*, Vol. I (Philadelphia, 1966), p. 338.
3 *Berachoth* 62b.
4 For an analysis of this problem and for older sources, see A. J. Heschel, *God in Search of Man*, pp. 387ff.

not merely transient selfishness, or a miscalculation of moral values, but the permanent and radical direction of his spiritual eye onto himself. There can be no religion when man becomes his own God but, equally, there can be no ethics when man's self occupies the place properly taken by some transcendental or, at least, objective standard. No standard, no moral certainty; and only the passions remain, ever changing, to obfuscate the light of reason.[5]

Love is self-love in disguise. But La Rochefoucauld offered a ray of hope:

If there be any love pure and free from admixture with the other passions, it is that which lies concealed in our inmost heart, unknown to our very selves.[6]

A considerable number of philosophers have agreed that self-interest was the ruling principle of human nature. According to one of them, Jeremy Bentham (1748–1832), "there has been among moralists a vehement disposition to shut out the influence of the self-regarding principle from the mind." Bentham continued, "Why this reluctance to admit, as a motive, that which is and must be the strongest of all motives—a man's regard for himself? Why is not self-love to be brought to the field?" Believing that all human interests were interdependent, he taught "the harmony and co-incidence of duty and self-interest, virtue and felicity, prudence and benevolence." Bentham's *Deontology* identified egoism with virtue:

It cannot be a man's duty to do what it is his interest not to do; [the immoral action is only] a miscalculation of self-interest . . . Though the idea of virtue may sometimes be included in the idea of

[5] A. J. Krailsheimer, *Studies in Self-Interest* (Oxford, 1962), p. 89.
[6] Maxime LXIX. *The Maxims of La Rochefoucauld*, translated by Walter Scott (London, 1901), p. 15.

sacrifice, or self-denial, yet these are by no means synonymous with virtue, nor are they necessarily included in the idea of virtue.[7]

Other thinkers have also asserted that egoism and altruism tend to coincide, and that selfish and non-selfish motives are often difficult to distinguish. Bishop Joseph Butler (1692–1752) maintained that no action was consistent with human nature if it violated either reasonable self-love or conscience; we could not justify any course of action that might be contrary to our happiness.

Self-love and benevolence, virtue and interest . . . are not to be opposed but only to be distinguished from each other . . .

Conscience and self-love, if we understand our true happiness, always lead us the same way. Duty and interest are perfectly coincident.[8]

Even those who have not shared the extreme position of La Rochefoucauld realize how easily self-esteem (*amour-propre*) turns to pride, and self-love (*amour de soi*) to selfishness.

It is a generally accepted view that a major motive of human endeavor is the desire to gain respect for the self from oneself as well as from others. Self-esteem and esteem from others are necessary to personal well-being. Such esteem becomes questionable, however, when it serves as an inducement for moral or religious action. The *raison d'être* of morality is that we yield to imperatives that overrule self-interest, particularly in situations where serving one's own interests is harmful to other human beings.

The task of overcoming self-centeredness is not easy. On the other hand, to give supremacy to the rules of self-interest under all circumstances must lead to what Thomas Hobbes (1588–

[7] *Deontology* (1834), I, 158f.
[8] *The Works of Joseph Butler*, edited by W. E. Gladstone (Oxford, 1896), pp. 25, 76.

1679) described as "the state of nature": "No arts, no letters, no society, and what is worst of all, continual fear and danger of violent death and the life of man solitary, poor, nasty, brutish, and short." [9]

While self-love or self-interest may be regarded as a legitimate component in the love of one's fellow man, it is incompatible with the love of God. If purity of heart is to will one thing, and that is to be the love of God, then desires must be excluded, particularly erotic desire, the Kotzker and Kierkegaard agreed. "Desire has its absolute object in the particular. It desires the particular absolutely." [10]

To satisfy one's own needs is entirely legitimate. But Judaism expects man to satisfy one's own interests for God's sake and then to transcend self-interest for the sake of God. However, it is also a tradition in Judaism to disparage religious acts motivated by self-interest, for spiritual existence dominated by striving for a reward is easily degraded to opportunism.

Disinterestedness, worship, and service from which all self-centeredness is purged and in which man seeks nothing in return, faith unalloyed—these were the central concerns of the Kotzker. He maintained that self-love as a motivation for religious acts was idolatry. The choice between love of God and love of self constantly confronts us, and the only way to steer clear of the latter is to live in militant opposition to the ego.

An important principle taught by the Kotzker was therefore to lead life incognito: spiritual existence was to be concealed. One had to will to conceal any spiritual effort. Piety was essentially to remain secret. The Kotzker urged his disciples to exert

[9] *Leviathan* (1651), Pt. I, Chap. 13.
[10] Kierkegaard, *Either/Or*, 1843, translated by David F. Swenson and Lillian Marvin Swenson (Princeton, N.J., 1944), Vol. I, p. 68.

themselves to the utmost, to be inventive and intrepid in preserving their incognito state.

Striving for inner anonymity was also emphasized by the great Hasidic sage Reb Pinhas of Koretz. The following tale about one of his disciples exemplifies the master's teaching:

Reb Raphael of Bersht was very holy, very humble, and very poor. His entire family lived in one room, which had to serve as kitchen, living room, bedroom, study, and reception hall. Many people who adored him came from various communities to ask him for guidance and blessing, to be taught and purified by his presence. He never shunned a soul and performed all services, study, prayer, and meditation while other people were around. There was one exception. He needed solitude for the Feast of Tabernacles service, when a prayer is said over the four species of plants.[11] This ritual is to bring about the union of the scattered Divine forces in the universe. On the eve of the festival he would prepare a corner in his room and isolate it with pieces of furniture. Then, on each of the seven days, he would seclude himself there to spend an hour with his Father in Heaven. This he did for many years.

One day Reb Raphael married off his daughter, and the young couple lived in the room too. The young son-in-law admired his father-in-law, watched his every action and habit, and tried to follow his ways. When he saw how he hid himself on the Feast of Tabernacles, he became curious. Knowing that all his religious duties were performed in the open, the young man concluded that this particular service must be of great significance. As Reb Raphael entered his private area, the young man followed him and peered through a crack.

The Rebbe, noticing this, came out to him and said, "My child, if I do not want to be present while I am saying the blessing over the plants, do you want to be present?"

11 The four different plants—the ethrog, the branch of the palm tree, the myrtle, and the willow of the brook.

The task was important, not who did it, asserted the Kotzker. If there should be a situation in which either you or I could do a *mitzvah,* I should let you do it. Personal salvation was of no concern.

When the Maggid of Mezeritch heard a voice from the Beyond say that he had dared to challenge a Heavenly decision and would therefore be deprived of his share in the life to come, he was overjoyed. He knew that from now on he would be certain to serve "for the sake of Heaven." "One hour spent in repentance and good deeds in this world is better than all of life in the world to come." [12]

"If Abraham," said Reb Aaron the Great, "were to suggest changing places with me, I would decline. What would the result be? I would acquire holiness as the great patriarch, and he would become a plain man called Aaron. Who would benefit from it? I. But what would it mean to God? Nothing, for in sum He would not have more than the one saint and the one simple man."

In praise of this principle Kierkegaard wrote: "Most people have no notion at all of the superiority by which a man transcends himself." And they have no inkling of the superiority that willingly assumes an incognito of such a sort that one seems to be something "far lowlier than he is." This is really self-abnegation in the service of God. Kierkegaard cites a Socratic maxim, that "in order to will the Good truly, one must avoid the appearance of doing it." [13]

[12] *Sayings of the Fathers,* IV, 22.
[13] *Training in Christianity,* 1850, translated by Walter Lowrie (Princeton, N.J., 1944), pp. 128*f.*
   Lowrie cites from Plato's *Republic,* Book II, Glaucon's argument: "There must be no seeming; for if the just man seems to be just, he will be honored and rewarded, and then we shall not know whether he is just for the sake of justice."

Subjectivity

In opposition to the Hegelian claim of objectivity or personal non-involvement in speculative thinking, Kierkegaard is an avowed subjective thinker, concerned with Truth for himself and for his concrete situation. He reiterates the assertion that Truth is subjectivity, that it can be acquired only through reflection, never as a finished product from somebody else's mind. Yet Truth thus arrived at may prove to be useless if it does not shape the thinker's existence, transform his personality. Once a religious man ponders religion, his thoughts reflect back upon the reflector. What about yourself? they seem to ask. It is one thing to think and another to exist in what is thought. The latter involves what Kierkegaard means by "double reflection": to become aware on second thought that the truth one has acquired "interests" one's existence. By "reduplication" he means *to exist in what one understands,* to be what one says—specifically, to reflect the truth in one's life. "The truth consists not in knowing the truth but in being the truth." [1]

Subjectivity, in Kierkegaardian terms, then, means an inner transformation, an actualization of inwardness. [2] Kierkegaard's "subjectivity" did not refer to the ancient principle of the Sophists that the individual or his judgment was the measure of all things. His intention was to stress that the authentic thinker was

[1] *Training in Christianity,* p. 201.
[2] See Kierkegaard, *Concluding Unscientific Postscript,* 1846, translated by David F. Swenson and Walter Lowrie (Princeton, N.J., 1941), pp. 553*f.*

the man who was concerned with the Truth for himself and his own concrete situation, not he who judged by objective standards. The mind is not a computer, we might say today, but, rather, the core of a person whose existence derives from and depends upon a transcendent God.

Kierkegaard did not mean to say that there was no objective standard of Truth. By stressing that Truth was subjectively conceived, he was insisting that the individual must appropriate Truth for himself. The category "for thee" with which *Either/Or* concludes—"Only the truth that edifies thee is truth for thee"— was basic to his thinking. In the same way, the *for me* or *unto me* was important to the Kotzker. The central act at a Jewish wedding ceremony is the groom's saying to the bride: "Behold thou art consecrated *unto me* with this ring according to the Laws of Moses and Israel." Said Reb Mendl, "If the groom repeats this formula without saying the two words *unto me,* the whole wedding ceremony including the feast, the music and the dancing, are devoid of meaning. The essence of the entire celebration is in the words *unto me*." Concern for doctrine retreats in the face of the concept "for me," of its assimilation and place in life.

Kierkegaard's principle of subjectivity may be regarded as a turning point in the history of Western philosophy and thought, a shifting of the balance from object to subject, from the objective world of ideas to the person who has those ideas. For both Kant and Descartes the self, the subject, was merely an abstract, thinking self, and all significance was derived from the objective system. To Kierkegaard the subject is the concrete, the whole person.[3]

[3] See Theodor Haecker, *Søren Kierkegaard,* translated by A. Dru, (London and New York, 1937), p. 24.

Similarly, the Hasidic movement, and particularly the Kotzker's teachings, mark a critical point in the history of Judaism, a shift of balance from object to subject, from emphasis upon mere action to the person who performs the action and is involved in study.

While most Jewish scholars were preoccupied with the subtleties of Law and ritual conduct, and most Christian theologians were intent upon the subtleties of dogma and the right content of beliefs, the Kotzker and Kierkegaard reflected on the individual's inner life.

There is a story about a learned man who came to see the Kotzker. No longer young—he was close to thirty—the visitor had never before been to a rebbe.

"What have you done all your life?" the master asked him.

"I have gone through the whole Talmud three times," answered the guest.

"Yes, but how much of the Talmud has gone through you?" Reb Mendl inquired.

The Kotzker was deeply distressed that those who claimed to be absorbed in the study of sacred literature did no more than flit across its domains like butterflies. He contended that the purpose of sacred study was to be transformed by it. An untransformed life was not worth living. "Choose life" meant "choose to be transformed."

In his criticism of learned professors of science, Kierkegaard maintained that the most distressing way to live was to be capable of explaining nature without understanding oneself. The Kotzker criticized learned Jewish scholars in the same way: what purpose was served in knowing the sacred text if one could not understand oneself?

It is this inward life of man, this inward deed, this human aspect relating to the deity about which everything revolves, and not large amounts of particular knowledge. For the latter will surely follow, and will not appear then as accidental or without coherence, without a point of heat wherein all radii have gathered.[4]

Kierkegaard's existential philosophy took the actual existence of an individual as the basis for its approach to reality. It contrasted with the conception of philosophy as a logically consistent world view. Analogously, the Kotzker, not satisfied with the conception of Judaism as a comprehensive view of God and man within a system of norms and generalizations, considered the concrete existence of individual man as the basis of his approach to everything. The whole tenor of both men's ideas was practical and challenging to life as well as to thought.

The Kotzker and Kierkegaard revealed how twisted man's inner condition was and suggested a way out of it that was straight if hard. Both were passionately concerned with the problem of what man means to himself. Beckoned to soar to infinite heights through his spirit, he proves too earthbound to make the voyage.

Faced with this predicament, neither thinker expressed much concern with social issues. The Kotzker looked with irony upon the activities of his friend, Reb Yitzhak of Vorki, who worked for the betterment of Jewry's economic status in Poland. Kierkegaard was blamed for taking no part in the political events that agitated Denmark during his lifetime. Thus lack of involvement with the sociopolitical dimension of religious existence, this tendency to regard individual choice in its purest form as the key issue has been severely criticized.

---

[4] Kierkegaard, Letter to P. W. Lund, June 1835; quoted in *The Concept of Irony,* translated by Lee M. Capel (London and New York, 1965), "Historical Introduction," p. 19.

Either/Or

The Kotzker did not make it his task to develop a *modus vivendi* between religious dedication and the needs of daily life, as the Baal Shem did in the spirit of the verse "In all your ways know Him" (Proverbs 3:6). He declared that there was a gulf between service of God and involvement in the world, between piety and expediency, between sanctity and self-interest.

According to Kierkegaard, the central dilemma in the life of man is Either/Or: the need to choose between the aesthetic life and the ethical. The term "aesthetic" is not limited to the appreciation of the beautiful but is used broadly to refer to satisfaction. As opposed to the stringently ethical orientation, the aesthetic life sees moral obligations as related to the pursuit of happiness. Kierkegaard claims that "everything brings one up squarely against the dilemma."

The most tremendous thing which has been granted to man is choice, freedom. And if you desire to save it and preserve it, there is only one way: in the very same second unconditionally and in complete resignation to give it back to God, and yourself with it. If the sight of what is granted to you tempts you, and if you give way to the temptation and look with egoistic desire upon the freedom of choice, then you lose your freedom. And your punishment is: to go on in a kind of confusion, priding yourself on having freedom of choice, but woe unto you, that is your judgment.[1]

[1] Kierkegaard, Journal entry, quoted in E. J. Carnell, *The Burden of Søren Kierkegaard* (Grand Rapids, Mich., 1965), p. 27.

Thus freedom of choice, Either/Or is to Kierkegaard

the token which insures entrance into the unconditional . . . the key to Heaven! . . . Just as every officer who belongs to the king's personal entourage bears a sign . . . whereby he is recognized, so were all those who truly have served Christianity marked by either/ or . . . Everything which is only to a certain degree has not served Christianity, but perhaps itself . . . What is in God's service is either/or.

In his lifetime he was given the nickname "Either/Or," and he once said, "I who am called 'Either/Or' cannot be at the service of anybody with both-and." [2]

"True worship of God consists quite simply in doing God's will," said Kierkegaard. "But this sort of worship has never been to man's taste." So "priests and professors of theology" have continued "another sort of divine worship,"

which consists in . . . having one's own will, but doing it in such a way that the name of God . . . is brought into conjunction with it, whereby man thinks he is assured against being ungodly— whereas, alas, precisely this is the most aggravated sort of ungodliness.

What every religion in which there is any truth aims at, and what Christianity aims at decisively, is a total transformation in a man, to wrest from him through renunciation and self-denial all that, and precisely that, to which he immediately clings, in which he immediately has his life.

Similarly, "What I am essentially concerned about with regard to *Either/ Or* as a whole is . . . the fact . . . that everything brings one squarely up against the dilemma."—Journal entry, quoted in Walter Lowrie, *Kierkegaard* (New York and London, 1938), p. 242.

[2] *Kierkegaard's Attack upon "Christendom," 1854–1855*, translated by Walter Lowrie (Princeton, N.J., 1944), pp. 81f., 91.

Professor Martenson eulogized the deceased Bishop Mynster by calling him "one of the genuine witnesses to the truth." This provoked Kierkegaard's public protest. He had long felt that Bishop Mynster's preaching

soft-pedals, slurs over, suppresses, omits something decisively Christian, something which appears to us men inopportune, which would make our life strenuous, hinder us from enjoying life, that part of Christianity which has to do with dying to the world, by voluntary renunciation, by hating oneself, by suffering for the doctrine, etc.

To see what Kierkegaard complained of, one only has to put the New Testament alongside of Mynster's sermons.

"A witness to the truth," Kierkegaard insisted, "is a man whose life from first to last is unacquainted with everything which is called *enjoyment*." "Christianity is heterogeneous to the world, wherefore the 'witness' must always be recognizable by heterogeneity to this world, by renunciation, by suffering." He concluded, "Bishop Mynster's preaching is related to the Christianity of the New Testament as Epicureanism is to Stoicism." [3]

The Kotzker's preaching also fiercely opposes those who soft-pedal, slur over, suppress, and omit something he regards as decisively Jewish, a voluntary renunciation, though it would make life strenuous. Only he is a Hasid who discards the old, who casts it away, said the Kotzker.

"To keep oneself pure and unspotted from the world is the task and doctrine of Christianity," [4] wrote Kierkegaard. Whoever wants to struggle against falsehood must first divorce himself from the world, taught the Kotzker.

The Kotzker did not demand nonconformity to society out of

[3] *Ibid.*, pp. 219, 221, 7, 11, 19.
[4] Kierkegaard, *Works of Love*, 1847, translated by Howard and Edna Hong (New York, 1962), p. 84.

melancholy or the view that the world was inherently evil. His exhortation was based primarily on the conviction that God exacted direct and undivided commitment, and that anything that lessened such an allegiance should be shunned. What he called for was not the sacrifice of all life's comforts, ascetic self-denial, or the mortification of the body for the good of the soul. He urged a recognition of the sham, the emptiness, and the folly of mundane pleasures, and therefore their depreciation, leading to independence from the world. One must stay away from the world's noise, its distractions and dangers. Then, and only then, can one serve God.

Every man ought to make up his mind whether man or God is the measure of all things.[5] If he accepts the former, he will always be subject to a multiplicity of standards as a member of society. But God is One, and there can be only one Truth and one standard for right and wrong.

To Face the Unconditional

Most of all, man is in need of a sense of the unconditional. Otherwise he will perish. "Without relating himself to the unconditional," Kierkegaard says, "man cannot in the deepest sense

[5] Cf. Protagoras, Diels, II, 1952, 263, and Plato, Laws, 716c 4ff.

be said to 'live' . . . that is, he may continue perhaps to live, but spiritlessly." [1]

Both Kierkegaard and the Kotzker felt that man's gravest danger lurked in the loss of his sense of the unconditional, the absolute. We conduct our lives according to conditionals, compromises, and concessions—all relatives. In faith an individual commits everything to the Absoluteness of God. But the Absolute is cruel: it demands all.

I have already mentioned that, in defining man's horizontal obligation, Biblical ethics introduces self-love as the normative justification for love of others: *Love thy neighbor as thyself* (Leviticus 19:18). For man's vertical obligation, for the love we direct toward God, it is sufficient reason that He is God.

There is only one whom a man can . . . love above himself—that is God. Therefore it is not said: "Thou shalt love God as thyself," but rather, "Thou shalt love the Lord thy God with all thy heart, with all thy soul, and all thy mind." A man should love God in unconditional *obedience* and love him in *adoration*. It would be ungodliness if any man dared love himself in this way, or dared to let another person love him in this way . . . God you are to love in unconditional obedience, even if what he demands of you may seem to you to be to your own harm. [2]

The basic message that both Kierkegaard and the Kotzker proclaim is that the life of faith is hard to enter upon and maintain, difficult to understand or explain.

[1] Kierkegaard, "My Position as a Religious Writer in 'Christendom' and My Tactics," 1850, in *The Point of View, etc.*, 1859, translated by Walter Lowrie (London and New York, 1939), p. 164.
[2] *Works of Love*, p. 36.

PART III

❖⦅❖⦅❖⦅

The Power of the Will

Faith and Will

I S RELIGIOUS faith and experience connected with some particular faculty of the mind? Rationalist theologians, who have regarded reason as the final arbiter in the whole domain of thought, have sought the foundation by equating religious belief with intellectual knowledge. On the other hand, thinkers who realized that religious men are often attuned to non-rational forces in the psyche have seen faith as the product of feeling.

In opposition to the rationalist view that one should never admit anything that is not reasonable, Pascal (1623–62) stressed "the reasons of the heart," maintaining that "we know truth not only through reason but more so through the heart. It is in this latter way that we know first principles, and it is in vain that reason, which plays no part in this, tries to combat them." Both heart and reason yield results that are certain, but by different routes, and it would be ridiculous to require proof of the heart's intuitions.[1]

What about the power of the will in the life of faith? This is a question that relates not only to religion but to all of mental life.

Medieval philosophy debated the question, which of the soul's powers was pre-eminent, the will or the intellect? Did the will's decisions depend upon ideas, or did ideas issue from the

[1] Pascal, *Pensées* 110 and 292 (Brunschvicg numberings).

will? Augustinians and Aristotelians disagreed, for Augustine had considered the will the impelling power, in antithesis to the intellectualism of Aristotle. Was the intellect or the will, then, the spring of faith?

For Descartes (1596–1650) the will was supreme. Through his will, guided by the right use of reason, man can avoid error, achieve moral virtue, subdue and even control his own passions. Descartes maintained specifically that religious belief is not an act of the mind but of the will. God has given finite understanding to man, his finite creature, but He has also given him an infinite will; and it is when man exercises his will in the absence of adequate intellectual information from his intellect that error occurs.[2]

The will, according to Pascal, is one of the principal constituents of belief: *not that it forms belief,* but because things are true or false depending on the angle from which they are seen. The will, which prefers one aspect to another, turns the mind from considering those aspects it does not care to see, and thus the intellect, moving with the will, pauses to regard the aspect it prefers, judging by what it sees there.[3]

William James (1842–1910) contended that beliefs are the product of our willing nature, which include not only deliberate acts of will but "such factors of belief as fear and hope, prejudice and passion, intuition and partisanship, the circumpressure of our caste and sect."[4] James recognized "the will to believe" as an element in every philosophy. Rationalists have asserted that we ought to believe only what we can demonstrate, but where, he asked, have they found or given a demonstration of this principle

[2] See Descartes, *Meditations,* 1641, IV.
[3] *Pensées* 99.
[4] *The Varieties of Religious Experience* (New York, 1902).

itself? That is merely a prejudice like any other, dictated by personal preference, by purely subjective sentiment.

In the light of these ideas, we can understand the significance of Kierkegaard's approach. Once the idea of man's freedom to choose between alternative courses of action has been accepted, the problem arises whether freedom of choice applies to the religious sphere. Does the will or the power of choice extend to the realm of faith? Are we free to choose between belief and unbelief?

In opposition to the Hegelian view that human existence developed logically within and through conceptual schemes, Kierkegaard maintains that the individual constitutes himself as the individual he is through the choice of one mode of existence rather than another. Religious faith is a matter of choosing to accept or reject God.

The strict pigeonholing of the inner life is the product of sheer fancy. The inner faculties, at least under normal circumstances, constantly intermingle. Will without intelligence would be a blind and reckless drive, and intelligence without will a faculty deprived of power.

Rationalists have grossly exaggerated the extent to which behavior is motivated by reasonable considerations, while philosophers of religion have underplayed the role of will, intent, freedom, decision in arriving at religious commitment.

A Matter of the Will

Both the Kotzker and Kierkegaard gave the will predominance over reason. Religious faith was justified in the very act of faith itself, not in rational illustrations. Both denied that reason or rational evidence had any important place in it.

Under the influence of Kierkegaard, many contemporary thinkers have stressed the decisive importance of religious commitment, of self-engagement. They consider faith primarily a matter of the will and decision.

Reminiscent of Tertullian and Pascal, Kierkegaard maintained that what the individual did was conditioned by what he willed, not by what he understood.

Christianity in the New Testament has to do with man's will, everything turns upon changing the will, every expression (forsake the world, deny yourself, die to the world, and so on, to hate oneself, to love God, and so on)—everything is related to this basic idea in Christianity which makes it what it is—a change of will.[1]

Freedom of the will, responsibility before God for one's actions were Kierkegaard's presuppositions. Sin was not inherent in human nature but resulted from an act of the will.[2]

Only a man of will can become a Christian, because only a man of will has a will which can be broken. But a man of will whose will

[1] Kierkegaard, Journal entry in *The Last Years: Journals, 1853–1855,* edited and translated by Ronald Gregor Smith (New York and London, 1965), p. 226.
[2] See "Vigilius Haufniensis" (Kierkegaard), *The Concept of Dread,* 1844, translated by Walter Lowrie (Princeton, N.J., 1944).

is broken by the unconditioned or by God is a Christian. The stronger the natural will the deeper can be the break, and the better the Christian. This is what has been described characteristically as "the new obedience": a Christian is a man of will who has received a new will. A Christian is a man of will who no longer wills his own will, but with the passion of his broken will—radically changed— wills the will of another.

A man of intellect can never become a Christian, at most he can use his imaginative powers to toy with Christian problems. And it is this formation of Christians, if one may call them this, which introduces every possible confusion into Christianity. They become learned, scientific, they transform everything into long-winded discussions, in which they drown the real point of Christianity. But of course Providence in His compassion can do much for a man of intellect, to change him into a man of will, so that he may become a Christian. For the possibility of becoming a man of will is in every man. The most wanton, the most cowardly, the most phlegmatic man, a man who argues without beginning or end—bring such men into deadly peril, and perhaps they will become men of will. Certainly necessity cannot produce freedom; but it can bring the freedom in man as near as possible to becoming will.[3]

Here is Walter Lowrie's account:

This is an expression for the purity of heart he sought after: "to will one thing." He is no less evidently thinking of himself when he describes what he considers

The Most Beautiful Sight

If there were a man who had attained perfection in this art of being able to perceive a task, to perceive a task in every situation and at every instant (Socrates was the man who attained this in the, highest degree)

—if there were such a man, then to see him in relationship to

[3] Kierkegaard, Journal 23 September 1855, in *The Last Years*, pp. 358f.

God who knows how to set a task every second and in every situation—

that would be the most beautiful sight.

Kierkegaard spoke of his father as a prodigious example of a man of iron will. "No one would think of describing Søren in such terms at any period of his life," comments Lowrie. Yet in his last years he began to stress the cardinal importance of the power of the will in religious existence.

He had learnt from his father that one *can* what one will; and the father's life had not discredited this theory. This experience had imparted to Johannes' soul an indescribable sort of pride. It was intolerable to him that there should be anything one could not do if only one would.[4]

Similarly, the rock upon which the Kotzker built his teachings was the belief in the freedom and power of the will. The essential task, therefore, was its formation, a principle he adopted from his master, Reb Bunam. Reb Mendl was strongly convinced of the will's vast power to dominate one's existence, to shake off waywardness, indolence, or laxity.

Belief in the freedom of will is an old Jewish doctrine. It became particularly prevalent under the influence of Maimonides. As generally understood, it meant the capacity to make a choice between alternatives offered by either good or evil impulses. Man was not compelled to act in any particular way; he could choose his own goals and course of conduct.

Personal will was not merely the strongest of the several interests or inclinations that prevailed after a struggle. The will was an active power, making its own choices, taking its own leaps, setting its own goals, establishing precedents and forming a pat-

[4] Lowrie, *Kierkegaard*, p. 489.

tern. Its accumulated choices added up to the permanent dispositions that formed an individuality.

Fully aware of the countless obstructions, restraints, and inner coercions, the Kotzker believed in the power of choosing and acting on one's own decisions. He therefore demanded unabated alertness, continuous initiative. The will was to be sovereign over the self.

Convinced of man's capacity for full self-control, and even self-destruction, the Kotzker set forth, as it were, his motto:

Dare to use your own will!

He made exaggerated claims for the power of the will and overstated the importance of the individual's role. Knock your head against the wall, and break through!

Against the Emaciation of the Commandments

The Kotzker set the religious ideal very high, maintaining that a man must be prepared to renounce everything, all his attachments and relationships, in order to relate absolutely to God. In his eyes, as in Kierkegaard's, the life of faith had been made too easy; it had lost all sense of the heroic, had become a relative ingredient. Both men felt that everyone was yielding, faltering, and compromising. With people satisfied with things only half done, compromise was taken as the norm, the tentative was seen as final, and the vision was consigned to oblivion.

"You shall be holy" (Leviticus 19:2), "Keep far from falsehood" (Exodus 23:7), "You shall love your God with all your heart, with all your soul, with all your might" (Deuteronomy 6:5)—these are infinite requirements. They admit no compromise, no accommodation. Yet in daily life the infinitude of these requirements is ignored, forgotten. Judaism becomes an emaciated and attenuated mode of conduct. This discrepancy agitated the Kotzker, as it did Kierkegaard within the framework of Christianity.

Like the Kotzker, Kierkegaard knew that faith constituted a demand rather than a consolation or comfort. They both attacked the complacency of believers.

Against the emasculated and diluted interpretation of Christianity as represented by the Established Church, Kierkegaard set forth the nature of the Christian requirement. The Christian must be prepared to renounce everything, any attachment to temporal matters and human relationships, in order to relate absolutely to God. This was a sharp criticism of the Church, which sought to bring everyone, or at least as many as possible, into Christianity.

In 1859 Kierkegaard's brief summary of his writings, "The Point of View for my Work as an Author," was published. In this account (written in 1848), and particularly in its supplement (written in 1850), he defined his "position" and his "tactics."

When the infinite requirement is heard and upheld, heard and upheld in all its infinitude, then *grace* is offered, or rather grace offers itself, and to it the individual, each for himself, as I also do, can flee for refuge. And then it is possible. But surely it is not an exaggeration when . . . the requirement of infinity, "infinite" requirement, is presented infinitely . . . On the other hand, it is taking Christianity in vain when . . . in view of this consideration the infinite requirement is reduced to finite terms, or maybe entirely ignored.[1]

Kierkegaard's insistence upon the sustained strain and tension required for the venture into faith continues to be a major reason why his thought is unacceptable to many theologians.

This criticism also applies to the Kotzker. Opponents maintain that his way was meant for titans, not for ordinary men; that, within the limits of everyday life, moderate, unsophisticated piety is valuable enough, if certain aberrations are corrected or neutralized. A life of accommodation, compromise, and mild sensuality may even justify itself.

The argument against Kierkegaard and the Kotzer can be reduced to a fundamental question: what is the truth about the goal and expectation of faith? Should its requirements be adapted to the weaknesses of human nature, or should human nature be raised to a level of greatness?

[1] "My Position . . . ," p. 160.

Defiance of the Self

To the Kotzker and to Kierkegaard the central problem was not the world. It was the self. Defiance or depreciation of the world was possible only through defiance or depreciation of the self, the Kotzker said. "When I want to spit," wrote Kierkegaard, "I even spit into my own face." [1]

Unable to find consummation in mere outwardness, the Kotzker demanded inwardness, purity of heart. His re-evaluation or rediscovery of Judaism as a service of inwardness led him to disparage repetitiveness, routine, religious habit. He refused to accept the human condition with its quotidian quality and demanded continuous transformation and transcendence to the interior life. In the absence of Truth there were only imitation and pretense, which inevitably led to corruption. Such radicalism was far removed from quietism or pietistic spirituality. The road to Truth for both the Kotzker and Kierkegaard was through self-examination.

Only intense self-reflection—at least as powerful as the conditions and falsehood it sought to transcend—could alleviate corruption. As such, this cure arrived at Truth by way of authenticity; it required unrestrained introspection, reflection. This search for increasing, progressive intensity is usually distasteful to man, to whom the outward life appeals because it is familiar and secure. His inner self is allowed to remain vague and ob-

[1] *Either/Or,* p. 20.

scure, and only the challenge of an extreme peril compels him to investigate it.

In times of balanced living, the Kotzker's repeated cries to look within and to practice continuous self-inspection may be both unbearable and unnecessary. Yet in today's disintegrating world, where all inwardness is externalized, our inner selves face a wasteland. We may sense a new relevance in such a call.

The Kotzker would say that Judaism is Truth, Truth is inwardness, inwardness is authenticity, and authenticity is attained through intense, passionate inner action. Only integrity can save man and his faith.

Such radical self-inspection may disclose a vortex in the soul, an intermingling of Truth and self-infatuation. Is it not perilous to face the unfathomed vortex within the self? It is because of the risk such inspection entails that one may challenge Reb Mendl's counsel. Charity or love, not Truth, would be advanced as the supreme principle. With all the impurities and infirmities of human nature, convention and obedience are decisive rather than carefully examined attitudes. It is dangerous to perform surgery on the soul, but the Kotzker insisted that, *nolens volens,* man must live dangerously.

The Kotzker was not preoccupied with authenticity of human life as the ultimate goal. Given the nature of man, he thought, the emancipation or cultivation of authenticity might end in the release of destructive impulses. What he sought was the authenticity of transcending human nature in confronting and observing God's requirements. It did not occur to him to assume a dichotomy of Spirit and Law, of inwardness and observance. Inwardness was an integral part of the duties, an essential part of the Law. Yet he seems to have realized that the crust of outward observance was too frail to keep in check the inner fires, "the evil inclination," to cure inner corruption. Courage to descend and confront the vertiginous inner life was essential. He considered devotion to one's self the source of Truth's corruption. It perverted honesty and destroyed purity of heart.

In discussing the pitfalls of self-deception, Kierkegaard mentioned as an example "calling love that which is really self-love."

There is no deed, not a single one, not even the best, of which we dare to say unconditionally: he who does this thereby unconditionally demonstrates love. It depends upon *how* the deed is done . . . One can perform works of love in an unloving, yes, even in a self-loving way . . . something every honest man will confess about himself, simply because he is not unkind and callous enough to overlook what is essential, in preoccupation with *what* he does to forget *how* he does it. Alas, Luther is supposed to have said that not once in his life had he prayed entirely undisturbed by any distracting thoughts. In the same way the honest man confesses that never, however often he has willingly and gladly given charity, that never has he done it except in frailty . . . perhaps to save face . . . perhaps seeking alleviation by giving charity . . .

There is only one a human being should fear—that is God; and there is only one a man should be afraid of—that is himself . . . [The purpose of Christianity] is to wrest self-love away from us human beings.

Wherever Christianity is, there is also self-renunciation, which is Christianity's essential form . . . Christian love is self-renunciation's love . . . Consequently Christianity has misgivings about erotic love and friendship because [it] . . . is really another form of self-love . . . Self-love is condemnable . . . Just as self-love in the strictest sense has been characterised as self-deification, so love and friendship . . . are essentially idolatry . . . Take care that you are not led into the snare of self-love.

Love of one's neighbor is self-renouncing love, and self-renunciation eradicates all self-love by the "You shall" of the eternal.

Self-renunciation is precisely the way in which a human being becomes sober in an eternal sense. On the other hand, wherever Christianity is absent, the intoxication of self-feeling is most intense . . . Spiritual love, on the other hand, takes away from myself all natural determinants and all self-love.[2]

Severity, Tension Serve a Purpose

To live means to walk perpetually on the edge of a precipice. The human predicament is a state of constant and irresolvable tension between mighty opposites. Piety and prudence, Truth and self-interest, are irreconcilable. Tension and conflict can no more be eliminated from thought than from life.

In contrast, the conventional defense of Christianity, according to Kierkegaard, maintains: "Do not disdain Christianity, it is a gentle doctrine, it contains all the gentle consolations a man some time in his life may find himself in need of. Good Lord, life does not smile upon one."

In this manner of living, thinking, and teaching, the Kotzker and Kierkegaard were earnest and harsh, causing discomfort, even distress, to their contemporaries by their bitter derision of complacency and mediocrity. Both men felt that there was but one salvation: sternness.

In dealing with his disciples, the Kotzker indulged in question-

2 *Works of Love,* pp. 25, 30, 32, 34; 68, 65, 69f., 73; 68.

ing in order to bring about the shock of intellectual awakening of inward transformation. Man could not be saved by gentleness. Similarly, Kierkegaard wrote:

Severity is the only thing that can help a man. Hence a child, in comparison with grown-ups, is capable of so much, is far hardier, because there is still some severity in the upbringing of children: and what was a child not capable of when severity was greater!

The Romans always conquered in battle because severity was part of their creed; it helped them fear defeat more than death.

And so it was also with Christianity. Once there was a time when with divine authority it exercised dominion over men, when it addressed itself to every single individual briefly, laconically, imperatively, with the order "Thou shalt," when it dismayed every individual by a severity which never before was known, by the punishment of eternity.[1]

Spiritual tranquillity is not found in the thinking of either Kierkegaard or the Kotzker. Aesthetic living may afford a measure of peace of mind.

The religious life is a perpetual struggle, tension, and suffering. The last stage in this life is that act of self-annihilation in which the ideal task of being an existing individual and the impossibility of fulfilling it concretely are at war with each other. An awareness of this incompatibility is the root of religious torment. It is inevitable, Kierkegaard thought.

[1] *Training in Christianity*, pp. 225, 223f.

In Praise of Strict Justice

According to the Midrash, God first intended to rule with stern justice the world He created. Realizing, however, that it would not endure, He gave precedence to divine mercy, allying it with divine justice.

An old tradition maintains that the Holy One, blessed be He, prays. What kind of prayer? Abba Arika (Rab), a celebrated sage who died in 247, suggested the following:

> May it be My will that My mercy may suppress My anger, that My mercy may prevail over My other attributes, so that I may deal with My children in the attribute of mercy and on their behalf stop short of the limit of stern justice.[1]

Mercy rather than justice is regarded as the outstanding attribute of God. The rabbis speak of the "thirteen attributes of compassion" (Exodus 34:6–7). While one of the most often used synonyms for God is "Compassionate One" (*Rahmana*), no synonym has been coined to denote the Lord as dispenser of justice.

The Kotzker, however, demurred. He considered mercy an attenuation of Truth. To show mercy means to compromise with evil and to come to terms with delinquency. If the world were conducted according to the principle of Truth, justice, not mercy, would be administered.

Reb Mendl cited a rabbinic thesis that the greatness of God, the King of Kings, is disclosed in His being a lover of justice

[1] *Berachoth* 7a.

(Psalms 99:4). This was his will: to favor man with benefits based on justice because he deserved them. God should not have to resort to mercy and bestow the good undeservedly. In rabbinic tradition, the ineffable Name, "the Lord," denotes the attribute of mercy, while the word "God" (*elohim*) signifies justice.

In this sense, too, the Kotzker explained the words of the Psalmist as a prayer for justice rather than mercy. "My soul thirsts for God . . . When shall I come and behold the face of God" (Psalms 42:3). Consistent in his commitment to Truth as the supreme standard for right and wrong, the Kotzker felt that to accept mercy as the supreme standard was a sign of weakness. Justice is the way of Truth.

The dichotomy between Truth and mercy agonized Reb Shneur Zalman of Laydy, founder of the Habad Hasidism, during his last hours on earth. In a brief essay written shortly before he died, he referred to the homily cited at the beginning of this book and concluded that the world was created on the principle of "mercy devoid (or in disregard) of Truth." Therefore, since most of men's deeds are false, it is impossible to carry out an act of mercy and an act of truth simultaneously. In a world of falsehood, human mercy is tainted with falsehood; only the Torah is Truth.

Even exalted people often ignored the Truth, wrote Reb Shneur Zalman, for this was "a world of lies and mercies." Did he then equate mercies with lies? And did the Kotzker give no thought to God's love and mercy? Did he solely emphasize man's falsehood and corruption?

It is natural to feel uncomfortable when confronted with such austerity. Yet a sense of comfort is no standard for Truth. It is precisely the one-sided emphasis upon God's love and mercy that stands in need of a corrective. We must be reminded that God of the Bible is both Judge and Father, severe as well as compassionate.

The Kotzker's thought does not offer a pleasing interpretation of man. Its core is an urgent call for self-examination, a critical surveying of our claims, our pride, a call for candor and humility. The disasters Jews have experienced in the twentieth century substantiate the Kotzker's admonitions against man's unreliability, revealing the insecurity of freedom. His incisive insights should open our eyes to inauthenticity in the sphere of religion, to the outright deceptions in politics and social relations and in institutional operations.

To Disregard Self-regard

The most preposterous falsehood is the most common, most cherished one: self-centeredness. Man tends to act as if his ego were the hub of the world, the source and purpose of existence. What a shameless affront to deny that God is that source and purpose, the sap and the meaning. The twin themes of the Kotzker—how to discard falsehood and how to overcome self-regard—are essentially one.

Reb Mendl's goal was to cleanse religious existence of self-centeredness and to emphasize an inwardness that sought to serve

God without rewards, even of a spiritual sort. He expressed a much-needed protest against attitudes that had debased religion to a supernatural commercialism by introducing vested interests into the relationship with the Holy.

The Kotzker did not call for the annihilation of the self. Nor did he look upon self-denial as an end in itself. Opposed to asceticism, he regarded the satisfaction of natural needs and compliance with legitimate interests as proper. Basic to his thoughts was a fundamental disgust with falsehood, evidenced in his maxim: undeceive yourself! If your life is to be dedicated to God, relinquish your dedication to self-interest, renounce your striving for personal gain while claiming to worship Him.

From the viewpoint of psychological realism, which apparently dominated the Jewish mind at the time of the Kotzker, it was clear that the good deed would rarely come to pass if absolute purity of intention were made indispensable for doing it. Hence, the prevailing opinion held that man's good deeds should not be disparaged, even when motivated by self-interest or the prospect of reward. Many sages, particularly the Baal Shem and his disciples, felt uneasy about such an accommodation with the ego and sought to foster ways of cultivating disinterestedness, self-detachment.

Yet none of the Baal Shem's successors took as consistently radical a position as the Kotzker. He demanded that his disciples serve God without worldly return; more, that the soul should be dulled to all desire, even to its wishes for a spiritual return. He maintained that any religious deed that yielded personal pleasure, such as the satisfaction of vanity, thereby became an act of egoism, a contradiction in terms. In matters of faith, self-renunciation should be the goal.

In this respect the Kotzker came close to repudiating the

traditional religious pre-eminence of deed over motive, upsetting
the balance in the order of Jewish life. Were his teachings a
religious fad in the history of Judaism, based on the whims of an
eccentric personality? Or did they serve religious integrity? And
did they represent a ripening of principles working quietly in
the souls of many people?

The clamor for purity of the heart rings through the history
of Jewish thought and often sounds like a signal of distress.

> This people draw near with their mouth
> and honor Me with their lips,
> while their hearts are far from Me,
> and their fear of Me is like a command
> carried out by rote. (Isaiah 29:13)

To many thinkers the central problem was *how* one observed
the law, not *how much*. We are expected to serve Him "out of
love," to do every *mitzvah* "for its own sake," to act "for the sake
of Heaven, for the sake of His great Name, and not be motivated
by hope of praise or advantage, or by fear of people or by avertive
injury in this world or the world to come." [1] "My son, give Me
your heart" (Proverbs 23:26). But it seems to be easier to ex-
pend one's wealth, health, and comfort than to give one's heart
to God.

The distinction had long been made between the man who
served "for the sake of Heaven" and the one who served "for the
sake of a reward." In the Middle Ages a special term was coined
for impure motivation in carrying out a religious act: *penyyah*,[2]
a term widely used in Hasidic literature.

In the history of the Hasidic movement, there were many

---

[1] Bahya Ibn Paquda, *Hovot ha-Levavot* (*Duties of the Heart*), edited by
Haymson, part IV, p. 68.
[2] See Maimonides's *Commentary on Makkot*.

who wrestled with inner adversity. Some tried to outwit the self and, by fostering spiritual incentives, to stimulate roots of integrity; others compelled their consciousness into prolonged self-forgetfulness by study of distant intellectual subtleties in the Torah. Realizing that uprooting of inner diversions was utopian, some Jews were overcome by a type of contrition that was purer than pure.

The verse in II Kings 3:15, "As the minstrel played, the spirit of God came upon him," was rendered in this way by the Great Maggid:

When the minstrel was like the instrument—free of self-consciousness—*the spirit of God came upon him.* Only when, like the instrument, the minstrel is neither self-seeking nor self-conscious, can the spirit of God come upon him.[3]

In Search of the Few

Knowledge—like the sky—is never private property. No teacher has a right to withhold it from anyone who asks for it. Teaching is the art of sharing. There is no one in the world who does not deserve to partake of the riches of learning. It was said of the Torah that whoever so desired was free to acquire it. "Rear many disciples!" instructs an ancient Jewish maxim. Indeed, knowledge was spread indiscriminately.

[3] Solomon Maimon, *An Autobiography* (1888), p. 166.

And yet there were voices in Jewish history opposing the principle that teaching should be available to all. This was Shammai's (ca. 50 B.C.E.—30 C.E.) opinion: he favored the use of standards of excellence in admitting disciples, as against Hillel's lenient view. Rabban Gamliel (ca. 80), head of the famous academy in Jabneh, Palestine, once proclaimed that a disciple whose character did not correspond to his exterior ("whose inside is not as his outside") could not enter. Only after Rabban Gamliel was replaced by Rabbi Eleazar ben Azariah was the doorkeeper dismissed and permission given to all disciples to enter.[1]

Those who attached no conditions to the study of the Law insisted, nonetheless, that only carefully prepared individuals be initiated into the realm of esoteric lore, namely mysticism. Even Maimonides confessed that the book containing his philosophical and theological views was written for the few. In the introduction to *The Guide of the Perplexed,* he addressed himself to his disciple Joseph, "Your absence has prompted me to compose this treatise for you and for those who are like you, however few they may be." He then set forth his educational doctrine:

When I have a difficult subject before me—when I find the road narrow, and can see no other way of teaching a well-established truth except by pleasing one intelligent man and displeasing ten thousand fools—I prefer to address myself to the one man, and to take no notice whatever of the condemnation of the multitude; I prefer to extricate the intelligent man from his embarrassment and show him the cause of his perplexity, so that he may attain perfection and be at peace.[2]

While other leaders sought to expand the Hasidic movement,

[1] *Berachoth* 28a.
[2] *The Guide of the Perplexed,* translated by M. Friedlander (New York, 1956), p. 22.

the Kotzker preferred to arrest its expansion and to internalize the Hasidic commitment. Besieged by multitudes of people who sought his blessing and his guidance, he exclaimed, "What do I need the mob for: I want a score of young men to stand with me on the rooftops and to shout: 'The Lord, He is God! The Lord, He is God'" (cf. I Kings 18:39).

The Kotzker insisted repeatedly that he wished to influence only a small number of disciples. He regarded the thousands coming to his door as a misfortune. In abandoning any hope of transforming the whole people, he could cite as authority the Prophetic teaching regarding the saving remnant, a small minority in a faithless world (*she'erit Israel* or *she'ar*), as indicated in the name of Isaiah's son Shear-jashub (Isaiah 7:3). Because of their sins, the majority would be carried away, only a remnant would survive, those who remained loyal to the Lord.

A statement found in a classical work on Jewish piety, *Duties of the Heart* by Bahya Ibn Paquda (eleventh century), is often quoted:

Only the prophet by reason of his natural endowment, or the distinguished philosopher through the wisdom he has acquired, is able to worship the First Cause. But all the rest worship someone else since they cannot conceive of any being that is not composite.[3]

True faith, thought the Kotzker, was the yoke of the gifted few called upon to bear it for all mankind. It was through the individual that the many would be uplifted. A man who in his privacy deeply cared for his personal spiritual concerns, was, in fact, more involved with the community than he who mingled with the people in pursuit of material concerns, said the Kotzker.

In publishing his writings, Kierkegaard's intention was "to

[3] *Hovot ha-Levavot*, Pt. 1, Chap. 2.

stir up the 'crowd' in order to get hold of the 'individual' . . . *Religiously* speaking, there is no such thing as a public, but only individuals; for religion is seriousness, and seriousness is . . . the individual." [4]

Both Kierkegaard and the Kotzker were more concerned with man in relation to his own soul than with his relationships to other men. Their constant effort was to expose the individual to the absolute and its unconditional requirement. "The greatest proof of Christianity's decay is the prodigiously large number of Christians," argued Kierkegaard.[5]

Both Kierkegaard and the Kotzker were aware that the comprehension of their thought was not to be expected of everybody who thought. Neither had respect for the public. When regarded as judges of ethical or religious matters, "the crowd is untruth." [6] New Testament Christianity, Kierkegaard claimed, was no longer to be found anywhere in the world. The history of the Church showed increasing degeneracy. It had begun at Pentecost, when the Apostles had admitted three thousand persons to the Church on one day. How could so many truly attach themselves to it at one stroke!

"The realm of faith is not a class for numbskulls in the sphere of the intellectual or an asylum for the feeble-minded," [7] reprimanded Kierkegaard.

It is true in fact that in the eyes of the world I am a scoundrel. In the eyes of the world! What are the eyes of the world but blindness?

[4] "On My Work as an Author," 1851, in *The Point of View*, pp. 151, 153.
[5] See M. M. Thulstrup, "Kierkegaard's Dialectic of Imitation," in Howard A. Johnson and Niels Thulstrup, eds., *A Kierkegaard Critique* (New York, 1962), p. 277.
[6] Kierkegaard, "The Point of View for My Work as an Author," 1848, in *The Point of View*, p. 116.
[7] *Concluding Unscientific Postscript*, p. 291.

And what is the judgment of the world? I have not found ten men who have the strength to judge severely.[8]

Like Nietzsche, Kierkegaard wanted no disciples. He thought they could be only "the greatest of all misfortunes." Yet to find himself without sympathizers was a source of agony. In his writings there are many indications of his concern for the reactions and the judgments of the very public he professed to despise.

On the other hand, for all his appreciation of learning and intellectual sophistication, the Kotzker was often repelled by the pretentiousness of learned scholars, and even by the common folk who came to seek his advice or blessing.

Individualism

Both Kierkegaard and the Kotzker were deeply concerned about the achievement of religious authenticity and the excellence of the chosen few. They evinced little interest in the "common man," who might not be able to reach the levels of reflection and intensity of will required for the attainment of religious authenticity and purity of heart. Thus, they assigned a second-class religiosity to the many.

Their idea of individualism implied that a person's decisions

[8] *Stages on Life's Way*, p. 240.

and acts are the outgrowth of his personal preferences, not a matter of conformity. Everyone differs in his perspective and approach. Each goes his own way, his life in no sense a duplication. He often sets his own standards of conduct without considering whether they are pleasing or annoying to other members of society.

Central to both thinkers was the problem of how the individual relates to God. According to Kierkegaard, the Instant—an atom of eternity in Time—was present whenever a man ceased to be thoughtlessly dominated by the herd instinct and when, as an individual, he turned from exclusive care for himself to concern with God's majesty and holiness. Each individual could achieve his relation to God only in isolation from other believers.

Kierkegaard rejected Hegel's "folk religion," which taught suppression of the personal response or sublimation of it into something necessary and impersonal. The turning of mind and will toward God was an inalienable affair of "the single one."

How often have I shown that fundamentally Hegel makes men into heathens, into a race of animals gifted with reason. For in the animal world "the individual" is always less important than the race. But it is the peculiarity of the human race that just because the individual is created in the image of God "the individual" is above the race. This can be wrongly understood and terribly misused: *concedo*. But that is Christianity. And *that* is where the battle must be fought.[1]

Kierkegaard constantly emphasized his category of the individual; many of his books are dedicated to "that *individual* whom with joy and gratitude I call *my* reader." [2] For him the individual

[1] Journal entry, 1850, *The Journals of Søren Kierkegaard, A Selection*, edited and translated by Alexander Dru (London and New York, 1938), ¶ 1050.
[2] "The Point of View," p. 20.

stood opposed to the public and the crowd which embodied "untruth."

Kierkegaard's individual was not the exceptional man, the genius, but the "religious individual," the man who had to reach the third level of existence beyond the aesthetic and ethical stages. This idea included all men, since each was called to being an individual in the religious sense, and could reach this (third) stage by existential effort.

Like Kierkegaard, the Kotzker wanted man to discover himself as an individual, to free himself from the crowd. To ignore public opinion was an imperative, and the Kotzker shared Kierkegaard's inability to run with the pack. He scorned "the crowd" and did not want to belong to it.

And as Kierkegaard dissented from the official Church of his day, so did the Kotzker from some of the views held by great rabbinic authorities. When the Law did not clearly indicate a course of action, Hillel, the first-century Palestinian sage, declared: "Leave it to Israel: if they are not Prophets, yet they are the children of the Prophets." [3] What he meant was: see how the people act and follow their example. In similar circumstances, Abbaye, the Babylonian Jewish scholar (ca. 278–338), and Reb Ashi replied: "Go forth and see how the public are accustomed to act." [4] Joshua ben Levi, the third-century Palestinian teacher, declared: "If the application of a law is undecided in the courts, and you do not know what its nature is (how to act) see how the people act." [5]

The tradition of Jewish Orthodoxy, which accented impersonal learning and obedience to the Law, was bound to bring

[3] *Pesahim 66a.*
[4] *Berachoth 45a; Erubin 146; Menahoth 35b.*
[5] *Yerushalmi Peah*, VII, 5, p. 20c top; *Yerushalmi Maaser Sheni*, V, 2, p. 566 top.

about a crisis. The Kotzker offered a response by his eagerness to emancipate the individual.

In a famous passage, Kierkegaard remarked that we lose sight of the individual when we think only in terms of laws and universals. To cite an example: for centuries the philosopher has been declaring, "All men are mortal," without paying attention to the fact that he, too, was a unique individual who must die.

The same may be applied to the strictly observant Jew, who, in conforming to the Law, thinks in terms of general rules and neglects the spiritual problems he should face as a particular individual.

To the Kotzker, the individual was a person capable of re-creating things anew. "God loves novelty," he said. Mere repetitiveness was contemptible. Individualism involves newness, creativity.

He demanded that his disciples be individuals, that they stand out from the crowd. A Kotzker hasid did not simply belong to a group. By his individual decision he had become a personality apart, breaking with his background, his family, his environment. Kotzk had become his entire world.

An individual faces the continuous task of bringing pressure to bear upon himself, urging his mind to influence his heart. A man should keep his character in constant repair. Though the soul is born clean, man gradually learns to convert it into a chalice in which he mixes his own brand of poison.

Hasidism had become a mass trend, threatened with spiritual enfeeblement, even trivialization. The only possibility of renewal, thought the Kotzker, lay in the reinstatement of the individual's role. The movement that had come into being through stress of the personal aspect of Judaism could be reborn only by an emphasis on individualism.

Every individual has a unique vocation and task to perform. He must be his own master, not rely on other people's wisdom. Even when the Messiah and all mankind are redeemed, the Lord will still review each individual to ascertain whether he deserves to be redeemed on his own merit.

The Kotzker does not imply that each individual should be concerned merely with his own salvation; such a view would destroy his basic premise that to be exclusively concerned with oneself is idolatry. One needs to be within another's concern and to embrace others in his concern. The greatest lie one can live is self-centeredness, and to be authentically human is to be able both to surpass oneself and to fulfill one's special relevant role vis-à-vis God.

If I am I because I am I, and you are you because you are you, then I am I and you are you. However, if I am I because you are you, and you are you because I am I, then I am not I and you are not you.

This saying, ascribed to the Kotzker, brings into focus his concept of individualism. If an individual claims to be self, an "I," only for the purpose of differentiating himself from people, from other selves, his claim is nothing but an empty negation, the absence of an image, contrariety. However, individualism implies strong positive content, a matchless unique quality, and perspectives, experiences, or events not to be found in any other human being.

Neither Kierkegaard nor the Kotzker regarded the excellence acquired by an individual to be its own goal. According to the former, God "employs the individual to provoke the established order out of its self-complacency." [6] Reb Mendl would probably

[6] *Training in Christianity*, p. 91.

have concurred. The burden of being is all upon the individual himself.

The Kotzker's outlook must be sharply differentiated from secular individualism, since his whole teaching stresses the overriding importance of an individual's personal, intimate, and vivid relationship to God. His master, Reb Bunam, once said, "When I look at the world, I feel as if every human being were a tree growing all alone in a wilderness, and God had no one else to rely on besides him, and he had no one else in the world but God to depend on."

Reb Mendl took the following passage in the Torah as his lead: "Behold I set before you a blessing and a curse" (Deuteronomy 11:26). The verse begins in the singular and continues in the plural. The Torah was given equally to all Israel, but each individual had to interpret it in his own way. The Kotzker repeated one of Reb Bunam's sayings: though the Torah was given but once, it must be received every day. The giving was offered in equal measure to all of Israel, the acceptance was not the same for everybody, since each individual acquired it according to his spiritual capacity.

PART IV

❖❰❖❰❖❰

Radicalism

The Attack on the Establishment

TOWARD the end of his life Kierkegaard published a series of leaflets in which he vehemently attacked the Church. They were primarily directed against Professor Martenson, who had eulogized the deceased Bishop Mynster, calling him a "Witness to the Truth." Kierkegaard was incensed by the use of the term "witness" (meaning "martyr" in the Greek original) to describe a highly paid career minister.

Walter Lowrie describes Bishop Mynster as follows:

In all respects one of the most admirable bishops the Protestant churches can boast of, a man of imposing presence and persuasive eloquence, whose sermons were not only heard with acclaim but read with devotion, an orthodox theologian who at the same time was well abreast of the highest intellectual culture of his age, a wise ecclesiastical ruler, and withal a man of genuine piety.[1]

According to Ronald Gregor Smith, Mynster had for many years exerted "an immense and continued influence on the religious life of Denmark by his prudent, benevolent, shrewd and brilliant worldliness, by his promotion of what Kierkegaard called 'Sunday-Christianity' or, even more sarcastically, a religion of quiet hours in holy places."[2]

[1] Lowrie, *Kierkegaard,* pp. 504f.
[2] Introduction to *The Last Years,* p. 14.

Kierkegaard's diatribe was not meant solely as an attack on the person of Bishop Mynster. He hoped it would serve as a challenge to Christendom, based on a comparison between New Testament Christianity and the subsequent development of the Church.

When one considers the present state of the world and the whole of life, he is obliged Christianly to say . . . : It is diseased. If I were a doctor and someone asked, "What do you think must be done?" I would answer: "The first thing, the unconditional condition on which anything can be done, is: Silence! Bring the silence! God's Word cannot be heard. If, served by noisy mediators, it has to be shouted clamorously in order to be heard in the hubbub and racket, it does not remain God's word." [3]

The Danish theologian did not attack the Established Church simply because it and its clergy had failed. Kierkegaard was probably aware that neither they nor he himself could fulfill the stern demands imposed by Christianity. What provoked him most of all was their refusal to admit their failure.

He was fully aware of the unique role he had assumed.

The task of an Apostle is to spread Christianity, to win men to it.
My task is to liberate men from the conceit that they are Christians . . .
It is the illusions that must be got rid of, the ground must be cleared, and instead of bringing new life into the illusions, the little life they have in them must be starved out, so as to make it manifest that Christianity simply does not exist. [4]

Kierkegaard condemned the readiness with which the Establishment accepts its own condition. "The official worship of God

[3] For Self-Examination, 1851, translated by Edna and Howard Hong (Minneapolis, 1940), pp. 56f.
[4] Quoted in Lowrie, Kierkegaard, p. 557.

(with the claim of being the Christianity of the New Testament)
is, Christianly, a counterfeit, a forgery." [5]

Strangely enough it is precisely this deification of the established
order which constitutes the constant rebellion, the permanent revolt
against God. It desires, in fact, . . . to be everything, to have the world-
evolution a little bit under its thumb, or to guide the development
of the race. But the deification of the established order . . . is the
invention of the indolent worldly mind, which would put itself at
rest and imagine that all is sheer security and peace, that now we
have reached the highest attainment . . . Every individual ought
to live in fear and trembling, and so too there is no established order
which can do without fear and trembling. Fear and trembling signify that one is in process of becoming, and every individual, and
the race as well, is or should be conscious of being in process of
becoming. And fear and trembling signify that God exists—a fact
which no man and no established order dare for an instant forget.[6]

In Kierkegaard's words:

Whoever you are, whatever your life may be, my friend, by refusing
hereafter (if you have participated hitherto), to take part in the
public worship as it now is (with the claim of representing New
Testament Christianity), thereby you assume the burden of one less
guilty crime upon your conscience, for you take no part in making
a mockery of God.[7]

When he was dying, Kierkegaard refused to receive the sacra-
ment from a pastor. "Pastors are royal officials; royal officials have
nothing to do with Christianity."

"Establishment" means a settled arrangement, a permanent
organization, such as an ecclesiastical system or church. But the

[5] *Kierkegaard's Attack upon "Christendom,"* p. 59.
[6] *Training in Christianity,* p. 89.
[7] Quoted in David F. Swenson, *Something about Kierkegaard* (Minneapolis,
1941), p. 24.

word may also be used in the sense of a prevailing system of thought, an ideology, a routine of life.

Like Kierkegaard, the Kotzker attacked the establishment, not as an institution—the Church had no equivalent in Judaism—but as a style of living, as a satisfying routine of obedience to law and tradition, as piety that had become the well-worn track of habit.

To be a Jew now, people thought, required little effort, merely facile adherence. One was simply born a Jew and continued to live and act as a Jew to conform with the immediate environment.

Kierkegaard lamented the fact that countless numbers considered themselves to be Christians as a matter of course:

The greater part, so far as one can judge, live in categories quite foreign to Christianity! . . . People who perhaps never once enter a church, never think about God, never mention His name except in oaths! People upon whom it has never dawned that they might have any obligations to God . . . Yet all these people . . . call themselves Christians . . . are buried as Christians by the church, are certified as Christians for eternity! [8]

He also wrote: "Luther had ninety-five theses; I should have only one, that Christianity does not exist."

The mass condition that grieved the Kotzker was totally different. Jews who would never enter a synagogue, never mention the name of God, or never be aware of any obligation toward God, were either nonexistent in the environment in which the Kotzker lived or too few to arouse his concern. What upset him was the low quality of their religious commitment, the lack of depth and honesty, not the absence of piety.

In the words of Kierkegaard,

[8] "The Point of View," pp. 22f.

"Why," says the established order to the individual, "why do you want to plague and torture yourself with the prodigious measuring-rod of the ideal? Have recourse to the established order, attach yourself to it. There is the measure. If you are a student, then you can be sure that the Professor is the measure and the truth; if you are a parson, then the Bishop is the way and the life; if you are a scrivener, the Judge is the standard." [9]

Kierkegaard and the Kotzker were extremists, radicals who in the eyes of most people went too far in their views, their demands. Yet, in spite of opposition, they continue to have a catalytic effect on our obtuse, lumpy minds.

What Kierkegaard said about the priests, the Kotzker felt about the teachers of Judaism. They applied its message tranquilizingly, whereas its intention was to be arousing, disquieting in the deepest sense.[10] Kierkegaard's last work was an *Attack upon "Christendom."* The Kotzker devoted his active life to questioning the spiritual vapidity of his fellow Jews.

If Kierkegaard berated parsons, the Kotzker was critical of office-holding rabbis, of those who made a career of serving God and even expected honors in addition to salaries. He used to call them "the red collars," rednecks. Both Kierkegaard and the Kotzker looked askance at respectability. The disciples of the Kotzker openly defied social proprieties and conventions.

The Kotzker could not stand the pompous stuffed shirts, the so-called pillars of society. Those rabbis who took themselves so seriously because of their learning or status, put on airs and thought they were celebrities.

When Moses had to send men to scout the Promised Land, he selected the big-shots for the mission, "heads of the people of Israel" (Numbers 13:3). Seeing the land and realizing how

---

[9] "The Point of View," pp. 26f.
[10] See *Kierkegaard's Attack upon "Christendom,"* p. 262.

much self-sacrifice and how many ordeals the conquest would require, they brought back to the people "an evil report of the land."

This episode caused a rebellion that ended tragically. None of the men who migrated from Egypt were to see the Promised Land. That whole generation died in the wilderness. The Kotzker said that if Moses had sent simple Jews, less sophisticated people, they would have realized that the power of faith would help them acquire the land.

The spies, the leaders of the people, wore fur-trimmed hats and silken garments—like Hasidic rebbes, Reb Mendl said ironically. When Joshua and Caleb saw that men ceremoniously attired could slander the land of their hope, they tore the raiment off the spies (Numbers 14:6) shouting, "Why do you still wear fur-edged hats and venerable garments if you are able to vilify the Land?"

The Kotzker had spiritual ancestors in his opposition to rabbinical and pedestrian communal leaders. Had not some of the ancient Prophets of Israel assailed the priests and the establishment of the sanctuary in Jerusalem?

Following a national disaster, the Jews were exposed to an avalanche of hostility, and self-defense took priority over inner dissent. However, the Baal Shem, though averse to contention and most unpugnacious, could not suppress his reprehension at a critical hour in Jewish history.

One Yom Kippur Eve the Besht perceived a serious charge brought against the Jews that the oral tradition would no longer be theirs. He greatly grieved the whole Yom Kippur Eve. Toward evening when everyone in the town came to him to receive his blessing, he blessed only one or two and said: "I can do no more." He did not bless them because of his sorrow. He went to the synagogue and preached harsh words to them, and he fell upon the ark and cried: "Woe! They want to take the Torah from us. How will we be able to survive among the nations even half a day?"

He was very angry with the rabbis and said that it was because of them, since they invented lies of their own and wrote false legalistic premises. He said that all the Tannaim and Amoraim were brought before the heavenly court. Afterwards he went to the beth-hamidrash and said other harsh words, and then they prayed the Kol Nidre. After Kol Nidre he said that the charge had become more severe.[11]

Reb Yaakov Yosef of Polonnoye, a disciple of the Baal Shem Tov, testified vigorously against the establishment of his time. His attacks were undoubtedly a factor in the strong opposition unleashed against the Hasidic movement. Yet those who followed Reb Yaakov Yosef abstained from taking issue with the established order.

Kierkegaard felt impelled in the name of Christianity to mount an attack upon "Christendom." And yet his assault was not intended to destroy the Church. The Kotzker felt an impulse for the sake of Truth in his understanding of Judaism to dispel some hallowed aspects of Jewish thinking. Although his thrust was not intended to weaken the tradition, some Jewish freethinkers interpreted his intention as an attempt to destroy the heart of Jewish faith. They spread rumors about his having uttered blasphemous words and demonstrated his loss of faith by acting against Jewish law one Sabbath eve.[12]

These vilifications were in part due to the current straitlaced, narrow-minded concepts of religious integrity. The Kotzker's utterances were often unorthodox, deviative, out of tune with

11 *In Praise of the Baal Shem Tov,* translated by Dan Ben-Amos and Jerome R. Mintz (Bloomington, Ind., 1970), pp. 54–55.
12 A detailed analysis of these rumors is offered in my forthcoming book, *The Kotzker,* Chap. XVI.

religious conformity, but so were many of the statements uttered by the Prophets of ancient Israel. Some of his outcries may have had the ring of defying God, especially to the ears of homespun pietists and plebian rationalists. To speak against the name of God is, however, often the burden of the holy life.

As one might have expected, the derogatory rumors about the Kotzker found credence even among some Orthodox Jews who had held the Kotzker in suspicion for many years. Their suspicion was due in part to their serious opposition to his views and manners, and in part to the usual reaction of a middle class with its mediocre leaders to the presence of a genius.

An End to Falsehood

The embarrassing questions raised by the Kotzker and Kierkegaard in their criticism of religion seemed in their lifetime to be *lèse majesté*. Although the religious establishment and the popular standards of religious values were intensely censured by the great Prophets of Israel, it was rare in subsequent centuries for any critique of Judaism to be tolerated. The whole system of beliefs, rituals, and customs was regarded as faultless, implying a belief in rabbinic infallibility. Innocent changes introduced by the early founders of the Hasidic movement were, therefore, condemned as acts of heresy.

What must be done? asks Kierkegaard. Let there be an end to falsehood, says the Kotzker, an end to the illusion that one is serving God while one is really pleasing the ego, relishing pleasure and conceit. Or, in the words of Kierkegaard,

First and foremost, and on the greatest possible scale, an end must be put to the whole official . . . falsehood which well-meaningly conjures up and maintains the illusion that what is preached is Christianity, the Christianity of the New Testament. Here is a case where no quarter must be given.

In the eyes of both thinkers, things had gone from bad to worse with us men; yet we had not become so degenerate, so wretched, that we were unable to bear "this divine thing." The question must be put, wrote Kierkegaard,

whether perhaps it is the same with the human race as it is with the individual, who the older he grows the more good-for-nothing he becomes . . . that it cannot be altered, and it is not God's requirement of us that we should alter it, but we must put up with it, humbly acknowledging our wretchedness; whether the human race has not now reached the age when it is literally true that no longer is there to be found or to be born an individual who is capable of being a Christian in the New Testament sense. In this way the case must be stated: away then, away with all optical illusions! Out with the truth!

It cannot be proved that the Kotzker entertained a similar theory of resignation concerning Judaism and its future. However, with regard to the religious situation of his day, which he equated with the situation of truth, he might have said, "Truth does not exist in this world," just as Kierkegaard proclaimed that, in his country, "Christianity does not exist." [1]

The Kotzker was appalled by people's mendacity. His concern dated back to his childhood.

[1] *Kierkegaard's Attack upon "Christendom,"* pp. 28f.

He once saw a woman selling apples in the marketplace. Delicious-looking, ripe apples were displayed on the top of the basket, while rotten ones filled the rest. The nine-year-old boy turned the basket over, ruined her business, and brought anger and censure upon himself.

The harsh words meted out to Mendl did not inhibit him from uttering disgust whenever he sensed a lie. Throughout his life, he turned over the basket whenever he felt that faultless specimens were used to conceal foul ones.

Self-deception

What is one of the major roots of evil in our insane world? The answer offered in this book is: mendacity, falsehood, wantonness of words, perversion of the heart. Falsehood is a refuge, an asylum for the cruel, the violent, for consummate criminals. What begins in a lie ends in blasphemy.

Rarely does an individual's falsehood remain a private affair. It is so dynamic, so infectious and expansive that it bursts all secrecy, all privacy, affecting ever more people.

According to most religions, lying is regrettably no more than a venal sin. Jewish Law, halakah, maintains that the verse, "Keep far from a falsehood" (Exodus 23:7), is a commandment addressed to judges, meaning, "Beware of a false charge." Only the masters of *agada* interpret it as an exhortation to every individual: "Keep far from uttering a lie."

"When will the Messiah come?" Reb Pinhas of Koretz asked.

"When people will consider the utterance of a lie as sinful as adultery," the Reb answered.

Truth is not a feeling, a mere thought. Truth confronts us as a behest, an insistent summons, austere, uncompromising. Are we able to respond to it in the recesses of our souls?

Truth is often gray, and deceit is full of splendor. One must hunger fiercely after Truth to be able to cherish it.

Those who teach that God is the ground of being have been acclaimed. We need feel no discomfort when God is called the ground of being. But those who insist that He is above the ground of being, that He is the source of qualms, conscience, and compassion, find very few ears.

Truth is severe, harsh, demanding. We would rather hide our face in the sand than be confronted by it. "To live means to be indebted"—who wants to hear this? "I am commanded, therefore I am"—who knows how to cherish it?

A lie may be defined as an attempt to deceive without the other's consent. This definition assumes that there is a silent contract among men to speak the truth. Correct as this assumption is on one level, it is occasionally challenged on another. Publicly we all pay homage to honesty; privately, however, we rarely resent flattery. We are indignant when we are fooled by others but live comfortably with our unconscious desire for self-deceit, being effusive when we flatter our own selves, deriving pleasure from wishful thinking. *Mundus vult decipi*: the world wants to be deceived.

To live without deception presupposes standards beyond the

reach of most people, whose existence is largely shaped by compromise, evasion, and mutual accommodation. Could they face their weakness, their vanity and selfishness, without a mask? Could they bear the discovery that they had lived for goods they had never believed in or cherished, that they had been committed to ideas they had never been convinced of?

The Kotzker realized these difficulties; and this is why he was concerned only with the few. He surely recalled the outcry of Rabbi Shimon ben Yohai, the master in whose path he had decided to lead his own disciples: "I have seen men of greatness, and they are but few." [1]

Flowers turn toward the light and grow. Owls avoid it and sleep. We are part flower, part owl. When light comes to us as a challenge and a demand, the owl in us is shocked and we turn away. When the urge to grow prevails, we welcome the challenge and the demand.

The Kotzker sought to live by the unconditional challenge and dared to utter it. But this privilege was bought at a price: estrangement from his community.

[1] *Sukkah* 456. This translation conveys the meaning of the passage as generally understood.

I Want Honesty

Kierkegaard's article "What Do I Want?" written in 1855, the last year of his life, begins with the words: "Quite simply: I want honesty." It then goes on:

I am not, as well-intentioned people represent . . . I am not a Christian severity as opposed to a Christian leniency.

By no means. I am neither leniency nor severity. I am . . . human honesty . . .

This is in my opinion the falsification of which official Christianity is guilty: it does not frankly and unreservedly make known the Christian requirement . . . to hate our own life in this world. Is there then a single one among us whose life in the remotest degree could be called even the weakest effort in this direction? . . . If then by "grace" God will nevertheless regard us as Christians, one thing at least must be required: that we . . . have a true conception of how infinitely great is the grace that is showed us . . . Honesty to Christianity demands that one call to mind the Christian requirement of poverty . . . because only in poverty can it be truly served.

"I want honesty"—this is the battle cry of both the Kotzker and Kierkegaard. The latter went to the utmost extreme to make people understand what he wanted.

If . . . this generation . . . will honorably, honestly, openly, frankly, directly rebel against Christianity, if it will say to God, "We can but we will not subject ourselves to this power"—but note that this must be done honorably, honestly, openly, frankly, directly—very well then, strange as it may seem, I am with them; for honesty is what I want, and wherever there is honesty I can take part.[1]

Here, then, is a position of decisive importance shared by the Kotzker and Kierkegaard: they regard honesty as the central or supreme religious virtue. It is a position that can be challenged. Is Truth or honesty the highest virtue, one that must be unconditionally observed? Indeed, there are situations in which our commitment to love and compassion would be violated if we acted according to this principle. Confronted with such a conflict, one is forced to admit that moral rigorism is not always a tenable position.[2]

Yet Kierkegaard insisted:

Far from impatiently and hot-headedly urging someone else impatiently and hot-headedly to attempt to forsake all things, which God perhaps does not demand of him, we would extol honesty, which God demands of everyone.[3]

Theodor Haecker cites an example of human honesty as understood by Kierkegaard:

That I shall do what I say, or that I shall say that I will disregard on weekdays the Christian ideal to which I subscribe or which I my-

[1] *Kierkegaard's Attack upon "Christendom,"* pp. 37f., 39.
[2] "Human honesty is not a specifically Christian concept . . . it is certainly not a religious concept . . . Human honesty is something great and always of great value; it means everything in purely *worldly* human affairs as well as in philosophy and science . . . Yet it is not everything in matters which do not concern man alone, but also God and faith . . . For instance, human honesty is much less than human conscience, since the latter is always in communion with God himself, however much it may be falsified. Human honesty belongs to a purely human ethic, to its immanence and autonomy; the human conscience transcends this immanence in all circumstances."— Theodor Haecker, *Kierkegaard the Cripple,* translated by C. Van O. Bruyn (London, 1950).
[3] Quoted in Paul R. Sponheim, *Kierkegaard on Christ and Christian Coherence* (New York, 1967), p. 148.

self preach on Sundays, and which I contemplate on Sundays; that I shall honestly and truthfully say *what I do* personally.[4]

In other words, "To God in heaven it is infinitely dearer that [the people] honestly admit, as the condition precedent to becoming Christians, that they are not and will not be Christians." [5]

In 1847 Kierkegaard published *Three Discourses in Various Spirits*. The first of these was entitled "Purity of Heart." Its theme was "Purity of heart is to will one thing." Writing of himself in the third person, Kierkegaard explained: "His purity of heart was *to will only one thing* . . . He did not abate the price, did not give in." [6] This of course applies to the Kotzker as well.

Some people preach continuously and complain about the deceitfulness of others. Yet truthfulness does not prevail in their own lives either. According to Proverbs (23:23), "Buy truth, and do not sell it," and as the Kotzker said, "Acquire Truth for your own consumption, not for export."

To Be Truth

The truth, [wrote Kierkegaard] consists not in knowing the truth but in being the truth . . . Knowing the truth is something which follows as a matter of course from being the truth, and not conversely;

4 *Kierkegaard the Cripple*, p. 508.
5 *Kierkegaard's Attack upon "Christendom,"* p. 84.
6 "The Point of View," p. 103; italics added.

and precisely for this reason it becomes untruth when knowing the truth is separated from being the truth, or when knowing the truth is treated as one and the same thing as being the truth, since the true relation is the converse of this: to be the truth is one and the same thing as knowing the truth.[1]

In stressing Truth as Judaism's supreme concern, the Kotzker also did not think primarily in terms of theoretical attainment of Truth but, rather, in terms of living the Truth. Human existence should be compatible with living in confrontation with God. Truth was the coincidence of thought and God, he maintained, or the coincidence of the individual's life with the will of God.

Being Truth, according to the Kotzker, like being *in* Truth according to Kierkegaard, implied a never-ending process. Man was always in a situation where he had to strive. The complete coincidence could only hover as "a creative longing." The Kotzker's passionate craving for Truth was a hunger and thirst after the Lord. Many ask, What quality, without reservation, may be identified with the Divine? Some reply, Love, or compassion, justice. The Kotzker maintained that it was *Truth*.

Truth leads to love, whereas love may be blind and yield to untruth.

In the Hebrew Bible there is no equation of God with any of His attributes, such as love, justice, or compassion. In Jewish liturgy (based on Jeremiah 10:10), however, the equation can be found: God is Truth. Love, justice, compassion are merely expressions of the Divine, not its highest manifestation. Truth is always with God. It is the mystery of being. Therefore, the way that always leads to God is Truth.

Yet Truth is buried and remains hidden. In a world full of

[1] *Training in Christianity,* p. 201.

falsehood, Truth can survive only in concealment, for lies lie in wait everywhere. As soon as Truth is disclosed, it is surrounded by forces seeking to destroy it.

Truth is not within man's reach. It is only in God. It is a peak of insight. One must strain to attain it. There are no proofs to validate ultimate Truth, since perception and reason say one thing and Truth may reveal the opposite. The only alternative is to eliminate the self, to grow in faith. Faith is more perceptive than reason.

Truth, bound to the existence of God, is possible only to the degree that those human acts which contradict God are recognized and eliminated. The test of Truth can take place only through the soul's confrontation with God, in moments of disregard for self-regard, confronting oneself as one is confronted by God. The result is not an arbitrary private judgment. One is overcome by the certainty that to express God's existence is like affirming the existence of other human beings.

Kierkegaard says, "The truth is a snare: you cannot have it, without being caught. You cannot have the truth in such a way that you catch it, but only in such a way that it catches you." [2] In "Purity of Heart" he maintains that only he who wills the good can be said to will one thing. For all is transitory; this alone abides. To will the good, one must end double-thinking and everything within that tempts man to seek some other end instead of the good, or by means of it. Man must rid himself not only of the hope for reward and the fear of punishment, but even of that self-esteem which is content only when the good wins through ourselves. Above all, he must be aware of reducing life to a series of partial interests, of willing the good to a certain extent, but not its ultimate.

[2] Journal entry in *The Last Years*, p. 133.

Mahatma Gandhi, one of the twentieth century's great seekers after justice, shared the insight of Kierkegaard and the Kotzker. On this point, he wrote, at the end of his autobiography, "My uniform experience has convinced me that there is no other God than Truth." [3]

Religious Radicalism

What are the epithets that accurately describe the conspicuous attributes of religious existence as commonly observed? Half-hearted, perfunctory, moderate, mediocre. Yet such a state is an untenable contradiction. The meaning of religion is that it is a culmination, a climax; not an ornament, but the heart, the chief meaning of existence; not a fraction, but a completion; not shallowness, but depth. The demand is for "service of the heart"; what is offered is lip service.

In *Training in Christianity* Kierkegaard conceded that the ideal goals of religion could not be attained. Nevertheless, he wanted to rouse people to higher ideality. Did the Kotzker entertain a similar reservation?

Both the Kotzker and Kierkegaard were outsiders, anguished by the moral and spiritual predicament of societies satisfied with their own stability. Their dark premonitions, their radical attacks

[3] *An Autobiography, or My Experiments with Truth* (Boston, 1957), p. 503.

and demands, were regarded as exaggerated, bizarre, or downright fantastic. Did the Kotzker intuit the coming triumph of Satan that brought the Holocaust to his people a few generations later? "I am not worried about hunger; what worries me is human cruelty," he exclaimed.

Opposition to the Kotzker—and to Kierkegaard as well—is easily explained. Cradled as most people are in optimism, believing in the wisdom of the golden middle course, they can hardly sympathize with such harsh and exacting concepts.

The Kotzker was provocative and irritating—most disagreeable in unmasking falsehoods, hypocrisy, cant. His demands were excessive. Was it not enough to live a normal, decent life, conforming to the laws and standards of Judaism? No, for conformity was deformity in the eyes of the Kotzker; observance without understanding and inner involvement was like a body without a soul. Indeed, a life of normal decency was an impossibility. Life was threatened with extraordinary dangers, always on the brink of abnormal indecency. Acute problems cannot be handled with bland solutions.

The Kotzker would maintain that a form of piety that stressed exclusively external compliance with the Law and disregarded the need for purity of heart, for inner motivation and devotion —thus evading the necessity of dealing with the problems of the person—was a truncation of the heart of Judaism.

Both Kierkegaard and the Kotzker, then, accused their contemporaries of not living up to their commitments. Kierkegaard called the Church a sham. The Kotzker hurled denunciations even at those who came to seek his guidance.

Their radical demands showed that the two thinkers had little compassionate consideration for the human condition and its natural limitations. The Kotzker's demands of extreme self-denial and perpetual self-examination went beyond the norms set forth by classical Jewish authorities. In a sense he sought to mold Judaism in his own likeness.

Common sense dictates moderation. Do not be excessive, whether in earthly or in religious affairs. "Too much" is always unhealthy. And so religion operates as the art of compromise. The fallacy lies in our not realizing that by serving the self, by being addicted to the ego, we impudently indulge in excessiveness.

The Kotzker's message was a protest against undue interest in trivialities, against a life style in which ritual consisted of cursory, hasty acts, against the sentimental twaddle that was concealed within pious orations.

Judaism as an order of living stresses the necessity of outward acts as well as inward moments—despite the threat that the first may gain primacy over the second, that observance may deteriorate into mere habit, that the religious act may become commonplace, stale, and vapid.

There must be no mere repetition, the Kotzker demanded. Even a religious custom must be carried out in an unaccustomed spirit. The Jewish order of living requires an abundance of ritual acts and prayers to be performed daily, and such a demand involved prodigious spiritual vitality, discipline, and spontaneity.

This was a central problem to the Kotzker. "I came into the world to discriminate between holiness and outwardness," he said. Giving priority to the person, to the inner life, he stressed that service to God must be eventful, a happening within the person.

The Kotzker's radicalism moved along the line of the old principle, *fiat iustitia pereat mundus*. The Torah, as we have said, set forth extremist demands: You shall be holy, love your God with all your heart, with all your soul, with all your might; stay far away from a lie. Yet Jewish tradition has sought to reduce these demands to moderate norms. The Torah had not been given to angels, it was said. Man was called upon to make an effort that he was capable of. And his power was conditioned by the circumstances of history.

The call for spontaneity and the denigration of mere outwardness in ritual observance have reverberated throughout Jewish history since the time of the Prophets. But the Kotzker carried this demand to an extreme. "He who prays today because he prayed yesterday—a complete rascal is better than he." Inordinate and excessive as this statement seems to be, one must not forget that the smugness it sought to unsettle is equally so. Were these words meant to be taken as a norm or as an alarm?

This was the way of the Kotzker. Just as there is a difference between day and night, there must be a distinction between one day and another. A man should not even imitate himself. Self-renewal must be constant. To repeat oneself is to commit forgery; one becomes mired in routine. Therefore, avoid the trodden paths! At least one day a week—on the Sabbath—keep away from sameness.

The Kotzker treasured rituals, the performance of the traditional commandments. He did not minimize their importance. Yet he disparaged those who set aside certain deeds or times for communion with the Holy, not seeking to maintain such communion in daily life. To the people who gathered around him on the Sabbath, he said:

I do not understand what they expect of me. All week long each person acts as he pleases. When the holy Sabbath arrives, these same people put on the silken robe, the pious sash, and the pompous headgear, and claim to be in communion with the spirit of the Sabbath. I say, as a person lives all week long, so will be his insight on the Seventh Day.

Kierkegaard similarly criticized the place and the use Christendom had assigned to the sacraments.

It is very true—probably the truest statement about Christendom—that, as Pascal says, it is a union of people who, by means of the sacraments, excuse themselves from their duty to love God.[1]

Traditionally, Jewish teachers have stressed the preciousness of doing a *mitzvah,* the good deed, even if it was not accompanied by an inner commitment to God. Yet, despite all the emphasis on the importance of deeds, the Kotzker insisted upon the decisive importance of inwardness. If a person had an inner living commitment to God, his *mitzvoth* and good deeds were precious; they were regarded as having been carried out by God. If, however, such commitment was lacking, *mitzvoth* and good deeds were of no value whatsoever. Such deeds were regarded as if they were "carried out by a machine."

[1] Quoted in Louis K. Dupré, *Kierkegaard as Theologian* (London, 1963), pp. 106–7.

A Little Heaven

In his later years the Kotzker seemed to have modified some of the radical views he had preached earlier in his career. While he disapproved of those who indulged in physical pleasures, he also knew that complete severance from the world was impossible. What was the right way?

The Talmud reports that when King Solomon instituted the laws concerning "the mixing of realms," private and public, and the washing of hands, a Heavenly voice declared: "My son, if your heart is wise, my heart too will rejoice."

What great wisdom in those laws impressed the power of Heaven? The Kotzker answered that this wisdom suggested that one ought to be mixed up with the world and to be able to wash one's hands of it —to be part of the world and also outside it. One had to be both involved and detached at the same time.

Let us remember that this Talmudic story does not come from some disenchanted or bitter recluse who had never enjoyed this world's delights. It involves a king who had tasted luxuries to the full.

To eat, to drink, to be active in the world, and to remain detached from it—here is wisdom. To abstain completely from all enjoyments may be easy. Yet to enjoy life and retain spiritual integrity—there is the challenge.

The higher flavor of living on earth is experienced when a

taste of Heaven is added to it. The danger is that a man may mistake worldly gratifications for the highest good he thinks he may achieve.

As a young man the Kotzker made a pilgrimage on foot to see his rebbe in a distant town. It was wintertime. The journey was tiring and the weather grim.

Suddenly, a rich man from his town came by in a sumptuous carriage drawn by four horses, with two extra horses in the rear. When he saw Reb Mendl trudging along, his bundle on his shoulders, he ordered his coachman to stop and asked, "Where are you going?"

Reb Mendl told him.

"Well," said the rich man, "get in. I will take you there."

"Why not?" said Reb Mendl.

Sitting in the carriage was a genuine pleasure. There was no lack of warm, woolen blankets. The rich man even asked whether he would like something to drink.

Reb Mendl warmed himself with some vodka and ate a piece of cake as well. Then he took a piece of roast goose and another sip of vodka. He felt most comfortable.

Suddenly he turned to his host. "Tell me please, what are your worldly pleasures?"

The man looked at him in astonishment. "Can't you see? The carriage and horses, the expensive food I can have even on the road. Do you mean to say that all of this is not enough for a fellow like you?"

"No," teased Reb Mendl, "these are your heavenly pleasures, the acme of your pleasures, but where are your worldly pleasures?"

In the *Sayings of the Fathers,* we are told, "More beautiful is one hour of tranquillity in the world to come than all of life in this world." The Kotzker was asked: "What sense is there in cherishing the promise of bliss in the life to come? Is it not realistic to enjoy this world's pleasures here and now? Did not even the sage Abbaye cite the proverb, 'A young pumpkin in hand is better than one full-grown in the field?'"

"That very proverb is a this-worldly argument," answered the Kotzker.

According to Reb Henokh, a disciple of the Kotzker, it was the ability to overcome the discrepancy between the worldly and the Heavenly that marked the major difference between Judaism and Christianity. For Christians this world is one realm and Heaven is another. To the Jews this world and Heaven are not separate. They are one and the same thing.

According to an ancient Hebrew law, he who owns no land in Palestine is not obliged to go on a pilgrimage to the sanctuary in Jerusalem. Since he has no property ties, he is *eo ipso* tied to God wherever he may be.

Poverty or Property

Poverty, the condition of having little or no wealth or material possession, was regarded in various religions as a spiritual good, as an adornment of saintly life. Man ought to be as self-sufficient as possible and reduce his dependence on things. In Hinduism poverty is praised because it brings freedom from the burdens and temptations of wealth. Traditionally, a Hindu, having discharged his family obligations, is supposed to end his life as a wandering ascetic.

In the Christian tradition, poverty was commended and ideal-ized as a counsel of perfection.[1] It was extolled not because lack of material possessions, when freely accepted, meant liberation from worldly interests but primarily because of the teaching that "the Kingdom of God is not of this world." Thus, the treasure of a Christian could not be found in this world but only in the after-life. The call to poverty also had an eschatological meaning. The present age was about to pass away, and he who remained bound by earthly ties was not free to embrace the coming age whole-heartedly.

The abandonment of material goods was an essential ingredi-ent of the renunciation involved in the monastic vocation from the very beginning. Protestantism, on the other hand, has gen-erally thought in terms of stewardship of wealth, with an aware-ness of its dangers rather than a demand for renunciation.

In the Hebrew Bible poverty is regarded as a misfortune. God's blessing is meant to include material prosperity. In this spirit we read in the Wisdom Literature, "All the days of the poor are evil" (Proverbs 15:15), "The poor man's wisdom is despised, his words are not heard" (Ecclesiastes 9:16), and "The life of the poor is a curse of the heart" (Ben Sira 38:19).

Consistent with the view of material prosperity and wealth as a divine blessing are various utterances in post-Biblical Jewish literature. Prayers for sustenance and prosperity are part of the liturgy. It is, however, incorrect to claim that Judaism has never seen anything meritorious in self-imposed poverty.[2]

The early masters of Talmudic literature, Rabbi Ishmael and

[1] "If you wish to be perfect, go and sell what you own and give the money to the poor, and you will have treasure in heaven" (Matthew 19:21). Sim-ilar appeals to give away all one has in order to study Torah or to help the poor are frequently reported in rabbinic literature.
[2] See Max Joseph, *Sittenlehre des Judentums* (1902), p. 52.

Rabbi Akiba, held diametrically opposed views concerning poverty. While the first deplored it as a misfortune, the second maintained, "Poverty is becoming to Israel as a red ribbon on the nape of a white horse." On the prophetic words "I have tried you in the furnace of affliction" (Isaiah 48:10), the Talmud comments, "This teaches that the Holy One, blessed be He, went through all the virtues in order to bestow them upon Israel and found none more becoming than poverty."[3]

While legally the right to property is recognized, we are told again and again that God, not man, is the owner of everything there is, that what we claim to possess is merely held by us in trust. "For Mine is the earth," says the Lord (Leviticus 25:23).

In the words of Henry George,

Everywhere in the Mosaic institutions is the land treated as the gift of the Creator to his common creatures which no one had the right to monopolize. Everywhere it is, not your estate, or your property, not the land which you bought, or the land which you conquered but "the land which the Lord God gives you . . . [Moses] not only provided for the fair division of the land among the people, and for making it fallow and common every seventh year, but by the institution of the Jubilee, he provided for a redistribution of the land every fifty years.[4]

In this spirit we are told in rabbinic literature that he who derives enjoyment without first uttering a blessing is considered guilty of sacrilege.

Ownership holds a secret malice in store. The usual justification for having property is that it safeguards a person's inde-

---

[3] *Hagigah* 9b.
[4] Henry George, *Progress and Poverty* (1879). Similarly, "There is on earth no power which can rightfully make a grant of exclusive ownership in land . . . For what are we but tenants for a day?"

pendence from other people. In reality, however, one may become easily bewitched by what one owns; things possessed take possession of the person who owns them. He forfeits his freedom and falls victim to avarice and niggardliness.

While the earliest Hasidic masters were concerned about the oppressive poverty of their flock and sought to offer help by means of counsel, prayer, and blessing, some of the masters of the third generation of the Hasidic movement were not in agreement about the effect of prosperity on the religious life. The Maggid of Kozhenitz maintained that being prosperous was detrimental to the life of piety, while the Seer of Lublin insisted that material well-being enhanced one's ability to live a saintly life. The Kotzker, we may recall, was first a disciple of the Seer and subsequently joined the dissenters led by the Holy Jew, who quietly established an opposing trend.

Money, Pfui!

It upset the Kotzker that people were passionately engrossed in business activities. A person must work for a livelihood, but why should the mind and heart submit to the amassing of profits? "You shall eat the fruit of the labor of your hands. You shall be happy and it shall be well with you," says the Psalmist (128:2). The hands should be used in making a living, but one's head should be in Heaven.

The Kotzker thought that the pursuit of wealth tended to demean a person. The universal passion for ever more possessions was an abomination to him. As long as it was voluntary, poverty was a preferable goal to strive for. He apparently thought that it was never despicable. Poverty released a person to go his way unobtrusively, uprightly, serenely, humanely.

Very early we are trained to develop a keen sense of property rights. Mine and yours! It begins when we are infants. In what follows the sense of possessiveness is continuously strengthened.

The Kotzker called for a revision of fundamental concerns. The separating wall between the sacred and the secular, worship and ownership, had caused a division between the conscience and God. In the Pentateuch the relation of man to things in space, to money, to property, is a fundamental religious problem. Avarice is often more obscene than lechery, for it feeds on self-centeredness. Its goal is the acquisition of property, implying its exclusive possession by the owner, mindless of course that "the earth is the Lord's" (Psalms 24:1).

The Kotzker was disgusted with the debauchery of making money. Outraged by the scandals of the world, he refused to join the people in the pursuit of material goods. "Discard the world!" Money—Pfui!

Recall that when the great sage Rabbi Shimon ben Yohai and his son emerged from the cave in which they had lived twelve years and saw the people plowing fields and sowing the seeds, whatever they looked upon was immediately consumed by the fire of their eyes. Thereupon a voice from Heaven exclaimed, "Have you emerged to destroy My world? Return to the cave!"

Reb Mendl, upon assuming leadership as a Hasidic rebbe, announced that he would lead his disciples in the path of Rabbi Shimon ben Yohai. Did he, too, hear a voice from Heaven and therefore withdraw from the world, spending the last twenty years of his life in solitude?

The Kotzker was poor most of his life. There were times when he could not afford to buy stamps in order to mail a letter. He seemed to have no appreciation for money. Once he was offered some coins by a disciple, and when he started to count them, he became flustered and could not add them up. His friend Reb Feivl of Gritze reported: "We were all young disciples in Pshyskhe, and very poor. Often we could not afford to buy a loaf of bread."

Fortunately a lady, called Temerl (died 1830), the wife of the very wealthy Berek Zbitkower—and grandmother of Henri Bergson—greatly admired Hasidim. Whenever possible, she offered Reb Mendl and his disciples opportunities of part-time employment that would not interfere with their studies.

Once Temerl arrived in Pshyskhe and Reb Feivl said, "Mendl, why you are starving! Why don't you go and see Temerl? She will give you a job and you will earn some money."

"Money? Pfui!" he exclaimed.

"I was nauseated for six weeks when the word 'money' was mentioned," added Reb Mendl.

Who does not know that often man sells his soul to gain riches? "It is not hunger I fear, it is the cruelty that comes from hunger that frightens me," the Kotzker said.

In an avowedly business society like ours, success is normally equated with material rewards. Money tends to be the yardstick with which we requite achievement, and not in commerce alone.

We were wisely counseled long ago of the danger in the inordinate love of money. On the other hand, to be poor in an affluent society is to bear a crushing load. Seeking to escape the shame and ostracism that such a condition entails lures many of us into a trap.

William James wrote:

The prevalent fear of poverty among the educated classes is the worst moral disease from which our civilization suffers. Among us English-speaking peoples especially do the praises of poverty need once more to be boldly sung. We have grown literally afraid to be poor. We despise any one who elects to be poor in order to simplify and save his inner life. If he does not join the general scramble and pant with the money-making street, we deem him spiritless and lacking in ambition. We have lost the power even of imagining what the ancient idealization of poverty could have meant: the liberation from material attachments, the unbribed soul, the manlier indifference, the paying our way by what we are or do and not by what we have, the right to fling away our life at any moment irresponsibly,—the more athletic trim, in short, the moral fighting shape. When we of the so-called better classes are scared as men were never scared in history at material ugliness and hardship; when we put off marriage until our house can be artistic, and quake at the thought of having a child without a bank-account and doomed to manual labor, it is time for thinking men to protest against so unmanly and irreligious a state of opinion.[1]

The distinguished social and economic historian, R. H. Tawney, an authority on the close relationship between religious ideologies and economic growth, was intensely concerned with problems of social injustice and profoundly suspicious of money. Expressing this dislike, he wrote:

The burden of our civilization is not merely, as many suppose, that the product of industry is ill-distributed, or its conduct tyrannical, or its operation interrupted by embittered disagreements. It is that in-

[1] *The Varieties of Religious Experience* (New York, 1902).

dustry itself has come to hold a position of exclusive predominance among human interests, which no single interest, and least of all the provision of the material means of existence, is fit to occupy. Like a hypochondriac who is so absorbed in the processes of his own digestion that he goes to his grave before he has begun to live, industrialized communities neglect the very objects for which it is worth while to acquire riches in their feverish preoccupation with the means by which riches can be acquired.

That obsession by economic issues is as local and transitory as it is repulsive and disturbing. To future generations it will appear as pitiable as the obsession of the seventeenth century by religious quarrels appears today; indeed, it is less rational, since the object with which it is concerned is less important. And it is a poison which inflames every wound and turns each trivial scratch into a malignant ulcer. Society will not solve the particular problems of industry which afflict it, until that poison is expelled, and it has learned to see industry itself in the right perspective. If it is to do that, it must rearrange its scale of values. It must regard economic interests as one element in life, not as the whole of life. It must persuade its members to renounce the opportunity of gains which accrue without any corresponding service, because the struggle for them keeps the whole community in a fever.[2]

[2] *The Acquisitive Society* (New York, 1920), pp. 183f.

PART V

The Battle for Faith

A Fighting Faith

BOTH KIERKEGAARD and the Kotzker contended that the essence of religion was warfare: a fight against spiritual inertia, indolence, callousness. To live with one's religious commitment was to face opposition, to dare, to defy. A lack of such commitment meant evading the challenge, drifting with the current.

Accepting the premise that the inner life was a constant battle, the Kotzker rejected the strategy of the defensive and insisted that the campaign be pushed to the extremes of human endurance, disregarding other considerations. All decisions had to be inspired by the will, which had to seize and retain the initiative.

The Kotzker's life was a dramatic combat on more than one front: with himself, with his disciples, even with Heaven. He wrestled with God and with men, as Jacob did, from the setting sun "until the breaking of the day" (Genesis 32:25).

In his individualism he was opposed to a recumbent Judaism which taught that the Torah was complete with finality, that obedience to it should be blind and inquiry stifled. The Kotzker avowed that the oral Torah had never been written: understanding and appropriating were of a higher order than obedience, and inquisitive reflection was a necessity.

Each believer, Kierkegaard said, could and should feel the

contemporaneity of the decisive event of Christian faith: the incarnation. Similarly, the Kotzker said that the event of the covenant and engagement of God and Israel should be experienced as a perpetual, ongoing, event.

Faith as a Leap

In his doctrine of the primacy of the will Kierkegaard was possibly influenced by Tertullian or Pascal. The individual constitutes himself as an individual through his selection of one mode of existence over another.

Central to Kierkegaard's thought is his insistence on the choice each person has to make between God and the world. And since there is no human existence without the making of moral decisions, it is a perpetual either/or.

There are no criteria, according to Kierkegaard, no logically compelling reasons why a man should opt for God rather than the world. But if he chooses a life of cultivated humanism or pleasure, he will inevitably be dogged by despair, consciously or unconsciously.

No humanism or hedonism can satisfy a mind so searching, a soul so tortured, an integrity so exacting. "Suicide is the only tolerable existential consequence of pure thought." [1] For such men the central issue is to trust in God or perish.

---

[1] *Concluding Unscientific Postscript*, p. 273.

Kierkegaard considered as essentially irreligious any attempts to provide Christianity with a rational justification. For, since the object of faith is an absolute paradox and an offense to the mind, faith cannot be an act of understanding or belong to the intellectual sphere. It can only be an act of the will. The certainty of faith can never come from rational proofs, but only by making a "leap of faith." And this leaping venture cannot just be made once and for all; it must be renewed continually, because objections to it continue to arise.

In this now famous metaphor, "the leap of faith," Kierkegaard expressed his repudiation of a smooth transition to new concepts through meditation, or of the arrival at new concepts by a progressive process of thought. Faith is attained, not by continuous and gradual approximations, but by a resolution of the will.

Immediate knowledge of God by the soul stands higher than knowledge attained by speculation. Faith stands outside the gradualism that is favored by those who are prisoners to the theories of evolution, interpreting all of the world's phenomena by means of it.

Beaten paths, thought the Kotzker, lead to quagmires. Routine threatens to ruin religious faith. There are no easy ways, no simple tricks. What is achieved without effort is not worth a tiny candle.

It is a fatal error to assume that the world is flat and that roads move horizontally. The main road is vertical, leading either up or down; one either rises or descends.

A Jewish maxim instructs that if you cannot win, give in. In Kotzk the maxim was altered: if you cannot win, you *must* win.

To be a Jew is a major enterprise. It means going uphill. No steps can be taken lightly. There are more impediments to leading a truly Jewish life than we realize. Yet the task urges one on, given one no rest, and progress is attained at the price of travail, by a "leap of faith."

This is how the Kotzker explained the plight of man: all souls descend a ladder from Heaven to earth. Once they have arrived, the ladder is removed. But then the souls are bidden to mount upward; they are called again and again. So they go about looking for the ladder . . . Some people give up, for how can one ascend to Heaven without a ladder?

There are, however, those souls that are resolved not to fail. They throw themselves toward Heaven but fall. They try repeatedly, until they too give up the struggle. Yet wise people maintain that since no ladder is to be found, there is no alternative; what we are called upon to do we must do. Whatever may happen, we must continue to strive upward, until God, may His Name be praised, has mercy and draws us to Himself. One must exert himself strongly to be worthy of God's aid. By the power of the leap alone, however, one cannot reach Heaven. It is only by an act of grace, or divine aid, that the goal is attained.

There is no ladder we can mount step by step, from the egocentricity that enthralls us to the surpassing of our self-regard, which is to say living for the sake of Heaven; from the confines of reason that can only comprehend what is within its scope to God, who transcends human reason; from the sensual faculties which are at home in the reality of this world to the insight that nothing is truly real except God.

God's transcendence over the mind of man is a necessary attribute of His being. "A God whom any dirty, little man could understand I could not believe in," said the Kotzker.

To commit oneself to God completely, then, requires a "leap," a suspension of man's inevitable self-centeredness. Kierkegaard attributed the idea of the leap of faith to Lessing, who maintained that accidental historical truths could never serve as evidence for eternal truths, so that a leap was necessary to arrive at the latter.[2] He also cited Moses Mendelssohn:

Zweifeln, ob es nicht etwas giebt, das nicht nur alle Begriffe uebersteigt, sondern völlig ausser dem Begriffe liegt, dieses nenne ich einen Sprung ueber sich selbst hinaus.[3] [To doubt whether there might not be something that not only transcends all concepts, but stands totally outside concept itself—I would call this a leap beyond oneself.]

Faith According to the Kotzker

The voice of the Kotzker—like that of Kierkegaard—was resonant with an awareness of power, with a certainty that faith was the answer to the human predicament. But faith was not easily won. Only through extreme spiritual anguish could it be gained, said Kierkegaard. The Kotzker agreed.

What does having faith mean? To follow the path of your ancestors? To carry out what is contained in a creed? Such simple faith is the backbone of all religions. After all, a hundred generations of Jews have borne testimony to the existence of God. So one may accept their words, their beliefs. Yet the Kotzker refused to be a follower, living on spiritual crumbs left by the

[2] *Ibid.*, pp. 86*ff.*
[3] *Ibid.*, p. 95.

princes of the past. Facile acceptance was not to his liking. Faith could not be inherited; each person had to earn it.

"This is my God and I will praise Him, the God of my father, and I will exalt Him" (Exodus 15:2). First one had to be able to say, "This is my God"; then one could add, "the God of my father." The Kotzker said, "Some of my Hasidim can point to Heaven and exclaim, 'This is my God!'" To be at ease was the reverse of living by faith. But to those who were in earnest, persistence in the pursuit of faith meant toil that also brought solace.

The Kotzker believed that ways of knowing God were not wanting. In the daily liturgy Jews declare, "The earth is full of Your possessions." The word for possession (*kinyan*) also means a way of making something your own, a mode of acquisition. And to the Kotzker the sentence implied that the world is full of ways of appropriating God, of making Him your own.

Effort and insight must precede the acquisition of faith. Only he who is a pioneer is worthy of being an heir. Even as a young man, the Kotzker stressed the importance of spiritual initiative. When his master, Reb Bunam, asked him, "Mendl, what source do you draw your faith from?" he replied, "It is written: 'Lift up your eyes on high and see who created these [Heaven and earth]'" (Isaiah 40:25). In other words, faith does not come from within but by raising our eyes. (Significantly, this verse from Isaiah is a major focus of speculation in the mystical Zohar.)

Reb Bunam disagreed: Jews did not derive their faith from the world, from creation, but from what happened in their history, their redemption from slavery.

Yet Reb Mendl would not budge. He insisted upon the necessity of personally acquiring insight leading toward faith. "The

Prophet," he argued, "still stands and calls: Do not be deaf! Do not be blind! (see Isaiah 42:18). It is entirely within your own power!"

"Understand and know Me" (see Jeremiah 9:24). Do not be a sluggard, man, there is no excuse for not knowing Me.

Though knowing God is not consoling but demanding, offering challenge rather than pleasure, it is both vital and urgent. The Kotzker never cherished learning because it led to power and distinction. In a deep sense, the more knowledge we acquire, the more uncomfortable we become. "He who increases knowledge increases affliction" (Ecclesiastes 1:18)—"Be afflicted and know!" [1]

Be Upset and Believe

Faith is deeper than knowledge. The latter is absorbed by our brains and remains there. When an insight of faith occurs, all limbs quiver and move, an upheaval agitates the whole man. The acquisition of scientific data causes no transformation of the person. Knowledge is knowledge, and the ego stays the same. But one cannot fail to realize that the ego is a trap when one experiences God's broad majesty intimately here and now.

Faith is the beginning of the end of egocentricity. "To have

[1] *Krenkn zolste un vissn zolste*—Yiddish saying.

faith is *to disregard self-regard,"* said the Kotzker. It involves the realization that, confined to our ego, we are in another man's house. Our home is where the self lives in fellowship with Him Who is all and Who includes us.

"I believe in God" does not mean that *I* accept the fact of *His* existence. It does not signify that *I* come first, then *God,* as the syntax of the sentence implies. The opposite is true. Because God exists, I am able to believe.

"What is faith?" Reb Bunam once said to his disciple Reb Mendl. Answering his own question, he said that faith meant faithfulness, integrity. Of God, the Psalmist says: "All His work is done in faithfulness (*emunah*)" (Psalms 33:4). He acts in order to aid. His acts are based on His integrity. "His faithfulness endures to all generations" (Psalms 100:5). To be faithful means not to act for private ends but as a messenger in loyalty to Him who has engaged us.

"To declare Thy steadfast love in the morning, and Thy faithfulness by night" (Psalms 92:3). In the brightness of the morning we sing praise; in the loneliness of the night we should have faith. This means being faithful to Him even in extreme misery. When we have every reason in the world to grieve, to lament, we shall be able to lean on faith.

Once again, man's faith cannot derive from rational evidence of the existence of God. The Kotzker repudiated attempts to establish such proofs and maintained that men must live by faith despite their agonizing subjection to arguments disputing its tenets. He interpreted Psalm 37:3 to mean: "Live in agony and survive by faith," or "Though life may be all hell, survive by faith." [1]

1 Yiddish lit. *Lig in der erd, un pashe dikh mit emune.* Reminiscent of this saying is Kierkegaard's statement that one must lie in the depths of over seventy thousand fathoms of water and still preserve one's faith.

Moses prayed, "Show me Thy glory." He was eager to understand God's presence, the meaning of what was happening in the world. And this was the answer he received: "You shall see My back, but My face shall not be seen" (Exodus 33:23). On earth everything looks topsy-turvy, confused, contrary to what human reason expects. The world stands with its back to reason. The face of God's presence is hidden.

The Talmud says: "When Nebuchadnezzar, the mighty King of Babylonia, wanted to sing praises to God, an angel came and slapped him in the face." Asked the Kotzker, "Why did he deserve to be slapped, if his intention was to sing God's praises?" He answered himself: "You want to sing praises while you are wearing your crown? Let me hear how you praise me after having been slapped in the face."

A higher level of faith is won when all acquired wisdom is set aside in order to believe in Him Who is One.

You do not attain faith by your own effort alone. Faith is a gift of God. Of Abraham it is said, "He believed the Lord, and reckoned it to Him as righteousness" (Genesis 15:6). Abraham considered that God's righteousness enabled him to believe in Him. He knew that his faith did not come from his own heart but from God.

Since faith stands higher than the reach of reason, one must strive for superhuman understanding. Saadia (882–942), the greatest scholar and author of the Gaonic period, introduced the distinction between the rational commandments, those that appealed to reason, and "the commandments of obedience," whose rational meaning remained hidden from man. The latter included the cultic and ritual laws of the Bible. Theologians have labored to find "reasons" for them, so that they might be looked upon as reasonable commandments, and thus become acceptable and easier to obey. But the Kotzker questioned the assumption that religious acts were discharged because they were intelligible. In the realm of faith, spiritual obedience stood higher than comprehension and should therefore determine the fulfillment even of reasonable commandments.

In contrast to classical Jewish philosophers, who defined faith in terms of epistemology, the Kotzker was concerned with it in terms of the total human situation. He also de-theologized faith, declaring that to possess faith simply meant *to disregard self-regard*.

In the history of Hasidism we come upon two types of faith: one is intimate personal attachment to God, the other self-centeredness overcome. Is there a way to correlate the two? The first is a promise, the second a challenge. The first is nurtured by wonder, song, poetry; the second initiates a process of self-scrutiny and alertness that can never end; there silence is the only refuge.

If faith is taken as the ability to disregard the self, the problem facing man is whether he is psychologically capable of attaining it. If, on the other hand, faith is ultimate personal attachment to God, is it metaphysically possible?

Faith is not a state of passivity, of quiet acceptance; to join others in assenting to certain principles will not suffice. Faith requires action, a leap. It is an enterprise, not inertia. It requires bold initiative rather than continuity. Faith is forever contingent on the courage of the believer.

Can he who is enslaved to his ego ever disregard self-regard? The Kotzker was aware of the sharp break with human nature that such conduct required and therefore suggested that faith involved a leap, a springing clear of the motives that usually feed the self.

A witness reported:

In the early years of his career as a rebbe in Tomashov, Reb
Mendl often took us to the forest and there talked to us for ten
hours at a stretch, imbuing us with his thoughts, so that everyone entered a trance in which our souls were no longer in their places . . .
One had to be very tough to endure it. Every word of his was abrupt,
tense, piercing, and uttered with such fervor that even those who had
hearts of stone were enthralled and held captive.

Other people looked for extraordinary or wondrous things to
impress them. The Kotzker claimed that everything anywhere
filled him with astonishment.

Reb Mendl's friend, Reb Yizhak of Vorki, once returned from a
journey to Chernobyl, where the famous Reb Motele taught.
"What did you see there?" asked the Kotzker.
"In Chernobyl I saw the table at which the Baal Shem studied."
"You have seen a table that is a hundred years old. Our rebbe
teaches things that are nearly six thousand years old and shows us
who created them.

"According to Kabbalistic tradition, the *ushpizin*—the seven mystical guests, Abraham, Isaac, Jacob, Moses, Aaron, Joseph and David
—visit a booth especially erected during the seven days of the Feast
of Tabernacles. Some rebbes say that they actually see the *ushpizin*
in the booth. I do not see them. I believe, and believing is more perceptive than seeing," said the Kotzker.

"And Israel saw the wondrous power which the Lord had
wielded against the Egyptians, and the people were overawed
by the Lord, and they believed in the Lord, and in His servant
Moses" (Exodus 14:31). Though they had seen the great miracles wrought in Egypt and in the parting of the Red Sea, they
were still in need of faith. For believing goes deeper than seeing.
One spark of awe is worth more than witnessing all the mir-

acles of history. It was the experience of awe that gave the people Israel the strength to believe.

Our hearts must be embedded in faith. We should expect nothing less than to face the truth through deep insight. We cannot be satisfied with half-learned views, half-baked truths.

Faith and Reason

In the Book of Proverbs and in Ben Sirach (Ecclesiasticus) understanding is extolled as a major and necessary virtue. Wisdom is equated with moral goodness and declared to be the first creation of God (Proverbs 8:22ff). But reservations about the role and attainability of wisdom have also found expression in Proverbs and elsewhere in the Bible: "the words of Agur" (30:1-4); Job 28; the Book of Ecclesiastes. To equate Judaism with rationalism, as has frequently been done in modern liberal thought, is an error. Even Maimonides, praised by many writers as a classical rationalist, has repeatedly stressed the limitations of inquiry by reason alone. The connotations of the term "reason," as he used it, set him apart from modern rationalism.[1]

On the other hand, we occasionally come upon the tendency in contemporary philosophy and theology to regard the irrational as the ultimate principle of all things. This is totally alien to Judaism.

[1] See A. J. Heschel, *Maimonides* (Berlin, 1935; Paris, 1936).

The Kotzker did not negate the validity of logical or rational thought. He insisted upon diligent study of the Talmud and was himself an admired master of its dialectics. He cherished the kind of reasoning cultivated by Talmud study as indispensable to spiritual catharsis.

In totally different circumstances, Kierkegaard initiated a revolt against the tyranny of rationalism. A twentieth-century disciple of his, Miguel de Unamuno, declared:

The truth is, in all strictness, that reason is the enemy of Life. A terrible thing is intelligence. It tends to death as memory tends to stability. The living, the absolutely unstable, the absolutely individual is, strictly, unintelligible. Logic tends to reduce everything to identities and genera, to each representation as having no more than one single and self-same content in whatever place, time, or relation it may occur to us . . . The mind seeks what is dead, for what is living escapes it; it seeks to congeal the flowing stream in blocks of ice; it seeks to arrest it. In order to analyze a body, it is necessary to extenuate or destroy it. In order to understand anything it is necessary to kill it, to lay it out rigid in the mind. Science is a cemetery of dead ideas, even though life may issue from them. Worms also feed upon corpses. My own thoughts, tumultuous and agitated in the innermost recesses of my soul, once they are torn from their roots in the heart, poured out onto this paper and there fixed in unalterable shape, are already only the corpses of thoughts. How, then, shall reason open its portals to the revelation of life? It is a tragic combat—it is the very essence of tragedy—this combat of life with reason. And truth? Is truth something that is lived or that is comprehended? [2]

The Kotzker and Kierkegaard were antagonistic, not toward the use of reason but to its abuse and presumptuousness. They never excluded intellect entirely from the act of faith. Kierke-

[2] *The Tragic Sense of Life* (London, 1921), p. 90.

gaard was opposed to philosophical idealism and pantheism, which held faith to be the outcome of speculative reasoning. The function of reason was not to explain the object of faith but to invite man and prepare him for faith.

"It was intelligence and nothing else that had to be opposed. Presumably that is why I, who have had the job, am armed with an immense intelligence," Kierkegaard wrote of himself.[3] He used reason to demonstrate its limitations. Reason could disclose eternal truths, including the opacity of existence to reason. Reason could validly deal with objective problems of being, but it could not grapple with existential problems.

Presumptuousness is intrinsic to human nature. All power corrupts, including the power of reason. When such corruption or arrogance sets in, it must be checked. Kierkegaard said:

If thought speaks deprecatingly of the imagination, imagination in turn speaks deprecatingly of thought; and likewise with feeling. The task is not to exalt the one at the expense of the other, but to give them equal status, to unify them in simultaneity; the medium in which they are unified is *existence*." [4]

The Kotzker, too, maintained that Judaism required the highest use of man's power of understanding and obliged us to examine our inner life. If understanding was missing, then all of observance became mere habit. While he spurned speculation on the cardinal tenets of Jewish faith, he insisted upon the use of reason to understand the Torah and the self. Beyond that, he was convinced that, just as contradictions found in the Talmud could be resolved by means of dialectical exegesis, perplexities that overwhelmed us concerning God's mysterious justice in dealing with man could ultimately be resolved. God's judgments

[3] Journal entry, 1854, Dru edition, ¶ 1335.
[4] *Concluding Unscientific Postscript,* p. 311.

could never be entirely understood. His ways could never be thought to the end, for they originated in His wisdom.

Faith According to Kierkegaard

In his *Philosophical Fragments* and *Concluding Unscientific Postscript,* Kierkegaard attacked Hegel's claim that he had demonstrated human history to be an intelligible plan in which God's will was manifest. It was ridiculous, he argued, that any human being should pretend to such knowledge, for he would have to be God to know it.

For how should the Reason be able to understand what is absolutely different from itself? If this is not immediately evident, it will become clearer in the light of the consequences; for if the God is absolutely unlike man, then man is absolutely unlike the God; but how could the Reason be expected to understand this? . . . Merely to obtain the knowledge that the God is unlike him, man needs the help of the God; and now he learns that the God is absolutely different from himself. But if the God and man are absolutely different, this cannot be accounted for on the basis of what man derives from the God, for in so far they are akin.[1]

Kierkegaard's rejection of any undertaking to find rational

[1] *Philosophical Fragments,* 1845, rev. ed., translated by David Swenson and Howard V. Hong (Princeton, N.J., 1962), pp. 57f.

proofs for the existence of God was due not only to the inability of reason "to understand what is absolutely different from itself" but, above all, to the presumptuousness inherent in such an effort.

For to prove the existence of one who is present is the most shameless affront . . . The existence of a king, or his presence, is commonly acknowledged by an appropriate expression of subjection and submission—what if in his sublime presence one were to prove that he existed? [2]

Kierkegaard rejected the traditional evidence for the existence of God and the assumption that intellectual certitude was necessary to faith. There was no direct transition from reason to faith. "Faith is over against understanding." There was a gulf between rational understanding and knowledge through faith. "Reason cannot grasp what faith believes." "In my relationship to God I have to learn to give up my finite understanding." Man had to make the paradoxical leap into faith which could yield him an existential certitude in God.

According to Kierkegaard, then, faith must possess the attributes of venture and risk, of choice and decision. Significantly, the Kotzker also demanded risk and abandon for a leap into the life of faith in God, whose way surpasses human comprehension. Reb Mendl interpreted Psalm 14:2 to mean: is it possible for a rationalist (*maskil*) to seek God? Faith cannot be won by speculation. Jewish faith comes about by doing, by living the commandments (*mitzvah*).

The meaning of faith is not to believe in an idea because it is incontestable. To believe is to contend against impediments, to defy refutation, and to accept embarrassment.

[2] *Concluding Unscientific Postscript*, p. 485.

PART VI

❖❰❖❰❖❰

Personality

Alienation

T HE TERM "alienation" as used here describes the situation of an individual whose goals or values diverge from those commonly held in his society. When Herman Melville said that he was a stranger in his own country, what he meant was that the things important and interesting to his fellow countrymen were trivial to him. Conversely, matters significant and valuable to him hardly concerned the people around him.

Satisfying human relations depend upon sharing identical values or having similar insights. But who else in Copenhagen shared Kierkegaard's sense of outrage at the shallowness of the prevailing religious mood? Though the Kotzker, unlike Kierkegaard, was surrounded by disciples and admirers, he too complained that he had no one to talk to. So both realized late in life that their road was the *via solitaria*. They had loneliness in common.

Alienation was a condition affecting the lives of the ancient Prophets of Israel, and it may have found an expression in the Psalmist's outcry "I am a sojourner on earth" (Psalms 119:19).[1]

One has the impression that the Kotzker's life, like Kierke-

[1] See Melvin Seeman, "On the Meaning of Alienation," *Journal of the American Sociological Association* December, 1959, pp. 783–91. On the alienation of the ancient Prophets of Israel, see A. J. Heschel, *The Prophets* New York, 1962, pp. 17–18, 408.

gaard's, was a long, painful self-inquisition. It was as if both men lived outside themselves, observing and examining what was going on within them. They were high-strung, hyper-conscious, living strenuously. There was nothing light or playful about them, and they used language as if it were a sledgehammer.

What Kierkegaard wrote about himself seems to apply to the Kotzker as well:

I have never had any immediacy,[2] and therefore, in the ordinary human sense of the word, I have never lived. I began at once with reflection . . . I am reflection from first to last.[3]

The Biblical words "an inquiry shall be held" (Leviticus 19:20) were taken by the Kotzker as a central imperative, with the self as the most important object of the inquiry. Almost all of his sayings are either calls for self-examination or the result of self-scrutiny.

Kierkegaard expressed this demand forcefully:

Now examine thyself—for that thou hast a right to do. On the other hand, thou hast properly no right, without self-examination, to let thyself be deluded by "the others," or to delude thyself into the belief that thou art a Christian—therefore examine thyself.[4]

The title of one of Kierkegaard's discourses is *For Self-Examination*.

It seems as if the whole of existence made the Kotzker anxious: nothing was good enough, true enough. Awareness of his estrangement from the world affected his thinking as well as his relations with other people. He could not conform or accept, he could only challenge and defy patterns of behavior around him.

[2] Kierkegaard uses this term to describe the sensuous life, relatively untroubled by reflection.
[3] "The Point of View," p. 81.
[4] *Training in Christianity,* p. 42.

Everything appeared alien, even recalcitrant to religious expectations. It created annoyance in him, disgust and phobias, and made him adopt certain tactics to keep the outside world at bay.

Kierkegaard described this painful condition in a striking manner:

My life has been brought to an *impasse*, I loathe existence . . . One sticks one's finger into the soil to tell by the smell in what land one is: I stick my finger into existence—it smells of nothing. Where am I? What is this thing called the world? What does this word mean? Who is it that has lured me into the thing, and now leaves me there? Who am I? How did I come into the world? Why was I not consulted, why not made acquainted with its manners and customs . . . ? How did I obtain an interest in this big enterprise they call reality? Why should I have an interest in it? Is it not a voluntary concern? And if I am to be compelled to take part in it, where is the director? . . . Whither shall I turn with my complaint? [5]

"The world stinks!" shouted the Kotzker, possibly foreseeing what Kierkegaard described as the "total bankruptcy towards which the whole of Europe seems to be heading." [6]

To people of our generation, Reb Mendl's exclamation does not sound like an overstatement. His agony over the falseness of man was a malaise from which he never recovered. Like Kierkegaard, he perceived the world around him as diseased and suffered much from the triteness of things. There was "a fundamental alienation, an ineradicable fissure sundering self from the world." [7] This explains the Kotzker's disquietude and unendurable tension. His life was filled with a *horror religiosus,* com-

[5] *Repetition: An Essay in Experimental Psychology,* translated by Walter Lowrie (Princeton, N.J., 1941), p. 114.
[6] Journal entry, quoted in Lowrie, *Kierkegaard,* p. 157.
[7] Thompson, *The Lonely Labyrinth: Kierkegaard's Pseudonymous Works* (Carbondale, Ill., 1967), p. 31.

pared to which the life of other believers looks like tranquillity itself.

Kierkegaard wrote:

Geniuses are like a thunderstorm: they go against the wind, terrify people, cleanse the air.

The Established Church has invented sundry lightning-conductors.[8]

The Kotzker and Kierkegaard were thunderstorms, and to this day their words give notice of danger.

From my youth onward I have been stirred by the thought that in every generation there are two or three who are sacrificed to the rest, in that they discover with terrible anguish something by which the rest profit; and sorrowfully I have found that the key to my own being was that I was destined to be one of these.[9]

The explosive energy of these minds, the eruptions of such blazing temperaments were not easy to bear. They were haunted by mysterious states of anguish, the price they had to pay for their penetrating insights. The Kotzker felt like a stranger in his own time: "My soul dates from the time before the Temple was destroyed." "I am not a man of today," he said. So, at the end of his life, he retired into the hermetic world of reflection and only occasionally received the vast numbers of people who came to seek his blessings. Kierkegaard, too, seems like "a lost wayfarer" who "has come into a strange land where the people talk a different language and have other customs."[10]

They were both conscious of being exceptional and of having to fulfill an extraordinary function. Kierkegaard believed that his

---

[8] *Kierkegaard's Attack upon "Christendom,"* p. 182.
[9] Journal entry, quoted in Lowrie, *Kierkegaard,* p. 181.
[10] *Stages on Life's Way,* p. 290.

was the work of "introducing the unconditional . . . to utter the cry of alarm." The same may be said of the Kotzker.

Both men were also moved by an awareness of a deep cleavage between their inner life and the world around them. The Kotzker's whole life was based on perpetual protest, dissent, repudiation; he called into question respectable attitudes and patterns of thinking, people's shifting emphases, their digressions from meaningful concerns. The interiority of these powerful human beings consisted of the gigantic struggles between Truth and falsehood besetting our bleeding world.

The Kotzker came closer to the meaning of religious expectation than many other thinkers who have veiled the inner condition of man and the urgency for his total transformation by focusing on compliance and obedience. But despite the awe his thoughts evoke, he cannot serve as a model. For it is surely not the will of God that man lead a tortured life.

Neurosis

A perplexing, obtrusive figure, the Kotzker cannot be reduced to a chapter in the history of Jewish theology, or to a set of ideas labeled as religious extremism. He returns as a person who, by his sheer being, painfully upsets our false sense of spiritual security.

One may, of course, neutralize his impact by means of psychological analysis that emphasizes the "abnormal" aspects of his character. He had suffered from bouts of melancholia since his youth. The Seer of Lublin had detected this, and, despite the Kotzker's efforts to hide it and his insistence that melancholy had no place in religious existence, he was unable to curb it.

Kierkegaard also complained that his whole youth, his childhood even, had been clouded by the deepest melancholy, which he had been unable to control. His relations with his father had a strong impact on his character. Similarly, the Kotzker openly defied his father's advice in spiritual matters.

Alas! Common prejudice is so hurtful that men of genius become dishonored when subjected to psychological analysis. The man of genius is often afflicted by insanity. Yet by what standards can we determine which of the Kotzker's and Kierkegaard's thoughts were the product of their genius and which the result of their insanity? Do creative insights ever come about under conditions of "normal" life? Is the psychological framework from which they emerge a test of their validity?

It would have been abnormal if a life possessed of such unbearable tensions had remained normal. And it required extraordinary strength not to subside into total mental derangement.

Is melancholy always a symptom of madness, or can it be a sign of deep anxiety about the madness that has overtaken so-called normal society? "Why are you cast down, O my soul, and why are you disquieted within me?" (Psalms 42:11).

The nature of melancholy is determined by its degree and quality. Melancholia as a state of depression that interferes with the proper functioning of the mind is not the same as pensiveness or sadness, however profound. One may be dejected because of personal frustrations or low self-esteem, or one may be overcome by feelings of hopelessness regarding the condition of the world.

It may be that both Kierkegaard and the Kotzker were afflicted with mental illness and that some of their thinking was conditioned by it. Yet it is just such a condition that enables a man to see through the falsehood of society and to come upon the burial place where Truth is entombed. Perhaps it was vicarious suffering that empowered them to express the agony of a sickness that afflicts us all. Their condition was not a personal idiosyncrasy; it represented a latent universal condition become explicit, apparent, a moment in the resurrection of stifled, buried Truth.[1]

The Kotzker and Kierkegaard pose a challenge to psychologists. What in others would be stark sickness leading to erratic actions produced outbursts of illumination in these men.

According to one authority, Kierkegaard apparently suffered from

a manic-depressive psychosis, marked by periods of dormancy interrupted by crises of extreme intensity, but never such as to overpower him completely. The peculiar characteristic of this psychosis is that it involves more or less frequent attacks either of excitement (mania) or of depression (melancholia) or of both alternately. Kierkegaard would appear to have been especially subject to the depression form, accompanied by deep emotional disturbance, with acute manifestations of grief and anguish . . . ochlophobia (horror of crowds) and desire for solitude.[2]

[1] Kierkegaard writes, "To elucidate the riddle of life has always been my desire . . . I want to go into a madhouse and see whether the profundity of madness will not solve the riddle of life for me." See Thompson, *The Lonely Labyrinth*, p. 53.
[2] Regis Jolivet, *Introduction to Kierkegaard*, translated by W. H. Barber (London, 1950), p. 69, quoting from Hjalmar Helweg.

Mutatis mutandis, this diagnosis may be applied to the Kotzker.

Both men were often filled with the despairing wish to withdraw from everybody and everything. An entry in Kierkegaard's diary for 1837 reads:

I will no longer speak with the world. I will seek to forget that I have ever done so. I have read of a man who kept to his bed for fifty years without speaking to a single human being. I will do likewise, and . . . go to bed after having quarrelled with the world. Or else I will seek to move to a place where no one knows or understands my language, nor I theirs, where I can stand like Kaspar Hauser—without really knowing how it has all come about—in the middle of Nürnburg Street . . .

No, I will not leave the world—I will enter a *madhouse,* and I shall see if *the depths of insanity* will not disclose to me the secret of life. Oh, fool, that I have not done so long ago, long ago understood what it means when the Indians honour the insane and go out of the way for them. Yes, to the madhouse—don't you think I can come in there.[3]

The Kotzker did indeed retire from the world and spent the last twenty years of his life in isolation.

Sarcasm

The unique pedagogy that the Kotzker used with his disciples was not simply to instruct or edify but to shock, to startle, to inspire dread. His consistent use of this method, explicitly de-

[3] Quoted in *The Concept of Irony,* "Historical Introduction," pp. 22*ff.*

cried in the Talmud and puzzling to his friends, reflected his
conviction of the importance of "stern education from . . . dread
to faith," as Kierkegaard expressed it.[1]

Learning to know dread is an adventure which every man has to
confront if he would not go to perdition . . . He therefore who has
learned rightly to be in dread has learned the most important
thing . . . The greater the dread, the greater the man . . .
Dread is the possibility of freedom. Only this dread is by the aid
of faith absolutely educative, consuming as it does all finite aims and
discovering all their deceptions.[2]

The Kotzker found dread an effective instrument in his desire
to subdue self-assertion in his disciples and to intensify their
estrangement from the world. A passage from Johann George
Hamann, quoted on the final page of Kierkegaard's The *Concept
of Dread*, sheds light on the meaning of this strategy:

This dread, which we experience in the world, is the only proof of
our heterogeneity. For if we lacked nothing, we should do no better
than the pagans and the transcendental philosophers who know nothing of God and like fools fall in love with this precious world; no
homesickness would attack us. This impertinent uneasiness, this holy
hypochondria, is perhaps the fire whereby we sacrificial animals must
be salted and preserved from the decay of the passing age.[3]

We all claim we want truth and integrity in our lives. Honesty in relation to ourselves and to other selves is a quality that
determines the attainment of basic virtues. But do we honestly
desire honesty, and is it easily attainable? The heart plays cruel
and bitter jokes on us; imperceptibly, almost unwillingly, we
become guilty of deceiving others as well as ourselves.

1 Quoted in Lowrie, *Kierkegaard*, p. 129.
2 *The Concept of Dread*, p. 139.
3 *Ibid.*, p. 145n.

Men need to be praised, but sometimes they also feel the need to be derided, denounced, even castigated. Satire serves to destroy falsehood by ridiculing foibles, pretensions, and delusions. In this manner, caricature may be the most effective way of loving Truth.

The Kotzker, like Kierkegaard, had a predilection for sarcasm, irony, satire, and polemic. No one in the history of Jewish piety was more biting than he in exposing the subterfuges of man. His language was abrasive. Kierkegaard and he were masters at stripping away religion's false fronts. They turned their invectives against arrogance and pride, against distortions and forgeries of Truth, against stuffed shirts and hypocrites. Their criticism is thus not confined to any one country or era. They are of special relevance today in exposing dishonesty as the disease underlying the political and social life of the modern world. Their diagnosis of man's predicament has become all the more striking as our people have borne the Nazi Holocaust and humanity has entered the feared nuclear age.

The Kotzker claimed that the view we held of our condition was a prodigious illusion. Jews lived with the blissful conceit that they were good. If authentic Judaism was to be reintroduced, the delusion must first be disposed of. Kierkegaard, too, served this goal in moving people "by means of the ideals, bringing them . . . into a state of suffering, stirring them up by the gadfly-sting of irony, derision, sarcasm." [4]

The Kotzker was incapable of uttering a cliché. His speech was terse and curt, never glib or rambling. Intensity and impatience drove him to seek extreme condensation of thought; his form of expression was epigrammatic. He never minced words, never softened a message by wheedling or smooth, be-

[4] *Kierkegaard's Attack upon "Christendom,"* p. 97.

guiling words. In order to jolt his disciples, he did not hesitate to use coarse language.

Dour and tragic, strongly introspective, grim, strange, deep, persistent, doubting, contradictory, despairing, hopeful, angry—the Kotzker's sarcasm reflected the intense sincerity of an explosive soul. I believe this brilliant spirit denied itself the joy of expression, for he wrote no books for posterity.

Neither Kierkegaard nor the Kotzker is an ingratiating figure. It is not the magnetism of their personality that attracts us. It is a recognition of our own ache that drives us to them.

Solitude

Both Kierkegaard and the Kotzker opted for a life of self-isolation. There were several reasons for their decisions, some of which were similar. We must keep in mind that Kierkegaard and Reb Mendl, like almost all wise and saintly men, considered solitude indispensable to spiritual living.

The Kotzker even rejected the argument that a lone life was antisocial. To him it did not mean exclusion of others, for it could embrace fellowship with like-thinking individuals. He maintained that men who were preoccupied with spiritual matters in solitude retained their affiliation with people, while those who were involved with many persons through mundane concerns acted each for himself, remaining essentially apart and alone.

Kierkegaard was shocked by the shallowness of the pseudo-Christian life he saw about him and the outright deceptive politics which churchmen had been made to serve. Out of scrupulous sincerity, he "excommunicated" himself. Similarly, the Kotzker was repelled by the inanity and subtle self-deceptions of the vast number of his pseudo-Hasidic "followers." So he, too, removed himself from his solemn vocation as charismatic leader.

Kierkegaard sometimes said his solitary state was a punishment visited upon him because his father had cursed God as a child. The Copenhagen street urchins used to shout, "Either/Or!" after him. A satirical paper published a series of cartoons depicting him successively as a magisterial hunchback, a thin-legged stargazer, and a rooster in a top hat surrounded by chickens.

In his early days the Kotzker was adored by both an intellectual elite and by Hasidim in general. He could have continued in his career as a renowned Hasidic rebbe and rejoiced in his impact upon so many people. But, as I have said, he isolated himself, because of his rigorous integrity, while other Hasidic leaders continued to offer guidance and hope and fostered joy in being Jewish among their flocks.

Though he suffered from disappointment and even frustration, it is doubtful whether these emotions alone drove the Kotzker into isolation. Was his self-imposed solitude due to his exacerbated sense of the difference between himself and everyone about him? Was he filled with anger and frustration because messianic redemption had not yet begun? Or did he arrive at the conviction that what was most important had never yet been said, never been revealed?

The thoughts he gave voice to made the Kotzker famous. Did he fear that external fame would accelerate inner decay? Did he suffer from contradictions within himself? Or did he bemoan the fact that those who came to see him were mostly admirers, not followers? He knew that he was lumined, but did he succeed in illumining others?

Did he expect pure devotion to God, impeccable inwardness, from man? Did he feel that in a world so degenerate, God Himself was alone? And did he withdraw from the world because he thought it his task to share the solitude of God?

According to Nietzsche, "The man is great who knows how to be most solitary, the man who is surrounded by loneliness, not because he wishes to be alone, but because he is what he is, and cannot find his equal."

A Christian [writes Kierkegaard] often feels a need for solitude, which for him is a vital necessity—sometimes like breathing, at other times like sleeping. The fact that he feels this vital necessity more than other men is also a sign that he has a deeper nature. Generally the need for solitude is a sign there is spirit in a man after all, and it is a measure for what spirit there is. The purely twaddling inhuman and too-human men are to such a degree without feeling for the need of solitude that like a certain species of social birds (the so-called love birds) they promptly die if for an instant they have to be alone. As the little child must be put to sleep by a lullaby, so these men need the tranquillizing hum of society before they are able to eat, drink, sleep, pray, fall in love, etc. But in ancient times as well as in the Middle Ages people were aware of the need of solitude and had respect for what it signifies. In the constant sociability of our age people shudder at solitude to such a degree that they know no other use to put it but (oh, admirable epigram!) as a punishment for criminals. But after all it is a fact that in our age it is a crime to have spirit, so it is natural that such people, the lovers of solitude, are included in the same class with criminals.[1]

Even as a child the Kotzker was inclined to loneliness. He preferred God's nearness, though it involved estrangement from people. He learned to extend his solitudes and to isolate himself. Life, he felt, should be lived apart from the self, for the sake of the greater One outside the self. The individual had to keep his head clear of all digressions that prevented the splendor of God's thought from centering in the mind. There were tremors below and dizziness above, but the intense love must grow in silence and with painful patience.

Was it not promiscuous to mingle with people who, by mendacity and effrontery, kept the Almighty in isolation?

Even while surrounded by disciples, Reb Mendl lived apart from others. When he closed his doors, it was not he who was suddenly alone but those who followed him. In this way he rid himself of flatterers and mediocre companions and was able to foster his contemplative impulses and insights undisturbed. His soul dwelled so long in the midst of alarms, was afflicted with such frustrations, that only in seclusion could he nurture some crumbs of hope. When decisive acts have to be carried out, even God says, "I have trodden the winepress alone" (Isaiah 63:3).

There is an old tradition in Judaism about holy men, such as Rabbi Shimon ben Yohai, who spent much of their time in solitude. It was this ancient sage's example that the Kotzker announced he would follow upon assuming the leadership of his Hasidic community. As a young man, Rabbi Yitzhak Luria, the founder of the Lurianic Kabbalah, removed to the banks of the Nile. For seven years he secluded himself for meditation, visiting his family only on the Sabbath, speaking seldom and then only in Hebrew, which was not commonly spoken in his time.

---

[1] *The Sickness unto Death*, translated by Walter Lowrie (Princeton, N.J., 1941); Anchor edition (Garden City, N.Y., 1954), pp. 197f.

Hasidic lore tells us that as a young man the Baal Shem Tov spent many years alone in the Carpathian Mountains.

Solitude was a common practice among mystically inclined Jews. Even the non-mystical Jewish writers of the Middle Ages seemed to agree that solitary living was indispensable to the attainment of spiritual purity. This view may be found in the writings of Abraham Ibn Ezra, Maimonides, Badarshi, Falaquera, Gersonides, Albo, Crescas, and Abravanel among others.[2]

What is there for one who seeks to save his authenticity other than withdrawal from the world's blaring lies and deceitful eyes? Proximity to the crowd, to the majority view, spells the death of creativity. For a soul can create only when alone, and some are chosen for the flowering that takes place in the dark avenues of the night. They may live on the brink of despair, alternating between a longing for fellowship and for privacy.

Even people who consider themselves moderately kind but also realistic tend to accept the use of God's name in association with falsehood or the daily murder of innocent people. How easily we develop indifference to evil and consent to mendacity as an indispensable fact of life.

Can a man of sense feel mercy if he himself has never experienced terror? The Kotzker is very close to us during the night —a night that lasts all day and opens up the horror that other people felt and saw, after which they died.

[2] According to the great-grandson of the Baal Shem Tov, Reb Nahman of Bratzlav, solitude is an indispensable prerequisite for spiritual living. He called upon his disciples to set aside an hour or more every day for seclusion and meditation, whether in an isolated room or in the fields. I recall that in the prayer rooms of his followers in Warsaw, there were narrow cells in which individuals could retire for an hour or more, since their homes were overcrowded and the surrounding fields offered no seclusion.

Sex

Kierkegaard's asceticism is the logical outcome of a conception which refuses to see in man, or even in nature, anything not fundamentally corrupted by sin. Going to extremes in this direction, Kierkegaard in the end even condemns marriage as incompatible with the Christian state. He bases this conclusion on a doctrine which expresses a kind of contempt for woman; according to him, she is egoism personified, and her destiny is to ruin the spiritual in man. Thus man degrades himself by being associated with the life of the other sex; marriage becomes an absolute obstacle to anyone who wishes to serve God. "It is an abominable lie," he writes, "to say that marriage is pleasing to God. From the Christian point of view it is a crime, and what is odious about it is that by this very crime the innocent individual is introduced into that community of criminals which is human life.[1]

These are hard words, and they justify one in speaking of Kierkegaard's "hostility to life."

Yet Kierkegaard's view was not always the same. In *Either/Or* he wrote that a man could not live a healthy human life without the fellowship of marriage. But if he was at first a champion of the wedded state, he came to look upon it in later years as a degradation of human nature and pronounced it a sin, mostly because the gratification of base desires was followed by the birth of children, who were almost certain to be eternally damned.

Family demands inevitably involved a man in worldly con-

[1] Jolivet, *Introduction to Kierkegaard*, pp. 157f.

cerns that prevented him from acting completely and solely for God.

It is quite certain and true that Christianity is suspicious of marriage . . . for . . . with woman and love all this weakliness and love of coddling arises in a man.

Christianity recommends the single state . . . Honestly, I am unable to comprehend how it can occur to any man to unite being a Christian with being married.[2]

Thus, in his last years Kierkegaard felt a strong attraction to, and became convinced that only a celibate could dedicate himself fully to, religious discipline. Monasticism fascinated him. "Back to the Cloister!" he was ready to cry.[3] He interpreted the passage on adultery in the Sermon on the Mount (Matthew 5:27–8) as a prohibition of any sexual cohabitation. These verses, he claimed, expressed a double opposition to the Mosaic commandment, a re-evaluation not only of adultery but also of sexual desire within the matrimonial framework as accepted by Judaism.[4]

Christianity founded upon such "severity" and a spiritual life that requires isolation, a sundering from the warm intimacies of human life and bodily happiness, necessarily inclines toward asceticism, celibacy, and even monasticism, Kierkegaard believed.

The religious abstraction desires to appertain to God alone, for this love it is willing to disdain, renounce, sacrifice everything . . . for this love it will not suffer itself to be disturbed, distracted, engrossed by anything else; with regard to this love it is not willing to have

[2] *Training in Christianity,* p. 119.
[3] Quoted in Lowrie, *Kierkegaard,* p. 500.
[4] "In paganism there was a god for love but none for marriage; in Christianity there is, if I may venture to say so, a god for marriage and none for love."— *Stages on Life's Way,* p. 106.

any double bookkeeping, all the turnover is to come about constantly with a clear relation to God, who is not related to him.[5]

The sexual is the culmination of human egoism . . .

In the Christianity of the New Testament God wishes to be loved, and therefore he wishes man to abandon the egoism of giving life.

The Fall is the satisfaction of his egoism—and this is where the history of temporality really begins, as the constant repetition of the same fault, constantly opposing or preventing what God has in view, which is to put a stop to this error—by means of celibacy. Every time we meet a celibate for love of God we see an effort to comply with God's intention.

But I almost shudder when I think how far along this way I have been, and how wonderfully I have been halted and sent back to celibacy; how too I have . . . known how to conceal what I knew from my contemporaries, till at long last I see how once more Providence has been with me, and wishes to have some quite definite result.

And then Protestantism comes and presents Christianity—in its connexion with marriage. It is marriage that is well pleasing to God . . .

The error in Catholicism is not that the priest is celibate; no, the error is that a qualitative difference between the layman and the priest has been introduced, which goes clean against the New Testament, and is a concession of weakness in relation to numbers. Certainly the error is not that the priest is celibate—a Christian should be celibate.

"But if you hold to this you will have no Christians at all!" If that is so, it is all one to me. "And on the other hand, if you make Christianity consist of marriage, then you will get millions of Christians!" It is all one to me.[6]

Celibacy, therefore, should not be limited to the clergy.

[5] *Ibid.*, p. 169.
[6] Journal entries in *The Last Years*, pp. 266f.

For it is not that the priest be unmarried, but that the Christians should be unmarried . . . For Christianity this is a sinful world, a child is conceived in transgression and sin. Christianity aims at calling a halt . . . not by beginning afresh . . .

To say that Christ has made satisfaction for original sin does not mean that Christianity desires the propagation of the species. For all reconciliation and atonement has surely always a retrospective and not a prospective reference. As in relation to actual sin, if one's sin was stealing, the atonement makes satisfaction for the past, but it does not mean that the man can now steal as much as he wants in the future. And similarly with satisfaction for original sin, which surely does not mean that now a man can enjoy himself as much as he wants with regard to the propagation of the species. No, Christianity blocks the way with celibacy. No, it says, your father's guilt, through which you exist—for that satisfaction has been made: but stop there: satisfaction does not mean that you now go off and do the same as he did; satisfaction does not mean that in this respect you can do as you please.[7]

The Redeemer was born of a virgin because marriage and the propagation of the species are intrinsically evil. Man is utterly bad by reason of his very birth; he lives under a perpetual curse and dies eternally damned. "I came into being through a crime against God's will. The offense, which in one sense, is not mine, though it makes me a criminal in the sight of God, was to give life."[8]

According to Christianity the world is a world of sin, the consequence of a fall.

Christianity is salvation, but at the same time it is a stopping, it

[7] Ibid., pp. 119, 299f.
[8] Journal entry, 1855, The Diary of Søren Kierkegaard, edited by Peter P. Rohde (New York, 1960), p. 239. Cf. pp. 31, 35 (both 1854). Cf. also Journals, Dru edition, ¶¶ 1337, 1385, 1399 (all 1854).

aims at stopping the whole continuation which leads to the permanence of this world.

And that is why Christianity holds by celibacy. By this the Christian gives characteristic expression to his relationship to this world, which is one of stopping. And that is why the New Testament too continually uses such words concerning the Christian as indicate this putting a stop to things: for example, to be salt, to be sacrificed, etc.

Yet it was not long before marriage was in full swing among the Christians—and this is where the confusing element enters in, that what is being fought against in the van is being encouraged in the rear. With marriage the Christian immediately has a different relation to the world than that of being a stranger and outcast, or salt, or being sacrificed, or putting a stop to things.

If anyone says that he is getting married in order to have children who may be brought up from their childhood in Christianity, in order to make true Christians for God, then I will answer, Nonsense! The fact is you feel the desire to beget children. But as for his method of creating true Christians, it is certain that, if there is any man for whom it is almost impossible to become a Christian, then it is that man who was brought up in Christianity from his childhood. There is nothing more opposed to Christianity than that it should be anticipated in this way and so become just nonsense.[9]

Kierkegaard maintained that marriage was the enemy of genius since it afforded a biological release of tension. He denounced Luther for encouraging the marriage of priests as a "concession to concupiscence." [10] He regarded himself as a signal instance of the sublimation of Eros. Yet what was required was more than a decision of the will; a strong sense of repugnance had to be cultivated.

What led the Kotzker to repudiate sexuality was probably the awareness that sensuality was the only powerful alternative to

[9] Journal entry in *The Last Years*, pp. 114f.
[10] Quoted in Lowrie, *Kierkegaard*, p. 524.

absolute religion. Insatiate desire, passion, love, excitement, and rapture are as organic to religion as they are to sexuality. He did not believe that our energies could be lavished equally on both.

Like Kierkegaard, the Kotzker saw human sexuality as the opposite of spirituality. Yet, by contrast, he did not discourage marriage, since Judaism sees celibacy as unnatural. It is not he who marries who sins; the sinner is the unmarried man who "spends all his days in sinful thoughts." [11]

Rabbi Eleazer said any man who has no wife is no proper man, for it is said, "Male and female created He them and called their name Adam" (Genesis 1:27). Adam equals man. Only when the male and the female were united, were they called Adam.[12]

He could not discourage marriage, which Judaism considers to be a divine commandment: "God blessed them, and God said to them: Be fruitful and multiply, and fill the earth and subdue it!" (Genesis 1:28).

Opposition to marriage would have implied a repudiation of nearly all the Biblical and rabbinic personalities, who were passionately attached to and never ceased to exalt marriage. They never maintained that love between man and woman is incompatible with love of God.

To summarize, the Kotzker demanded the sublimation of sexuality. One should go beyond the physical basis of life, since the conquest of the sexual drive alone can assure total commitment to spiritual pursuits. The libido was to be transferred to the realm of religious passion. Deprived of biological release, the body might weep, but the imagination would remain fresh and pure.

Whatever its ultimate validity, the Kotzker surely knew that such an intense, libido-defying spirituality could only be pre-

[11] *Kiddushin* 29b.
[12] *Yebamoth* 63a.

served by select individuals. The hiatus between such a rarefied life and the common ways of humanity would necessarily create painful problems. Only the celibate could follow his, and Kierkegaard's, uncompromising path.

In suggesting that abstinence freed a man's energies for spiritual pursuits, the Kotzker anticipated in a way Sigmund Freud's view of sublimation. While unable to oppose marriage, he called at least for suppression of sexuality, for waging a permanent intimate war against an exceedingly powerful part of human nature. To his extremist mind, man must make a choice: either to conquer the power of sex or to be conquered by it. If a complete victory is impossible, let one strive at least for a truce. He therefore demanded a discipline of continence, which he considered a possible mode of living, since man's power of will is capable of dominating human nature.

Kierkegaard noticed with approval, "Montaigne says somewhere that, remarkably enough, what we all owe our existence to is something to be despised." [13] Similarly, the Kotzker agreed with Maimonides, who also had a low estimate of human sexuality and praised a saying ascribed to Aristotle that "the sense of touch is a disgrace to us." [14] Indeed, disagreement with the Kotzker's hostility to the sexual life was probably one of the reasons why his favorite disciple deserted him and left Kotzk to establish a school of his own. [15]

[13] *Søren Kierkegaard's Journals and Papers,* edited and translated by H. V. and E. H. Hong (Bloomington, Ind., 1967) Vol. I A-E, p. 31.
[14] See *The Guide of the Perplexed,* II, p. 36.
[15] See my forthcoming book, *The Kotzker,* Chap. XVII.

PART VII

Resignation

No Reconciliation with the World

KIERKEGAARD asserted that there never can be a reconciliation between the world and the demands of Christianity. "But woe, woe to the Christian Church if it would triumph in this world, for then it is not the Church that triumphs, but the world." [1] He therefore exhorted men to renounce the world, the flesh, and the devil, for only through renunciation of the world and self-will could one become a true Christian. Unless a true Christian felt cut off from most men and women, he had to question his being a Christian with an uneasy conscience.

Whoever suffers for his doctrine also dies away from the world.

I can wish myself away from the vanity and corruption of the world, and, even if the wish does not avail, the hearty longing for the eternal avails to carry me away; for in the longing itself the eternal *is*, just as God *is* in the sorrow which is sorrow *unto* God.[2]

Following his own teachings, Kierkegaard practically lived like a hermit in his later years. Significantly his earliest and best-known work, *Either/Or,* was published under the pseudonym Victor Eremita.

[1] *Training in Christianity,* p. 218.
[2] Kierkegaard, "Discourse on Luke 22:15," *Christian Discourses,* 1848, translated by Walter Lowrie (New York and London, 1940), p. 267.

To Discard the World

The first lesson taught in Kotzk was to cultivate disgust for false-hood and to care nothing for what "the world" said. To hell with the opinions of society! "A Hasid is he who discards the world."

Here "world" does not mean nature or the earth. For no one could deny the Kotzker's love of nature, his feeling for Tyres, his sense of serenity in forests. He referred to the marvel of nature as a source of certainty that a God existed. Indeed, we may recall, that when his master Reb Bunam asked him what his source of faith was, his answer came: "Lift up your eyes on high and see who created these" (Isaiah 40:25). What he found abhorrent was what men did on earth; it was in society that he did not feel at home.

The Kotzker did not call for a retreat from the natural world. Nor did he demand that all forms of enjoyment be given up. By the term "world" he meant public opinion, all accepted modes of behavior and formalities, the ceremonialism that engulfed the average man, and particularly the conduct of respectable society, its customs and standards. "The whole world isn't worth uttering a sigh for," he said.

One of the sins reported by the men whom Moses sent to spy out the land of Canaan was that "All the people that we saw in it are men of great stature . . . and we seemed to ourselves like grasshoppers, and so we seemed to them, the inhabitants of the land" (Numbers 13:32–3). Never mind, said the Kotzker, that they felt small and puny. This was understandable. But why did they care how they looked to other people?

"Man was created single," said the Mishnah. You were single and alone when you were created, and alone and single you must remain, remarked the Kotzker. One must live in readiness to sacrifice the self as Abraham was ready to sacrifice Isaac, to subdue his own inclinations. Never show partiality either to yourself or to others.

Abraham stood the test twice: first when he placed Isaac on the altar, then when he helped him down from it. The second trial exacted greater strength than the first. God Himself had told him to sacrifice his son. Then an angel came and called out, "Stop, don't touch him." How could he listen to an angel and disobey God? It took great self-control to miss such a marvelous opportunity to make a supreme sacrifice, and to yield to the angel.

He who seeks to pursue the path of Truth will not make a good mixer or fellow traveler. Reb Mendl's Hasidim did not care about the world. They were taught to give "two figs," that is, to snap their fingers twice, once at themselves and once at the world. They paid no obeisance to anybody, showed no respect for those who expected it. Those who exacted deference deserved a headache. "One's vision must be directed upward; pay no mind to here and now."

Such disdain for public opinion conflicted sharply with authoritative Jewish scholars. Hillel taught, "Do not sever yourself from the community." Rabbi Hanina ben Dosa said, "Anyone who is liked by his fellow men is liked by God; anyone who is not liked by his fellow men is not liked by God." Great masters insisted, "It is a man's duty to be free of blame (to give no cause for suspicion) before men as before God, as it is said, 'and be guilt-less before the Lord and before Israel' (Numbers 32:22)." [1]

Yet the Kotzker taught: take no notice of society; do not be concerned with your rating in it. Indeed, if "the world" paid little attention to Judaism, why should Judaism please or flatter it? Since "the world" would not change, the only choice open was to discard it.

If you want to engage yourself to God, then you must sever yourself from the world as personified by society. Make no deals with it. You cannot be in love with both God and the world, dance at two weddings at once. What the world may endorse, conscience must often condemn.

The Kotzker deprecated material things. "Beauty and eternity belong to God"—objects may be beautiful in our eyes the first, second, and third time we see them. But only what belongs to God is eternally beautiful.

The whole conventional system of human conduct and cus-toms appeared to the Kotzker as a rigmarole, without validity. As discussed earlier, he particularly detested the obsession with mak-ing money. To him society was plagued by three maladies: dis-honesty, egocentricity, and avarice. Since his approach derived from a powerful affirmation of Truth, his negation of "the world" had its root in his realization that Truth and this world were contradictions. The more intensely we understand the integrity of God, the more horrendous will be our dismay at the deceit-fulness of the world.

One of his disciples spelled out the Kotzker's thought, allud-ing to the opening words of the book of Genesis:

At the beginning God created Heaven and earth. And the earth was *tohu-bohu* [without form and void]. He said, "When a Jew

[1] *Sayings of the Fathers* II, 5; III, 12; *Shekalim* III, 2.

gets up in the morning and thinks 'At the beginning God created Heaven and earth,' then everything that comes into sight reveals itself to be a world of *Tohu* and *bohu*, chaos and deceit."

The Talmud says, "Everyone of the House of David who went out to the war wrote a bill of divorcement for his wife." [2] To be a Hasid, according to Kotzker, was to be at war, and whoever was about to engage in battle must first divorce himself from other interests.

No Self-satisfaction

To afflict the body was a futile occupation, Hasidim thought. Amenities of this world were to be enjoyed as long as enthusiasm for them did not break all bounds.

Indeed, the Kotzker himself held ascetics in contempt. Mortification of the flesh was a cheap exercise and did not affect one's inner life. He had never disclaimed the thesis of the Baal Shem Tov that one was able to serve God with his body in the satisfaction of natural needs. Spirituality did not come about by severing oneself from the material world but, rather, by being related to it and transcending it.

A young man one day poured out his heart to his master, Reb

[2] *Shabbath* 5ba. The divorce was conditional; it became retrogressively valid if the husband fell in battle.

Bunam. For a long time he had submitted to ascetic exercises, fasting, mortifying his body, and yet after all this he did not feel that he was growing spiritually . . .

Reb Bunam told him the following story:

The Baal Shem Tov once called for Alexei his driver to harness the horses and make ready for a journey. Since the affair to be taken care of was urgent and he had to arrive at the destination as soon as possible, the Baal Shem brought about a miraculous short cut by means of his supernatural powers. A distance that normally required a great many hours was traversed in a short time. The horses moved as fast as arrows.

While racing through the countryside, the horses wondered why the driver did not stop at any of the inns along the road where they were usually given a chance to enjoy new-mown hay and fresh water. After reflecting for a while, they came to the conclusion that they were no longer horses but humans, who took their meals upon arrival at a town. But, having passed through many towns without pausing anywhere, it occurred to them that they were no longer humans either but angels, and angels did not eat . . .

When they arrived at the place where they were eventually fed, they threw themselves upon the fodder like horses.

Fasting alone never turned a person into an angel. The real test came after the fast.

The sacred vocation of a Hasidic rebbe involved many responsibilities. He was not expected to live in isolation but to be involved with the lives of those attached to him, to exalt and to inspire, to pray for and be open to them whenever they came for counsel in confusion or distress.

In his youth the Kotzker was among those who had gathered around the Holy Jew in rebellion against the Seer of Lublin. Hasidism had become a mass movement. Instead of sharing his marvelous insights with an elite, hungry for wisdom of the soul, the Seer had to give most of his time to a vast multitude who sought his blessing for the sick and the impoverished or his counsel in all sorts of mundane affairs. In the eyes of the young rebels, Hasidism had become trivialized.

Convinced that the perversion of Hasidism was due to its popularity, the rebels initiated a dissident movement first led by the Holy Jew, then by Reb Bunam of Pshyskhe, and finally by the Kotzker. Pioneers of renewal, they sought to condense all of Hasidism into one concern: to purify and to exalt an elite, and to prevent the dissipation of the spiritual gifts of the rebbe on the paltry concerns of the people.

When the Kotzker became rebbe in the year 1827, he was for some years able to maintain his unique style of leadership. Surrounded by a select few, he involved them in a way of living that called for a highly sophisticated and sober spirituality. These first years of his leadership may be called his "Tomashov phase."

In 1829 the Kotzker left Tomashov and settled in Kotzk. By this time he was finding himself trapped in the very situation he had sought to escape: his renown as a rebbe had spread like wildfire, and great crowds of people flocked to see him. Kotzk threatened to become another Lublin, a center for the trivialization of Hasidism.

His popularity was one of several issues that disconcerted Reb Mendl greatly. He sought escape from the multitudes that came to Kotzk and became unwilling even to celebrate the Sabbath meals in the fellowship of his disciples. He was torn: should he give up being a rebbe or continue and accept the threat of spiritual debilitation.

The year 1840 was his moment of decision. Reb Mendl detached himself from his community, discontinued his role as rebbe, retired to his study, and only rarely permitted the door to be opened to admit people. The effect of his withdrawal was grief and dismay among those who adored him.

The Kotzker's lifelong inner solitude had become external, visible to others. Did his seclusion proclaim the futility of spiritual leadership? Perhaps. But we must remember the words of Ezekiel 2:1–5:

> And he said to me, "Son of man, stand upon your feet, and I will speak with you." And when he spoke to me, the Spirit entered into me and set me upon my feet; and I heard him speaking to me. And he said to me . . . "I send you to them; and you shall say to them, 'Thus says the Lord God.' And whether they hear or refuse to hear . . . they will know that there has been a prophet among them."

In a piece written by Rabbi Zlotnik and published in Warsaw in the year 1920, the Kotzker was described as a philosopher who had intended to bring about a reformation in Judaism. According to this article, when he realized that his followers did not understand him, he decided publicly to transgress one of the laws of the Sabbath. A number of writers have inflated the importance of this story, describing his violation as a watershed in the life of the Kotzker. Yet the account is devoid of any historical evidence.[1]

Even if the story were true, it could be regarded only as petty and trivial. Seen in the context of the immensely turbulent life of this unequaled man, such an episode would hardly be in accord with the magnificence and audacity of his thought. He continued to live a life of traditional piety and holiness.

[1] See my forthcoming book, *The Kotzker,* Chap. XVI.

The Kotzker's Withdrawal

During the last twenty years of his life the Kotzker was disaffected, disillusioned, beset by many anxieties. We can only speculate which issues stirred him most. Perhaps the realization that Truth was a derelict and that the earth alone was willing to take it to its bosom. Or the thought that ultimately God Himself was responsible for the inherent falsehood of human existence.

Who could feel close to the Kotzker in his self-exile, a thunderbolt in solitude? And what did he seek to achieve by his retirement? To protest against the spuriousness of the world? Exclusive dedication to a battle with Heaven instead of dispersing his energies in battling human stupidity? Had he come to the conclusion that to be an effective leader of people one had to stay away from them? Or was it his intention to proclaim that the end of Hasidism had arrived, to finish off what the Baal Shem Tov had begun?

He had sought men whose hearts were of steel but discovered that most of them had stultified ears. He had been misunderstood by his closest friends. Did he blame them or himself for his inability to speak more lucidly, more explicitly? In any case, he decided to walk alone by the edge of the stream of possibilities, a vision ahead, despair behind.

After his virtual retirement in 1840, hearts were no longer smitten by the wonders of his mind, or shaken by the fury of his voice.

Once, during a Sabbath meal, Reb Mendl commented on the

verse, "And Jacob sent messengers . . . to . . . Esau" (Genesis 32:4). Suddenly he cried out, "How long will Jews be preoccupied with the question of how Jacob sent messengers to Esau." Then he suffered a nervous breakdown, used abusive language to his Hasidim, screaming, "Get away from me." On that occasion he also insulted his distinguished friend Reb Mordecai Yosef. He was carried to his room and remained sick in bed for several weeks.

From far and wide people came to see his face, to hear him speak. But the Kotzker rarely received them. He spent nearly all of his last twenty years alone behind closed doors. Once his venerable friend, Reb Yitzhak Meir of Ger, tore into Reb Mendl's room and shouted, "Jews are living in misery! And you shut your door!"

Was this withdrawal a form of self-imposed exile? In those years it was not uncommon for saintly Jews to banish themselves and spend years in strange little towns, unknown, unrespected, as a way of experiencing exile in solidarity with God, who is homeless in this world. Did the Kotzker too decide to experience banishment in his own home?

It is my hypothesis that his withdrawal was a shifting of the fronts, from waging the battle with man to a confrontation with God. Though it was most unlikely that his thought could be cast in the shape of other people's minds, he would suddenly appear in the House of Learning from time to time, exclaiming strange words full of daring. The assembled disciples, overcome with fear of this awesome man, would run away in consternation, instead of staying and permitting him to finish his utterance. So his voice remained enveloped in darkness, like a wind howling in the night. Yet some people will feel smitten some day, for those who ran away did not let him finish what he had to say.

His utterances remained cryptic, incomplete. Perhaps he had no courage to complete what he alluded to. The totality of his sayings looks like a torso; he did not voice his thoughts to the end. No one fully grasped what he said. He was like a wick burning out, and no one understood the pain in his glance.

Yet the Kotzker did not fail. He may have thought he had little impact, but the struggle he waged goes on; his words once again act as a battle cry.

PART VIII

Differences

Differences

THE FOUNDATION upon which the Kotzker's understanding of human existence was built differed from that on which Kierkegaard's insights rested. This fact is, of course, rooted in the fundamental differences between Judaism and Christianity. Indeed, their profoundly distinctive grasp of ultimate realities accounts for their respective insights, both similar and sharply divergent. In considering, therefore, the concerns and perspectives shared by the two men, we must not lose sight of the subtle but drastic differences in their thinking.

Furthermore, knowledge of the world in which a thinker lives is a necessary prerequisite for a full appreciation of his thoughts. We must keep in mind the cultural and social dissimilarity between Copenhagen and Kotzk; between Berlin, where the philosophy that deeply affected the mind of Kierkegaard was taught, and Lublin, where the Kotzker first groped his way to Hasidism; between Hegel, whose system occupied Kierkegaard's attention, and the Holy Jew, who inspired the Kotzker.

The intellectual atmosphere in which Kierkegaard grew up was Hegelian in philosophy and Romantic in literature. To be considered educated, a man had to think in Hegel's terms. Ordinary people appropriated the jargon of his philosophy, and discussions using the terms "thesis," "antithesis," and "synthesis" could be heard in the stores of Copenhagen.

The Kotzker, on the other hand, lived with Talmudic dialectics and the search for depth in religious existence. The personalities and teachings of the Baal Shem and his disciples held many people spellbound.

Kierkegaard was an author, passionately involved in writing and publishing. The Kotzker, we are told, was engaged in writing, but then threw his manuscripts into the fire.

Their respective modes of living were also in sharp contrast. Kierkegaard was one of the great masters in the history of philosophy, the Kotzker one of the most radical tzaddikim in the history of Hasidism.

Kierkegaard was no moral hero; he was even inclined "to waste his prodigious talents in a round of activities which would have to be conventionally classified with the sins of the flesh." Nor was he above accepting interest. His charitable contributions were rather modest in view of the fortune he had inherited from his father. Students of Kierkegaard speak of a lack of correspondence between his life and his writings.[1] Although he came ultimately to praise asceticism and the monastic life, he did not practice it; in fact, he lived in a somewhat extravagant style.

The Kotzker lived the life of a holy man and remained detached from the world, disdaining money and the pleasures of the flesh. Even his opponents did not question that he was a saint, and in the eyes of some of his disciples he seemed an angel dwelling on earth.

For all his awareness of life's darkness and all-pervading anxiety, the Kotzker maintained that a corner of light could always be found. He disagreed sharply with those who claimed that man was acting largely in the dark when attempting to serve God's will.

[1] See the literature cited by Sponheim, *Kierkegaard on Christ and Christian Coherence,* p. 16, n. 27.

His agony reached a limit in dismay, not in despair. He was baffled, not shattered. His misery defied explanation, yet it was not beyond hope or cure.

Kierkegaard's inner state was drastically different, both theologically and psychologically. He struggled against a sickness composed of melancholy and self-accusation. He attributed both these disorders to his father, "an old man, himself prodigiously melancholy . . . [who] had a son in his old age upon whom the whole of that melancholy descended in inheritance." In Kierkegaard's own words:

> If something is really to become depressing the foreboding that there is something wrong must first of all develop in the midst of the most favourable circumstances, one does not become conscious oneself of anything so wrong; but it must lie in the family history, then the all-consuming power of original sin shows itself, which can grow into despair.

His father, a deeply religious, passionate, austere, and guilt-haunted man was obsessed with his own sinfulness and the curse it brought upon him and his family. Most of his children died during his lifetime. He was tormented by the memory that as a boy he had once cursed God. His conscience was further plagued by an act of incontinence he had committed. At the end of his life he confessed all this to his son. Kierkegaard's knowledge of his father's guilty secret convinced him that he was accursed and helped to strengthen his sense of sin.

> How terrible about the man who once as a little boy, while herding the flocks on the heaths of Jutland, suffering greatly, in hunger and in want, stood upon a hill and cursed God—that the man was unable to forget it even when he was eighty-two years old.[2]

While the Kotzker shared Kierkegaard's melancholy disposi-

[2] Journal entries, 1846, 1837, 1846, Dru edition, ¶¶ 600, 100, 556.

tion, the sense of inherited guilt or curse was certainly absent in him and from his heritage. There is no indication of it in his personal life, nor is there a place for it in Jewish thought. Classical Jewish literature firmly rejected such a concept. The Targumim, the Aramaic translations of the Bible, render the words of the second commandment in this way: "visiting the guilt of wicked fathers upon their rebellious children . . . if the children continue to sin like their fathers" (Exodus 20:5; Deuteronomy 5:9).

Kierkegaard's thinking was Christocentric; the Kotzker's was preoccupied with One God, the creator of Heaven and earth. For Kierkegaard the primary fact attendant upon man's existence was his disengagement from God and his consciousness of it. The Kotzker, on the other hand, considered the disengagement a contingency rather than a necessity, rooted in the absolute difference between man and God. A Jew, the Kotzker held, was never absolutely separated from God, for in doing a *mitzvah* he united himself with His will. Disengagement was not a foregone necessity of his nature but a situation resulting from a failure of his will, and engagement could be restored by an act of return, *teshuvah,* or repentance.

For Kierkegaard the world we see and live in was not an open door toward God, but one closed off from Him. The door could be opened only by Him from the other side.[3] The Kotzker held that God was always waiting for man's initiative to open the door. "Where does God dwell?" he was asked. "Wherever you permit Him to enter" was his answer.

Kierkegaard stressed God's absolute self-sufficiency. Judaism

---

[3] See Kierkegaard, *Purity of Heart Is to Will One Thing,* translated by Douglas V. Steere (New York, 1938), p. 115; and *Purify Your Hearts!,* translated by A. S. Aldworth and W. S. Ferrie (London, 1938), pp. 109f.

teaches that God needs man to carry out His acts through history, that man depends in his very being on God, and that, within the dimension of history, the relationship between God and man is a covenant, a reciprocity, in which the partners have obligations toward each other.

True to the meaning of the covenant, God is in need of the cooperation of man. It is for this reason that the Kotzker stressed contrast and opposition as well as analogy and cooperation between God and man. He insisted upon the importance of both human enterprise and divine assistance, human initiative and divine grace.

For Kierkegaard, inwardness represented a clash between man the creature and the fearful judgment of God. The Kotzker saw inwardness as a struggle for inner purity, an endeavor to achieve it, sustained by hope. In Kierkegaard the tension never ceased, the conflict was beyond reconciliation, for vis-à-vis God man was always in the wrong.

While the Kotzker's life was dominated by an awareness that the falseness and egocentricity of men separate them from God, he was also profoundly open to God's love and forgiveness in the light of Judaism. The efficacy and preciousness of good deeds reveal an affirmation of the world. For all his severity, Reb Mendl stressed the spiritual health of joyousness and the ravages perpetrated by melancholy. He could not have shared Kierkegaard's view that "a witness to the truth is a man whose life from first to last is unacquainted with everything which is called enjoyment!" [4]

The dualism of body and soul is frequently expounded in Christianity, and the absence of such a dichotomy in Judaism is often cited as one of the outstanding differences between Juda-

[4] *Kierkegaard's Attack upon "Christendom,"* p. 7.

ism and Christianity. Yet one must not disregard the powerful ascetic trend that has captured the hearts of simple as well as intellectual Jews.

In fact, Augustine's frequently quoted statement that "the love of God, the love of our neighbor, is called charity; the love of the world, the love of this life is called concupiscence" [5] has its parallel in medieval and post-medieval Jewish literature. Young Maimonides, for example, wrote in his *Introduction to the Mishnah:* "The restoration of the soul is contingent upon the destruction of the body, and the destruction of the soul follows the restoration of the body." [6]

This theme has profound religious, moral, and psychological implications. Apologetic writers who have dealt with it have failed, to repeat, to be aware of some powerful trends in Jewish history that sharply diverged from what is parabolically called "normative Judaism."

Self-negation

Kierkegaard stressed that Judaism, unlike Christianity, does not preach about a cross and agony, about hating oneself. It does not teach that

[5] *Enarrationes in psalmos,* translated by E. B. Pusey, in Erich Przywara, *An Augustine Synthesis* (New York, 1958), p. 341.
[6] See Heschel, *Maimonides,* p. 36.

what God wills (out of love) is that a man shall die from the world . . . that what God then does (out of love) is to torment him with every anguish calculated to take his life.

In the New Testament, Christianity is the profoundest wound that can be inflicted upon a man, calculated on the most dreadful scale to collide with everything.[1]

Christianity, Kierkegaard insists, is heterogeneity and separateness from the world. Therefore, a man must renounce this world; he refers to it as a penal establishment. The meaning of life, according to Kierkegaard, then, is found in the possibility of suffering. One cannot avoid pain where the eternal and temporal meet each other. "It was because of Christianity's hostility toward life that paganism called it *odium generis humani* [hatred of the human species]. This charge is true, says Kierkegaard."[2]

Christianity is heterogeneous to the world, wherefore the "witness" must always be recognizable by his heterogeneity to this world, by renunciation, by suffering, and this is the reason why such a mode of being is little capable of being something else at the same time.[3]

Significantly, Kierkegaard himself was aware of this important contrast between Judaism and Christianity.

[He] once told Israel Lewin, his secretary, who was a Jew, that he envied him because he did not have to be concerned with Jesus Christ; meaning that he thereby escaped the suffering which is always the Christian's lot, because of the collision between Christ (and the Christian likewise) and the world.[4]

"Christianity means literally the end of the world," Kierke-

[1] *Kierkegaard's Attack upon "Christendom,"* pp. 224, 258. "Christianity and worldliness never come to an understanding, even for a moment."—*Works of Love,* p. 82.
[2] Thulstrup, "Kierkegaard's Dialectic," in *A Kierkegaard Critique,* p. 269.
[3] *Kierkegaard's Attack upon "Christendom,"* p. 11.
[4] T. H. Croxall, *Kierkegaard Commentary* (London and New York, 1956), p. 226.

gaard responded ironically to the objection that if everyone re-mained unmarried, man would become extinct. "What a pity!" he added. Christianity should act directly to terminate the continuation of the world; this was its task.

Kierkegaard reproaches Luther for de-emphasizing the require-ment [of remaining unmarried] and turning Christianity into Juda-ism . . . Fruitfulness and propagation belong to Judaism where those who fear God are happy and blessed and where the promises apply to this earthly life. But Christianity's kingdom is not of this world . . . The reason for this difference between Judaism and Christianity lies in their differing orientation to eternity. Essentially Judaism is the temporal without the eternal; in Christianity everything is directed toward eternity.[5]

Father and Mother

It seems that Kierkegaard's understanding of Christianity was strongly determined by Luke 14:26. "If any man come to me, and hate not his father, and mother, and wife, and children, and brethren, and sisters, yea, and his own life also, he cannot be my disciple."

[5] Thulstrup, "Kierkegaard's Dialectic," p. 274. The last sentence in this quo-tation echoes an unfortunate misinterpretation of Judaism common in Chris-tian literature.

This passage has puzzled many interpreters. *And hate not:* "the word repels."[1] It has often been understood to mean that he who wishes to follow Jesus must choose Him so unconditionally as Lord and Guide that he makes all other loyalties and ties absolutely subordinate.[2]

In the eyes of the Kotzker, such a saying contradicts Jewish tradition. Rabbi Shimon ben Yohai maintained that "the Lord put the obligation of honoring one's father and mother" before that of honoring Himself.[3] According to another version, "Great is the duty of honoring one's father and mother, since the Holy One, blessed be He, made the honor due to parents equal to the honor due to Himself."[4]

The only possible parallel in Judaism would be a rule derived from Leviticus 19:3. "Even though I have admonished you regarding fearing [your] father, if he shall say to you 'Profane the Sabbath' do not listen to him." But there is no injunction to hate a father who demands the transgression of a command in the Torah. It merely puts forward the one existing limitation to the obedience which the child must accord its parents.

An analogy may be found in the rule that if one's father and teacher are both in a house of captivity, he must ransom his teacher first (but only when he is more learned and receives no fee) and only then his father.

[1] *The Interpreter's Bible,* VIII, 259. Some commentators regard this as an idiomatic expression for loving less, as in, e.g., Genesis 29:31 and Romans 9:13. Matthew tones down the harshness of the saying: "He who loves father and mother more than me" (6:24).

[2] See, e.g., Norval Geldenhuys, *Commentary on the Gospel of Luke* (Grand Rapids, Mich., 1951), p. 398.

[3] *Yerushalmi Kiddushin,* I, 7.

[4] *Pesikta Rabbati,* translated by W. G. Braude (New Haven, Conn., 1968), Piska 23/24, p. 498.

Sin and Guilt

Kierkegaard writes:

Christianity rests upon the . . . presupposition that the human race is a lost race, that every individual who is born is by being born a lost individual. Christianity then would save every individual, but it makes no disguise of the fact that, when this is taken seriously, this life becomes the direct opposite of what is to man's taste and liking, being sheer suffering, anguish, misery.[1]

The forgiveness of sins cannot be such that God wipes out all guilt, with one blow, obliterating all its consequences. Such a desire is only a worldly longing which does not rightly know what guilt is. It is only the *guilt* which is forgiven, the forgiveness of sins is not more. It does not mean to become a new man under happier circumstances, but to become a new man in the consoling assurance that the guilt is forgiven, even though the consequences of sin remain. The forgiveness of sin must not be a scheme whereby a man who has tried his hand at many things ends by wishing to be a new man, and hopes to stumble through with the help of the forgiveness of sins. No, only the man who has understood that guilt is something absolutely different and far more terrible than the consequences of sin (looked upon as misfortune, suffering), he alone repents.

This is how I understand the relation between *satisfactio vicaria* and man's expiation of his own sins. On the one hand it is of course true that through Christ's death sin was forgiven; but on the other hand man is not lifted from his former state, the "law of sin" as St. Paul says (Romans viii. 25), as though by magic. He has to return

[1] *Kierkegaard's Attack upon "Christendom,"* p. 226.

along the road he went whilst the consciousness that his sins are for-given buoys him up and gives him the courage to defy despair.

To be sure, I believe in the forgiveness of sins, but I understand it as hitherto, that I must bear my punishment all my life, of remain-ing in the painful prison of my isolation, in a profound sense cut off from communication with other men—nevertheless softened by the thought that God has forgiven me.[2]

Perennial guilt deriving from a state of sin was certainly absent from the Kotzker's thoughts. A sense of irreparable disorder caused by sin or of a catastrophic and final loss of God are in-conceivable in Jewish thought; nor is inherited guilt, as already stated, a part of the Jewish consciousness. Even the mystics who have believed that Adam's sin or some other cosmic disaster cor-rupted the original order of creation and who have seriously sensed its consequences to their own day, did not place the burden of guilt upon the individuals of subsequent generations.

Judaism maintains that human existence is a state of involve-ment. Man is involved with the Creator by his very being; for in being he obeys the command, "Let there be!" Just to be is holy.

Being is not a predicament of guilt but rather a triumph, a tribute to Him Who has created the world. Just to be is a blessing. Being is a continuous bestowal of blessing. The problem is not being. How to be is the dilemma.

[2] Journal entries, 1846, 1837, 1848, Dru edition, ¶¶ 606, 116, 749.

Suffering

The concept of faith as a leap, which the Kotzker and Kierkegaard shared, can have different connotations. Predicated upon the ultimate repudiation of reason, the leap of faith causes mental offense and suffering, according to Kierkegaard. Yet the Kotzker never taught that the burden of faith caused suffering, stressing the contrary, the joy of faith.

Kierkegaard regarded *suffering* as the prerequisite for Christian existence. One could become a Christian only by experiencing acute consciousness of sin and remain one through constant penitence. The central object of Christian faith was not God in Himself but God in human form. This was absolute paradox and therefore an enduring stumbling block and an offense to the human mind. Consequently, man could enter into a life of faith in God only by accepting with anguish a paradox against which the mind revolted. Furthermore, such torment was not merely experienced once, but was continually renewed by the repeated acceptance of the paradox. Thus, suffering had to be a pervading and ever-present element in the life of a true Christian; if it were not, it was proof that he could not rise to that level.

To be a Christian, then, meant to take up the cross and accept persecution, *imitatio Christi*. This did not mean merely enduring the trials that face all men; the prerequisite intrinsic to true Christianity was to be found only in the suffering a man voluntarily took upon himself. To be a Christian meant nothing less than being a martyr.

Kierkegaard was a sufferer. The shadow cast by his father's sin, his broken engagement to Regina Olsen, the ridicule to which he was exposed by attacks published in the Copenhagen journal *Corsair*, the disillusionment with Bishop Mynster and the Church in his closing years—all bore in upon him. What is significant about Kierkegaard is the use he made of this suffering. He refused to seek invulnerability. He accepted the pain, lived with it, searched it, and found its costly meaning for him—that he was to live as one called under God, to live as a lonely man, to live for an idea. Through suffering he found his vocation. A Journal entry in 1843 reads

The most important thing is to be honest towards God, not try to escape from something but to force oneself through until he himself gives the explanation, which, whether it is the one one wants or not, is still best.[1]

"Viewed religiously, it is necessary . . . to comprehend suffering and to remain in it, so that reflection is directed *upon* the suffering and not *away* from it." [2] In the last years of his life Kierkegaard thought himself a spiritual martyr, enduring ordeals comparable to those of the early Christians.

The Kotzker showed understanding for the meaning of suffering as a spiritual test that some people must undergo. However, he never explicitly maintained that it was indispensable to the life of faith. The Jew is never encouraged to hate life in this world, which Kierkegaard regarded as a Christian requirement. On the contrary, this life was to be greatly cherished, since it was only here that man could carry out a *mitzvah* in service to the Lord; no such opportunity would be offered in the life to come.

[1] Dru edition, ¶ 454.
[2] *Concluding Unscientific Postscript*, p. 397.

Original Sin

Kierkegaard's stress upon the infinite qualitative difference between God and man has its analogy in the Kotzker's awareness of the radical apartness of man from God. But there is a profound difference between the two conceptions, rooted primarily in their notions of the nature of man. Kierkegaard's insistence upon the infinite qualitative difference between God and man indicates that man is capable of nothing; it is God who gives everything, who even gives man faith. This is grace, and it is the primary focus of Christianity.

Article 4 of the Augsburg Confession (1530) rejected all righteousness through moral work by grounding man's salvation solely in his being justified by God's grace through faith alone. The central teaching of Paul (Romans 3:24) was thus afforded normative authority in the sixteenth century. Based on a repudiation of Mosaic law,[1] this doctrine sharply contradicts a central tenet in Judaism regarding the merit and basic importance of good deeds and obedience to the will of God the lawgiver.

Theoretically, Kierkegaard objected to that tenet. True devotion arises only when man sees that he has absolutely no means of pleasing God—this is the voice of Protestant piety. Jewish piety, on the other hand, is rooted in the consciousness that there are innumerable ways of pleasing God.

---

[1] The views in the Epistle of James—e.g. "What does it profit, my brethren, if a man says he has faith but has not works? . . . Faith by itself, if it has no works, is dead" (2:14, 17.)—led Luther to call it "an epistle of straw."

Jewish consciousness is not aware that the soul is buried under a curse or trapped by inherited guilt from which it must be saved. The doctrines of the Fall of man and Original Sin never became established tenets in Judaism. In the apocalyptic literature of the first century, they are expounded in one book [2] but rejected in another.[3]

The sin of Adam and his expulsion from Eden remained important to Jewish thought throughout the ages, but not all authorities regarded them as having decisively altered what God had originally brought into being. No act of man, however grave, could essentially change or distort what was created by an act of God. Significantly, there is no word for "Original Sin" in Yiddish, the language spoken by the majority of the Jewish people for nearly a thousand years. And the Hebrew term for it occurs as late as the thirteenth century, when it presumably appeared under the impact of medieval Christian–Jewish disputations.

In his daily prayers, the Jew confesses, "The soul Thou hast given me is pure." The sins each individual commits defile his soul. "Blessed shall you be when you come in, and blessed shall you be when you go out" (Deuteronomy 28:6) has been interpreted to mean, "May your exit from the world be as your entry into it; just as you entered it without sin, so may you leave it without sin." [4]

Kierkegaard regarded the problem of sin as central to the religious view of life, and as the starting point for the Christian heart. Particularly in *The Concept of Dread* and *The Sickness unto Death,* he maintained that the consciousness of sin was the

[2] II Esdras 7:118; 3:20; 4:30–1
[3] II Baruch 34:15–19.
[4] *Baba Mezia* 107a.

most concrete expression of the subjective self, the deepest self-awareness the human mind was capable of.

Though the Jewish view of life also embraces the profound consciousness of sin, it focuses on sin in a concrete sense, as a personal act committed against the will of a personal Creator. And though the sins may be grave and many, the evil done is not irremediable. The Christian reference to an ineradicable and comprehensive sinfulness in the nature of every man can never strike root in the Jewish mind. A mighty evil impulse there is in him, but in opposition to it there is also the good impulse. The Psalmist who confesses, "For I know my transgression, and my sin is ever before me" (51:3), is also able to sing, "Bless the Lord, O my soul . . . who forgives all your iniquity" (103:2f.). There is a dialectical relationship between sin and forgiveness. The more sensitive one's awareness of his sins, the more gracious is God's forgiveness.

According to the Kotzker, the leap is the soul's response to a divine call. This presupposes human readiness for such a call. And if the soul is capable of listening, it cannot be maintained then that there is an infinite, qualitative difference between God and man.

The self-analysis Socrates calls for leads the individual to discover his ignorance. The self-reflection demanded by Kierkegaard directs a man to the discovery of his guilt. The self-examination the Kotzker cries out for makes a person face his inauthenticity, his lack of truthfulness, his impurity of heart.

The Torah was not given to angels, says the Talmud; men were not intended to live like angels. But according to Kierkegaard, man feels he is asked to do the impossible. This awareness is central to what he calls "hidden inwardness," a consciousness of a tension. The obedience demanded by the divine imperative is experienced as guilt or sin, owing to a man's slowness or complete inability to respond. He can never measure up to God's overwhelming demand that he place his own life infinitely and passionately in His hands.

Inspired by the teachings of the Bible, the sages of Israel maintained that man was capable of acquiring merit in the eyes of God.

There are two ways of accumulating merits: negative and positive ones. The Church Fathers speak of the former, the Rabbis of the latter. Since man's life "is justified by faith apart from the works of the law" (Romans 3:28), he can obtain merits only by avoiding the *indulgentia dei*, i.e. what is forbidden. The Jews, however, have been taught how to obtain positive merits. Men and women can rise by positive deeds to such a height . . . that they are regarded as meritorious before God.[5]

For Kierkegaard man is saved by the grace of God, regardless of personal merit. Yet if man does not himself say "yes" to the love of God he is not saved, even though he performs the works of love. In this Kierkegaard follows Luther.

The Kotzker was fully aware of the defectiveness of human intentions; nevertheless, he did not question the presence of holiness in even imperfect deeds. He knew of God's promise to abide with Israel in the midst of "their uncleannesses" (see Leviticus 16:16). Only vulgar minds regarded the accumulation of merits as promissory notes. The consciousness of one's deficiencies in the service of the Lord was as important an aspect of Judaism as the doctrine of merit. The Kotzker, committed to both, knew that what was needed was a sense of insecurity rather than complacency.

[5] A. Marmorstein, *The Doctrine of Merits in Old Rabbinic Literature* (New York, 1920), p. 3.

Kierkegaard's famous utterance "As against God we are always in the wrong" is a paraphrase of a verse in the Book of Psalms (143:2), "Enter not into judgment with Thy servant, for no man living is righteous before Thee." Yet this truth about an individual's personal relationship to God does not vitiate his right to argue with the Supreme Judge about His possible injustice toward other people.

True to his intense awareness of man's guilt, Kierkegaard seems not to have been troubled by problems of theodicy, of the need to vindicate a God who permits evil to exist.

The Kotzker was a man of spirit as well as faith. His questions endured even in deep faith. Even in defeat, he continued to demur.

Though he was not, of course, plagued by a sense of guilt due to the Original Sin committed by Adam, the Kotzker was tormented by a more radical agony—the awareness that God was ultimately responsible for the hideousness of human mendacity. It was this concern with the paradox of divine responsibility that finally plunged his soul into the dark grief of his last years.

Did the Kotzker's demand for integrity derive from a view of the depravity of human nature, from an assumption that all the deeds and thoughts of man were tainted by the Original Sin? Such an interpretation would be entirely wrong. On the contrary, his demands were so radical because he believed in man's potential purity and spirituality. He presumably shared the view held by the Hasidic masters that the soul is "a part of God, having come down from above." [6] His entire thinking seemed clearly based on confidence in man's own powers. He overestimated them, in fact, for he expected man to achieve what may be called greatness of soul.

[6] Rabbi Shabbetai Sheftel ben Akiba Horowitz, *Shefa Tal,* beginning.

Kierkegaard's books, together with his journals, all his direct and indirect communications, are an unbroken narrative of man's desperate, frenzied, convulsive struggle with original sin and the horrors of life which arose from sin.[7]

It is highly instructive to note that for all the affinity of the Kotzker and Kierkegaard, this entire issue remained alien to the former. What upset him was *the myth of the buried Truth* rather than that of the fallen man.

Guilt and Expectation

There are two basic concepts with which we attempt to decipher what is at stake in our existence, final possibilities beyond which we cannot go in trying to order our lives. These concepts are not derived from experience; they are ultimate categories of the spirit. One is that man must atone for a guilt; the other that he has a task to carry out, an expectation to fulfill. The first has found expression in the Fall of man, his sinful nature, while the second has laid stress upon the *mitzvah*.

The first interpretation arises from the Orphic conception, which correlates man's guilt to the captivity of the soul within the body. The whole of human life is a penance for some heavy

[7] Lev Shestov, *Kierkegaard and the Existential Philosophy,* translated by Elinor Hewitt (Athens, Ohio) p. 311.

guilt that the soul has incurred in an earlier existence.[1] It found its powerful echo in Augustine's translation of Original Sin into a sense of universal guilt. Adam's Fall was the loss of real being; all future generations derived their corrupt nature from him and therefore inherit his guilt. According to Calvin, "being perverted and corrupted in all parts of our nature, we are merely on account of such corruption deservedly condemned by God . . . this is not liability for another's fault."

G. van der Leeuw explains that sin is enmity against God.

We offend God, even when we ourselves neither know nor desire this; we are enemies of God, and indeed for no other reason than that he is our enemy . . . Conscience cries out to man that he hates God. The will that is hostile to God arises from man's deepest being . . . The distinctive peculiarity of the Christian idea of sin is to be perceived in the concept of general sin as general guilt.[2]

According to Paul Tillich, existence itself is a state of estrangement. Man is alienated from the ground of his being, from other beings, and from himself. The transition from essence to existence, a universal quality of finite being, results in personal guilt and universal tragedy.

Each child inherits Adam's guilt. Man's problem, then, is not basically his own transgression of God's law. "His primary guilt lies in the fact that he is a prodigal in a far country."

> We have no choice but to be guilty.
> God is unthinkable if we are innocent.

writes the contemporary Christian poet and dramatist Archibald MacLeish.[3]

---

[1] See Werner Jaeger, *Aristotle,* translated by Richard Robinson (London and New York, 1934), Chap. IX *passim.*

[2] G. van der Leeuw, *Religion in Its Essence and Manifestation* (London, 1938), p. 520.

[3] *J. B.* (Boston, 1958), p. 111.

The heart of man asks: what is expected of me? Or in the language of the Bible: what is required of me? Insight is awakened by the awareness that one must answer. Beyond personal problems there is an objective challenge to overcome helplessness, carelessness, inequities, oppression, suffering. Above the din of desires there is a calling, a demanding, a waiting, a sublime expectation.

We do not come upon only flowers, stars, mountains, rivers. Over and above all things there is a sublime expectation, a waiting-for. With every child born, a new expectation enters the world.

This is the most important experience in life, a mysterious waiting which every human being senses at moments: something is being asked of me. Meaning is found in understanding the demand and in responding to it.

We are indebted by virtue of being human because we cannot simply be; we are constantly being created. Thus, as mentioned earlier, the "ought" precedes the "is." The world is such that in its face one senses owingness rather than ownership. In its presence one must be responsive as well as responsible.

Indebtedness is not derived from abstract concepts; it lives in us as an awareness before it is verbalized or its content is clarified. It is the sense of having a task, being called upon, an urge to experience living as receiving as well as taking. Its content is gratitude for a gift received. It makes for more than a biological give-and-take relationship.

Indebtedness expresses the pathos of being human, an awareness of the self as committed. Man cannot think of himself as human without being conscious of his indebtedness. Thus it is not a mere feeling but a constitutive feature of being human. To eradicate it would be to destroy man's humanity.

This sense of indebtedness is translated by people in a variety of ways: duty, obligation, allegiance, conscience, sacrifice. And the content and direction of each of these terms are subject to interpretation.

There is no authenticity in human existence without a sense of indebtedness, without an awareness that man must transcend himself, his interests, and his needs, without the realization that existence involves both utilization and celebration, satisfaction and exaltation.[4]

Antithesis to Luther

Though Kierkegaard's thought showed a marked leaning to Catholic ideals in its ascetic tendencies, it reflects its Lutheran ancestry in decisive aspects—for example, in its opposition between faith and reason, and in the stress it lays on the relation of the individual soul to God, almost to the exclusion of the community of believers. Indeed, Kierkegaard's spiritual wrestling would have been inconceivable if Lutheranism had not stressed the continuous witness to the truth of the Gospel as developed and applied through centuries by believing individuals. Yet as a witness himself, he was forced into collision with the Lutheran Church of his day.

[4] See A. J. Heschel, *Who Is Man?* (Stanford, Cal., 1965), pp. 107ff.

PART IX

❖❰❖❰❖❰

The Kotzker and Job [1]

To Exalt the Heavens

WHAT WERE the problems that troubled the Kotzker during his last twenty years, which he spent in seclusion? No answer can be posited with certainty. From his utterances on those occasions when he left his chamber, we can only surmise that he was tormented by the ever-present enigma: why did God permit evil in the world?

What was the Kotzker searching for all along, and what did he expect to achieve? A score of young men who would shout from the rooftops, "The Lord is God!"? But what, after all, could mere individuals accomplish? Would so few be able to reshape the world? The Kotzker's vision was more daring. A balancing of reverence and intrepidity, of awe and audacity, was an ongoing activity in Reb Mendl's soul.

"Who is like you, O Lord, among the silent, who sees the abashment of His people and remains silent!" was the outcry of Rabbi Ishmael in an age of martyrdom. According to an old Jewish tradition, tzaddikim, holy men, have a power to which God himself is willing to yield. God may issue a decree, but if it is too severe, the tzaddik has the power to annul it. At a time of grave adversity, his disciples pleaded with the Kotzker to act accordingly.

"Yes," the Kotzker responded, "but how about reverence?"

Underneath his reverence, however, was dissent and contentiousness, a sense of outrage at the depth of falsehood afflicting the world as well as silent animadversion. For who was responsible that we hurried about in a world of phantoms? Was only man to blame? The Kotzker uncompromisingly castigated his fellow men. But did not castigation itself cast reproach upon their Maker? What about the Heavens above that permitted, or even ordained, that the predicament arise and persist? The affliction over this issue was even deeper than the predicament itself. Something had gone awry in Heaven.

Had there been no alternative to burying Truth when man was created? Ultimately the Kotzker arrived at the austere conclusion that the goal and purpose was not to purify man but to exalt the Heavens.

During a visit to Kotzk by Reb Yankev Arye of Rodzhimin, Reb Mendl asked him, "Yankl, why was man created on this earth?"

"He was created in order to restore the purity of his soul," Reb Yankl replied.

The Kotzker Rebbe roared back at him, "Yankl, is that what we learned from the rebbe in Pshyskhe? Surely man was created to exalt the Heavens!"

If man was created to seek the purity of his soul, then his entire worship was for his own benefit. And if serving God meant to serve the self, what happened to faith? Did not the Kotzker insist that the meaning of faith derived from disregard for the self? To do what was Holy in order to please oneself was an act of idol worship. Thus, the doctrine that man was born in order to strive for personal salvation would signify that he was intended to worship an idol . . . No, the supreme purpose could not be personal salvation.

I Am Choking

Severity may be allowed where gentleness is futile. Yet few men can afford to express anger without causing harm to their own souls. The Kotzker carried anger as a flint bears fire. His silence was grim, his speech an outcry, his indignation a moment in which unmixed agony, unceasing bitterness blasted all restraint, corroding every comfort. His way was not to explain and elucidate but, rather, to protest, to contradict, to reject in the name of higher visions, of hidden sufferings.

But could a creature of flesh and blood overturn the Heavens? Could he reach that high and bring order into the upper spheres? Besides, how dare he challenge God? Reb Mendl drew his conviction both from Scripture and from the Talmud and Midrash. Since the day Abraham argued with God over the fate of Sodom and Gomorrah, and Jacob wrestled with and overcame the angel, many Prophets and rabbis had occasionally engaged in similar arguments. The refusal to accept the harshness of God's ways in the name of His love was an authentic form of prayer. Indeed, the ancient Prophets of Israel were not in the habit of consenting to God's harsh judgment and did not simply nod, saying, "Thy will be done." They often challenged Him, as if to say, Thy will be changed. They had often countered and even annulled divine decrees.

As mentioned earlier, the Heavens were open to the great tzaddik; he could accomplish great things if only he would raise himself high enough. If he struggled out of holiness and in Truth, he might break through all the way to Heaven.

The Kotzker once said, "If I were told by Heaven that there was no way for me to repent, I would overwhelm the Heavens." He also interpreted the verse "This is the law of the guilt offering. It is most holy" (Leviticus 7:1)—as follows: "Where is the guilt to be found? In the most holy." A Hasid is he who discards the world, declared the Kotzker. Underlying this statement was an awareness of the contradiction between the world and Truth. Only by saying "no" to the world could one live Truth.

The Kotzker conceived of living as an ongoing encounter, a fighting to the end, in which thought of surrender was inconceivable. He held moral cowards in contempt, disliked pusillanimous souls. The battle waged was fierce: it was an encounter with the ego and its treacherous delusions.

This was the Kotzker's position as expressed in his teaching. But privately, beyond the ken of his disciples, in his passionate solitude, he was also engaged in another battle, a battle with God, a battle for the sake of God.

The disaster was greater than people imagined. If the fault were only in the nature of man, restoration would be so much easier. But the calamity had occurred even before man was created.

"Show me Thy glory," Moses implored, and the Almighty said to him, "and you shall see My back, but My face shall not be seen" (Exodus 33:18, 23). This meant that everything appeared back to front in the world, that what prevailed was the reverse of what, according to man's conception, ought to be. The world stood with its back to reason; the face of Providence was hidden.

One could endure such a world only with a heart of iron. One was overcome with nausea when he started thinking about mendacity, cruelty, malice. That was why the Kotzker maintained that a Hasid is he who discards the world. The fate of the entire world did not deserve a single moan, he said, for it was a world of phantoms. "The world is putrid, it makes me choke!" he cried.

The Kotzker felt the agony, knew the tragedy, but what was the remedy? There was only one way to survive: to be Holy in challenging God, to pray militantly, to worship heroically, and to wait. Above all, not to be fooled by false concessions from Heaven.

Such audacity was not to overshadow man's awareness of his pettiness. Reb Henokh of Alexander, Reb Mendl's disciple, once said, "Do you know what we learned in Kotzk? 'That man should know that he is a stinker.'" Here lies the ambiguity of man and the paradox of his destiny: although he is utterly trivial, he is called upon to elevate the earth to the level of the Heavens.

Reb Henokh interpreted a passage from the Psalms, "The Heavens are the Lord's Heavens, but the earth He has given to the sons of man" (Psalms 115:16), as follows: the Almighty created the Heavens for Himself, while He handed the earth over to man to make it into a Heaven. The Kotzker, then, had a tremendous task—to convert the earth into a Heaven.

Reb Henokh believed that Moses succeeded in this, for when the Torah was given at Sinai, a miracle happened: even dulled hearts became Heavenly. "While the mountain burned with fire unto the heart of heaven" (Deuteronomy 4:11)—the mountains burned until the Jews received "a heavenly heart."

Perhaps this explains Reb Mendl's bitterness. He was himself encompassed by flames, like Mount Sinai. Ablaze, he carried a vision of transforming earthly men into Heavenly people. Then came the realization: their hearts were cast in clay; no fire ever burst from clay.

Submission?

The Kotzker himself was involved in the paradox of man's triviality and audacity on the ultimate level of his existence. Though certain of the power of the tzaddik to affect decisions made in Heaven—"the tzaddik decrees and the Holy One fulfills, the Holy One decrees and the tzaddik annuls"—he refused out of reverence for a higher Truth to make use of it in particular cases. On the other hand, God's consigning of Truth to the tomb exceeded the limits of the Kotzker's acquiescence. Though he cloaked his accusations in silence for the most part, occasionally he would shout out biting words. Was it fitting for a tzaddik to have complaints against God, and even to voice them?

This problem had aroused a controversy among Jewish sages in antiquity. Rabbi Akiba held that one ought always to acknowledge the justice of God's ways. Even if a man was consumed by utter darkness, he was to accept suffering lovingly; to complain against God was impudent. Rabbi Ishmael, on the contrary, refused to consent to the sufferings of Israel without remonstrating. He dared to challenge the Almighty. "Who is like you, O Lord, among the silent, who sees the abashment of this people and remains silent!" was the outcry of Rabbi Ishmael in an age of martyrdom.

Most sages of Talmud and Midrash regarded Job as one of the few truly God-fearing men of the Bible. To others he was a blasphemer. One scholar said of his orations: "Stop him! Put earth into his mouth." [1]

In the Jew of our time, distress at God's predicament may be a more powerful witness than tacit acceptance of evil as inevitable. The outcry of anguish certainly adds more to His glory than callousness or even flattery of the God of pathos.

Reb Mendl adopted Rabbi Ishmael's position. A man who lived by honesty could not be expected to suppress his anxiety when tormented by profound perplexity. He had to speak out audaciously. Man should never capitulate, even to the Lord.

Did a man who argued with God have the slightest hope of winning? The thought of a victory over God was totally incongruous in the Kotzker's view. No matter how painfully palpable the perplexity, any possible solution to it was hidden. A man of flesh and blood was simply not meant to comprehend the divine response to the deepest of human problems. Divine secrets were not compatible with the human intellect. Did we have to conclude then that all controversy between man and God was futile?

The Kotzker loved the ruthless turbulence of protest and anger. Such turbulence, he thought, should never cease to defy the Heavens. It was apparently God's will that man not surrender but confront the Heavens and storm them. Nature, God's creation, provided him with an example.

"Thou dost rule the raging of the sea, when its waves rise, Thou praiseth them" (Psalms 89:10). There seems to be an inherent con-

[1] *Baba Batra* 16a.

tradiction here. For the Creator had "placed the sand as the bound for the sea, a perpetual barrier which it cannot pass; though the waves toss, they cannot prevail; though they roar, they cannot pass over it" (Jeremiah 5:22). Why then do the waves rage and beat against the shores, trying to break the barriers with violence and flood the land? Why does the sea rebel against God's will and fight so fiercely, spewing forth foam like a dragon without end. Surely it knows it cannot destroy God's established order? It cannot possibly prevail. The land will not be flooded. Nevertheless, the Almighty praises its passionate desire to ravage the boundary. The sea knows that it has not the power to win, yet it struggles on.

Submission and blind obedience repelled the Kotzker. He hated the milksops who knuckled under, the docile, pious yes-men. A man must be a rebel in his very existence; he must refuse to be what he is. Reb Mendl's teacher, Reb Bunam, had no end of praise for the revolutionary spirit of Rabbi Abraham Ibn-Ezra. "I simply cannot make out how his shoulders did not crack with fear of the Lord," he once said. One ought not to be servile even before God. Even in defeat, continued courage was essential.

The Kotzker had tremendous respect for dissenters who refused to be pushed around. Did not Jewish tradition consider offensive those who flatter God? He admired the rebels in the Bible, such as Korah and Pharaoh.

Korah, leader of the revolt against the authority of Moses, Reb Mendl once explained, was not just someone off the streets. Of Pharaoh, King of Egypt, he said, "Pharaoh was a man of mettle; were even half a plague to strike anyone today, he would be yielding in no time. God is just and His judgment is just! he'd cry. Pharaoh was hit by a host of plagues, yet he remained true to himself."

In describing the last plague sent against Egypt, the Scripture says: "And Pharaoh rose up in the night . . ." (Exodus 12:30). In his commentary, Rashi adds, "He arose from his bed." What difference does it make whether he rose from a chair or a bed?

The Kotzker explained that Rashi had added a crucial insight to the passage. Freethinkers of today brag about their heresy though they are actually faint-hearted cowards. The moment one of them has a headache, he immediately begins to recite Psalms or runs off to a witch [doctor]. They are not heretics, just sissies.

Pharaoh was of another breed altogether; he was a full-scale heretic. He saw all the plagues Moses prophesied come true, and that same day Moses warned him: "About midnight . . . all the first-born in the land of Egypt shall die . . . And there shall be a great cry throughout all the land of Egypt, such as there has never been, nor ever shall be again" (Exodus 11:4ff.). Even though Pharaoh was himself a first-born son, he was not perturbed and lay down as if nothing would happen. He slept like a man after a heavy meal and awoke only when all of Egypt was deafened by weeping. Thus "He arose from his bed" takes on an extra dimension of non-acquiescence.

Unlike some other rebbes, the Kotzker did not teach that man should under all circumstances be meek because he was a nothing, that he should be quieter than calm water and flatter than mown grass. On the contrary, he should hold his head up high; for a feeling of meekness and inferiority was the worst possible trait in the fight for Truth. Even if he were to lose the battle, he should not fall like a dog.

The heathen prophet Balaam once said of Israel, "He couched, he lay down like a lion" (Numbers 24:9). Even when he fell, he lay like a lion.

There are some forms of suffering that a man must accept with love and bear in silence. There are other agonies to which he must say no.

"I will bring you out from under the burdens of the Egyptians" (Exodus 6:6). Why does Scripture say "burdens" rather than "slavery"? To this Reb Bunam replied that the greatest evil of the Egyptian exile was that the Israelites were able to tolerate anything. No matter how tough the work, they gradually got used to it. When the Lord saw them toiling away with mortar and bricks and patiently resigned to their slavery, He said to Moses, "If they can tolerate this, things are bad, and we have to get them out of Egypt soon, otherwise they will be slaves the rest of their lives." Their redemption began when they ceased to tolerate their slavery: "who has brought you out from under the *burdens* of the Egyptians" (Exodus 6:7).

This inner attitude is what counts—how one feels about suffering.

Problems with God

Time and again the Kotzker returned to this issue: was it conceivable that the entire world, Heaven and earth, was a palace without a master?

Whenever an exceptionally knotty Talmudic problem was raised, just one person's interjection, "Lord of Abraham!" would force the opposition to change its course. Reb Mendl often referred to the following parable:

A man once wandered from city to city and came upon a palace that seemed unattended. He wondered: Could it be this palace has no lord? Finally the lord of the palace peered out at him and said, "I am the lord of this palace."

Similarly, Abraham looked around at the world and thought: Could it be that this world has no lord, no master? Then the Lord of the universe peered out at him and said, "I am the master, the sovereign of the world."

In the original Hebrew the phrase describing the palace, *birah doleket,* is ambiguous. It could mean "a palace full of light" or "a palace in flames." According to one interpretation, Abraham saw a world of infinity, beauty, and wisdom and thought: is it possible for such grandeur to have come into being accidentally, without a creator? The second interpretation is that he saw a world engulfed in the flames of evil and deceit and thought, Is it possible that there is no Lord to take this misfortune to heart?

Apparently, Reb Mendl accepted the latter meaning. He also considered Abraham's question to be the central issue in the search for faith.

"Could it be that this palace has no lord?" This problem tormented Reb Mendl. He, who never ingratiated himself with anyone and spoke the truth to everyone's face, did not delude himself with facile solutions.

Once a man came to Reb Mendl and poured out his heart. His wife had died in childbirth, leaving him with seven children and an infant. He himself was in rags.

"I cannot console you over such cruelty," said the rebbe. "Only the true Master of Mercy is able to do it. Address yourself to Him."

Difficulties always arise during Torah study. While other people are merely bothered by these problems, they were a source of pain to the Kotzker. For instance, before his seclusion in 1840, Reb Mendl sat at the table in the House of Study, surrounded by his Hasidim, on the Sabbath of the weekly portion Toledot. He asked, "How could Isaac at first have intended to give his blessing to evil Esau?" He became so engrossed in the matter that he fainted. All his Hasidim were seized with fear. Their rebbe was unconscious, his head thrown back over his chair. Then one of the leading Hasidim carried him out and laid him down on his bed. Reb Mendl lay sick in bed for several weeks.

The Talmud relates the experience of a sage.

Rabbi Yose says, "I was once walking along the road, and entered one of the ruins of Jerusalem in order to pray. Elijah of blessed memory appeared and waited for me at the door till I had finished. Then he said, "Peace be with you, my master!"

And I replied, "Peace be with you, my master and teacher!"

And he continued, "My son, why did you go into this ruin?"

"To pray."

"You ought to have prayed on the road."

"I feared that passers-by might interrupt me."

"Then you ought to have said a shortened prayer."

Thus I learned from him: one ought not go into a ruin to pray, one may recite his prayer while walking on the road, and if one is on the road, he recites an abbreviated prayer!

It was an act of grace from Heaven to send Elijah to teach Rabbi Yose that one ought not go into a ruin to pray, for one must not expose oneself to danger. But why did he not appear to him *before* he entered the ruin? "Indeed," said the Kotzker, "this is how God deals with man. First he lets him act the way he pleases, then he appears and criticizes him, saying, "What have you done!"

Once, when the Kotzker heard that someone had died, he posed the question: "Lord of the universe, what trouble would it have been to you to let him live out his years?" Sometimes he was tormented by serious doubts. "Yitzhak Meir," he once said to his best disciple, "if only I could be certain that there is punishment in the world to come, I would go out into the streets and dance for joy. If only I could be certain . . ."

The man who has doubts about serving the Lord and eventually clarifies them stands above the man who insulates himself from all doubt. This idea is to be found in the writings of one of the Kotzker's disciples, Reb Mordecai Yosef, who later left the master. He added, however, that this principle applied only to certain souls.

Perhaps all doubts can be mitigated by the metaphor alluded to in the Pentateuch. The Heavens that God created had open gates, but man's heinous sins caused the gates to lock and the Heavens to become like copper. No man on earth, however virtuous, can penetrate them. Since copper is cold and indifferent, calling on Heaven is like knocking your head against a wall.

Of all the terrifying curses threatening the people when they stray from the path of righteousness, Reb Mendl considered "And the Heavens over your head shall be copper" (Deuteronomy 28:23) the most dread-filled curse of all.

One Foot in Heaven, the Other in Hell

Doubts and uncertainty did not evoke any shock in Kotzk. Fundamental certainty could be achieved only after experiencing radical uncertainty, after crossing the gulf of disbelief. The mind must be kept open. Each thought called for deliberation. There was no censor of rebellious thoughts.

Once a Hasid came to Reb Mendl with a problem.

"Rebbe, I have terrible thoughts."

"Well?"

"I am afraid to utter them. I am appalled to have such thoughts. Even Hell could not atone for them."

"Out with it."

"What a wretch I am. Sometimes I think there is neither judgment nor Judge, that the world is lawless, God forbid."

"Why does it bother you so?"

"Why?" shouted the Hasid. "If there is no judgment and no Judge, what purpose is there to the whole world?"

"If the world has no purpose, what concern is it of yours?"

"Rebbe, if the world has no purpose, of what use is the Torah?"

"Why should it bother you if the Torah is of no use?"

"Woe is me, Rebbe. If the Torah is of no use, then all of life is meaningless! That troubles me enormously."

Reb Mendl replied, "Since you are so deeply concerned, you must be an honest man, and an honest man is permitted to harbor such thoughts."

The Kotzker knew well that his path was treacherous. One day he said of himself, "I stand with one foot in the highest Heaven and with the other in hell." [1] Again, "Do you think this is a light matter? It is easier to jump into a burning furnace."

"I am honest!" he cried. "I was created to be honest!" Another time he said, "Even in Heaven I have no true friend. The angels

[1] *Siah Sarfe Kodesh,* III p. 32. Reb Ephraim of Sudlikov, at the end of his *Degel Mahane Efrayim,* reports the following from the Baal Shem Tov: I swear to you that there is a man in the world who hears Torah directly from God and the Shekhinah, and not from an angel or a seraph . . . and he does not believe that he will not be pushed aside by God as he can easily be plummeted into the deep abyss of evil.

and the seraphim are against me. Yet I have no fear of them, for I am honest . . ."

Why did he think the angels and seraphim were opposed to him? Reb Mendl apparently felt that his temerity bordered on impudence. His thoughts were presumably even more offensive than his words.

One view expressed in the Talmud criticized Job on similar grounds: "With his lips he did not sin, but he did sin within his heart . . . Job sought to turn the dish upside down [i.e. to declare all God's works worthless] . . . dust should be put in the mouth of Job!"

Dramatic, cryptic, Reb Mendl's voice occasionally revealed the turmoil of his soul. "Though the heart may burst, the shoulders may crack, heaven and earth may crumble, still man must stand firm and not capitulate," he once exclaimed. These words sound as if, in the midst of a bitter battle, he had to address a call for unyielding determination to himself.

The contestant with whom the Kotzker wrestled remains visually anonymous. To put into words what the soul could hardly bear would have been blasphemous. The precarious dividing line between righteousness and presumption was better couched in silence.

It was after midnight on the closing evening of Rosh Hashanah. Some of the Hasidim were ardently engaged in study, while others, exhausted, lay dozing on the wooden benches in the House of Study. Suddenly the Kotzker threw open the door and burst in upon them.

"Faces! Tell me, is there a face that can challenge the face of the Almighty?" [Meaning "Who is there who would dare to confront God?"]

The disciples, overcome with consternation, leaped up from their benches while Reb Mendl continued.

"Do you know what I want? This is what I want. Heaven should bend, the earth should crumble, and man should refuse to capitulate." And all the disciples exclaimed, "Yes, yes."

And the Kotzker continued. "Seek [demand of?] the Lord while he may be found!" (Isaiah 55:6) he cried, leaving his disciples stunned.

The Eloquence of Silence

Job had many successors. The Kotzker was one of them. His mind did not, however, follow traditional ways of asking Job's questions. The Kotzker never imitated or repeated. In his eyes all imitation was forgery, all repetition spurious. To challenge God's judgment or His failure to exercise judgment without restraint would have been foolhardy. The Kotzker reasoned with audacity but walked in awe.

Job was provoked by suffering, by apparent injustice; the Kotzker by falsehood, by lies. To him untruth was the cardinal evil, not suffering. He interpreted "Even the darkness is not dark to Thee" (Psalms 139:12) to mean: knowing that darkness comes from Thee, even the darkness is not dark. But one thing remained dark without redeeming comfort: falsehood.

We find that the Holy One, blessed be He, created everything in His world, only this stuff of falsehood He did not create, did not fashion. Out of their own hearts did mortals conceive false words, as it is said: "They conceived and uttered from the heart lying words" (Isaiah 59:13).

So we read in a medieval Hebrew work.

"Many are the pangs of the wicked" (Psalms 32:10)—the evildoer is in great pain; he is full of complaints and nothing is to his liking. "But he who trusts in the Lord, mercy encompasses him." Said Reb Mendl:

He who trusts in the Lord sees everything around him as a great mercy. "Those who seek the Lord lack no good thing" (Psalms 34:11). Why? Because they see each of God's deeds as for the good.

Suffering can be accepted then. Falsehood, however, cannot. For generations people had answered Job's terrifying question by saying that all of God's deeds are just, though His ways cannot always be comprehended. One must trust in the Lord.

The liturgical poems recited on New Year's Day say that His justice is hidden, we do not see it. Reb Mendl maintained in faith that "the ordinances of the Lord are true, are righteous altogether" (Psalms 19:10). Though in this world it might seem at times that God's ways were unjust, ultimately all His ways would be revealed as just.

A Jew is called "Yehudi" after Judah, about whom Leah, his mother, said, "This time will I praise the Lord." Rashi commented, "I have reason to praise, for I have taken more than my share." Indeed, every Jew should know that whatever the Almighty does for him is more than he deserves. According to this view, then, there are no grounds for complaint against God.

The Kotzker certainly never thought of measuring devotion in terms of reward and punishment.

Even if a reversal were to occur in the divine order, whereby I would be punished for observing a divine commandment and rewarded for transgression, even so I would not swerve from my path and would serve God as before.

These were the words of a Kotzker Hasid, Reb Avrom of Porisov.

I have already mentioned that Reb Mendl was most troubled by the problem of why God had buried Truth *before* creating man. The whole world trembled when God proclaimed, "You shall not swear *falsely* by the name of the Lord your God" (Exodus 20:7). How, then, could He have cast Truth into the ground?

This was a terrifying question, especially since men were allowed to dance upon the grave of Truth. Why did man accept the diabolical role of dancing in preventing Truth from being resurrected?

There was yet another difference between Job and the Rebbe of Kotzk. Whereas Job thought aloud, Reb Mendl's thoughts mostly remained in his heart. He was a man of few words, realizing that man could make a fool of himself by questioning, challenging, or criticizing the Creator. The phrases that a man thrust against Heaven could easily boomerang.

In his wisdom and awe, Reb Mendl knew full well how the most fiery accusations could sound like gibberish when articulated. One of the Kotzker's disciples said, "To think a thought is easy but to express it is no mean feat. That is why we pray: 'Open the mouths of those who put their trust in Thee.'" In Kotzk they cultivated the eloquence of silence.

Reb Mendl Vorker, another disciple, kept silent for several hours at a time surrounded by the Hasidim. Complete stillness. They sat in dread and awe. One could hear a fly crawling along the wall. After the concluding grace, one of the leading Hasidim exclaimed: "That was some gathering! He took me to task and pumped me with questions, but I held my own. I answered every single question he put to me."

The less spoken, the better. It is better to put off uttering a word, even a syllable, as long as possible. *Wayelekh haranah*— Jacob left Beersheba and went "toward Haran" (Genesis 28:10). Rashi commented that whenever the Hebrew preposition *lamed* is called for to denote "to" or "toward" a certain place, the Torah prefers to place the letter *hay* at the end of the word (as in *haranah*): this has the same meaning as the letter *lamed* preceding. Reb Mendl asked what advantage there was in using the letter *hay* at the end instead of *lamed* at the beginning of the word? It teaches us to restrain our speech; and to delay articulating a syllable even for a second is worthwhile.

A lock ought to hang over one's mouth. He who reveals what he knows has little to say. "Let your heart burst before uttering so much as a moan."

"When a man has reason to scream, and cannot though he wants to—he has achieved the greatest scream." This was Reb Mendl's interpretation of the Talmudic passage "If one enters [a house] to visit a sick person [on the Sabbath], he should say, 'It is the Sabbath, when one must not cry out, and recovery will soon come.'"

In Kotzk one did not cry. Even when in pain, one did not weep. "Silence," the Kotzker said, "is the greatest cry in the world."

"When she opened it, she saw the child, and lo, the boy was crying. She took pity on him and said: 'This is one of the Hebrew children'" (Exodus 2:6). When Pharaoh's daughter opened the basket, she was amazed. The Scripture says she saw rather than heard the child weeping. Then she said, "This must be a Hebrew child, because only a Hebrew child could weep so softly."

Job's mistake consisted in his crying out when in pain but keeping silent when all went well. Real questioning should occur in both cases. Why are things so good for me, as well as why are they so bad?

Mankind may be compared to chains that shackle the hands of God. Job's outcry today ought to be to free God from our chains.

A teaching of the Baal Shem Tov.

The Romans had issued an edict forbidding Torah study. When Rabbi Akiba, one of the great masters of the Talmud, defiantly continued to teach, he was imprisoned and then tortured to death by having his flesh torn from his body with "iron combs." He bore his suffering with fortitude, welcoming his martyrdom as a unique opportunity of fulfilling the precept, "You shall love the Lord thy God with all thy heart and with all thy soul . . . even if you must pay for it with your life."

"All my days I have been troubled by this verse 'with all your soul' —namely, even if He took my soul. I said, 'When shall I have the opportunity of fulfilling this? Now that I have the opportunity shall I not fulfill it?' "

He stretched out the word *ehad* ["One" in "Hear, O Israel, the Lord is our God, the Lord is One"] so that he was still saying it when he expired.

When the Holy One, blessed be He, was asked by Moses, "Is this your reward for the study of Torah?" God replied, "Silence! Thus it has risen in Thought" [Meaning "such is My decree"].

What was the meaning of this answer? The Baal Shem continued:

The answer is ambiguous. Its true meaning is: Silence! Thus *he* has risen in Thought. There is a spiritual realm to which one can only rise (or attain) through martyrdom. The Almighty loved Rabbi Akiba deeply and wished to uplift him to this realm of Thought, where there was an answer to every question.

The Cossack Wants a New Song

As discussed earlier, the Kotzker suffered from an inability to overcome his melancholy. He himself did not consider silence the ultimate response; this can be inferred from the following saying, which he cherished:

> Three ways are open to a man who is in sorrow. He who stands on a normal rung weeps, he who stands higher is silent, but he who stands on the topmost rung converts his sorrow into song.

In this spirit, a contemporary of the Kotzker, Reb Shloymo of Radomsk, maintained that the degree of excellence achieved by Aaron, Moses's brother, was surpassed by that of King David.

Of Aaron the Priest it is said, "And Aaron was silent" (Leviticus 10:3). Two of his sons had perished in a gruesome manner, and he had remained silent. King David, on the other hand, went further than holding his peace. "That my soul may sing praise to Thee, and *not* be silent" (Psalms 30:13).

The fact that this utterance by Reb Shloymo made a deep impression on the Kotzker is indicated by the latter's search for a more powerful response to his human quandary than silence. Did he achieve it?

Those were difficult times. Grief was no rare commodity. Each person carried his own burden of sorrows, knowing that no final blessing would come his way. When the heart was heavy the eyes flowed. But the Kotzker Hasidim, I repeat, did not weep. "Let the faithful [Hasidim] exult in glory; let them sing for joy upon their couches" (Psalms 149:5). Said Reb Bunam, "Hasidim, even when they are bedridden, manage to sing."

Hasidic song expressed exultation in the Lord. It seemed to celebrate Israel's marriage to God. One must make merry at a wedding; moreover, a gift was called for. But what kind of gift would be suitable? A song, for life was a song. The Almighty wanted to hear a good song.

Answers to the ultimate perplexity cannot be expressed in words. Response is facilitated by song. Singing is not the mere repetition of notes, or even the expression of joy or sorrow. Singing means uplifting all of existence to the level of perfection. Singing means raising oneself above all words and all ideas, to the realm of pure thought. "Thus has [Rabbi Akiba] arisen in Thought." One cannot truly sing by repeating an old melody. "God loves novelty," said Reb Mendl; one must sing a new song each time.

Reb Henokh, his disciple, loved telling piquant stories. Those who did not know him well broke into laughter. Reb Yekhiel Meyer of Gostinin remarked, however, "Henokh is lamenting the destruction of Jerusalem, and they are laughing."

When Reb Henokh lay on his deathbed, his friend Reb Avrom of Porisov came to visit him. Reb Henokh told him the following tale:

When Russia occupied Poland in 1792, few Jews knew the Russian language. Once a Cossack visited a Jewish homeowner and asked him, "Are you the *khazyayen* [the owner]?"

The Jew did not understand. His wife translated wrongly: "The Cossack says: 'Are you a cantor [a *hazan*]? Sing for me.'"

So the Jew began singing the chant "The Sons of the Temple." The Cossack lost his temper and began to beat him.

So his wife explained: "He obviously doesn't like that song. He wants another one! A new song!"

With these words Reb Henokh breathed his last.

Did Reb Henokh feel that the Cossack, which is to say the Lord, was angry and therefore harsh with us? Was this an admission that he had failed to understand Him? Is it at all within our power to sing the song that the Cossack wishes to hear?

The Kotzker taught his disciples that to have faith in God was no game, for the Lord could carry out His words "with destructive force." Perhaps the Almighty directs the world by means of wrath because he dislikes our way of worshipping Him with our worn-out, old tunes. Was Reb Mendl, then, in search of a new song, a new path, which he could not find?

Barrels Full of Holes

The Kotzker hinted that all of human endeavor might be fruitless labor, that our finest convictions may be mere affectation. Surely moral attitudes depend upon a belief in the congruence between human values and the nature of the world. And if the world is in its very being devoid of Truth, is there any validity to man's moral efforts?

Reb Mendl struggled with this dilemma. Was it not self-delusion to think that we were accomplishing anything worthwhile on earth? Perhaps all our labors were worthless.

In a conversation with several of his disciples, the Kotzker quoted from an old Midrash:

"Wisdom is too high for a fool; in the gate he does not open his mouth" (Proverbs 24:7). "This reminds me," says Rabbi Yannai, "of a fool who once stood staring at a high pole, on top of which was a tempting loaf of bread. The fool was hungry; his mouth watered, but all he did was gape and exclaim, 'Who can bring this down? How tasty it looks!' His companion, wiser than he, answered: 'You, silly fellow! The pole is no higher now than when the loaf was first put up there. I will show you how to get it down.' He took a long ladder, mounted it, reached the top, and brought the loaf down."

Another sage said: "This reminds me of a thirsty fool at a well. The water looked fresh and most alluring, but the well was too deep for him to draw water. His companion, wiser than he, took pieces of cord, tied them together, attached a bucket and brought it up with water."

Rabbi Levi said: "This may be compared to the case of the punctured barrels. The king who owned them hired laborers to fill them with water. One of them was a fool. 'What good is all this?' he said. 'What goes into the barrels at one end, trickles out at the other.' The wise laborer, however, said, 'Surely I am to be paid for every barrel! I shall fill them; for this clearly means that my obedience is important to the king.'"

Reb Mendl explained the difference between these parables. The reasoning of the first wise man was simple: he saw the loaf of bread on top of the pole and realized that it could be reached since someone had placed it there. The wise man of the second parable was more perceptive than the first. Perhaps no one had been able to haul up water from the well. Some means had to be devised. Now he knew the goal, he needed only to devise the means of reaching it.

The third man was wise indeed. He saw no goal. Pouring water into a barrel full of holes seemed to make no sense. So he explained to the other workers that the object was not to fill the barrels; it was to fulfill the king's desire.

And the Kotzker concluded, "Do you understand what I think?"

What did he intend to convey? That all our efforts were as futile as pouring water into punctured barrels? What we achieved might have no meaning, life might be absurd, vanity of vanities. But act we must, it was the will of God.

The last parable is reminiscent of Sisyphus, the son of Aeolus, king of Corinth, noted in classical mythology for his trickery. His punishment in Tartarus was to push a huge boulder up a hill till it reached the top; but it always rolled back, so his work was endless. Sisyphus realized the futility of his task yet persisted in carrying it out with melancholy courage. Similarly, in Reb Mendl's parable the wise worker understood not only the absurdity of filling leaking barrels but also the point of carrying out the king's will.

Kierkegaard emphasizes the irrational in order to encourage the strongest possible faith. The Kotzker's parable also points up the absurdity of existence. All searching for rational meaning must yield to the reality upon which Judaism is built: to live is to obey.

So many of us are haunted by the ugly futility of human effort, the triumph of brute force, of evil, and man's helpless misery. Is not any form of hopefulness false, unreal, self-deceiving?

What is Truth as available to us? Is it a curse, a path toward defeat laden with torment? Are we doomed to live with delusion while searching for Truth in vain? We spend a lifetime looking for the key, and when we find it, we discover that we do not know where the lock is.

Is this how we should define our predicament? Man is called upon to regard Truth as his goal, but his own nature does not provide him with adequate means to attain it.

We are stunned by the discovery that *our* meaning may be meaningless, *our* purpose futility. What many had cherished as a utopia has turned out to be a nightmare. What we had acclaimed as purpose has turned out to be poison. Our designs become distorted in the process of being carried out. Our failure is greatest when we think we have succeeded. We think we have arrived, only to discover that we have gone astray. The means we use are unrelated to our vital goals. The acts we carry out are not designed to satisfy authentic needs. We are conscious of acting absurdly but seem powerless to bring about our emancipation from absurdity.

Reinterpreting the Kotzker's view, to the human mind the enterprise of living looks absurd indeed; yet, just as we must disregard self-regard in thinking about God, we must transcend our sense of values in evaluating the enterprise of living. In faith we can accept that there is *meaning beyond absurdity,* a meaning which is *supra rationem,* above reason, not *contra rationem,* against reason.

All moral action is subject to this deadlock. The world as we experience it fails to satisfy our hope that the good can conquer through our moral efforts. Nor are the guarantees offered by human reason capable of serving as a basis for an ethic. The validity of moral distinctions rests solely on obedience to God.

The supreme category accessible to man, then, is that of command. And the supreme response of which man is capable is obedience.

But is it possible that we misunderstand the king's assignment? that his intention was for us to repair the barrels rather than to continue pouring water into the shattered vessels?

The Solution Is in the Problem

Was this the last word, the ultimate conclusion the Kotzker reached: no sense, no hope, except obedience? Is it conceivable that he who always demanded audacity, defiance, should at the end advocate submission, surrender? Is it not a repudiation of all meaning to say "Amen" to the seeming absence of meaning? How ludicrous to build a paper bridge across the terrifying abyss that extends between hope and absurdity.

The barrel was full of holes, the whole enterprise absurd. Only one thing held significance—Truth—and to live truthfully meant, first of all, not to delude the self into believing that triumphs of falsehood are of lasting importance.

The essential point of the parable was that the laborers knew that they were hired and would be compensated for their toil.

Therefore, it had meaning in the king's eyes. Besides, he was responsible for having ordered the job to be done. Therefore, he alone was concerned about its purpose and ultimate effect.

Moreover, granting that their efforts were absurd, what alternative did they have? Would not the refusal to carry out the assignment have been equally absurd? And if everything was meaningless, so were men's statements that it was so.

Then how could one take anything seriously?

The complete failure of all consolation, the love of life despite its absurdity, holds out the certainty of a meaning that transcends our understanding. We encounter meaning beyond absurdity in living as a response to an expectation. Expectation of meaning is an *a priori* condition of our existence.

One thing we can be sure of: the king has hired us, and the original responsibility is his. What we must do is to remember Him Who has engaged us.

There is a strange contradiction in man's bringing charges in the name of Truth about the absence of Truth; such an argument can be meaningful only if it presupposes the presence of Truth. Is not our agony over the burial of Truth evidence of the life and power of Truth?

What lends meaning to our problem is the premise that God and meaning, as we understand them, are one. We would not, for example, ask how to reconcile the vast power of nuclear energy with its tremendous potential destructiveness.

It was faith in the mystery of God's justice that made Job's outcry possible. No Job arose in Hellas. Indeed, his outcry is part of the drama in which God and man are involved with one another.

Plato maintained:

God, if he be good, is not the author of all things, as many assert, but he is the cause of a few things only, and not of most things that occur to men; for few are the goods of human life, and many are the evils, and the good only is to be attributed to him; of the evil things other causes have to be discovered.[1]

It would have been simple for the Prophets of ancient Israel to say that evil issues from another source, that God is not responsible for it. The Supreme God of the Avesta is Ahura-Mazda, conceived as good, and the author of all that is good; contrasted with him is the Destroying Spirit, Ahriman, of later Persian literature.

Out of his absolute certainty that God is One and the Creator of all things, the Prophet proclaimed, "I am the Lord, and there is no other. I form light and create darkness. I make weal and create woe. I am the Lord, who do all these things" (Isaiah 45:6f.).

God is Truth. We carry out His orders, pour water into leaking barrels, believing in the activity for its own sake. Is it conceivable that God Who is Truth would be deceiving us? Truth cannot lie—there can be no doubt about that. There *is* meaning, though it is concealed from us. Truth is buried, and so, too, is meaning.

Jews have always believed in the resuscitation of the dead. The soul of Truth lives in concealment, and one day it too shall be resuscitated.

Reb Mendl wished to cultivate a sensitivity to higher concepts in his Hasidim. Abstract notions often assumed crude, earthy formulations. More exalted ideas were to be grasped in a wink, at a glance. Neither the senses nor simpleminded parables could help to achieve this. The Heavens did not spoon-feed; all they

[1] Republic II, 379c.

offered was a taste, an intimation. The focus of man's study was to detect what his senses and his intellect had missed. Reb Mendl interpreted, "Now . . . Jethro . . . heard . . ." (Exodus 18:1), as "Jethro's ear detected"; it absorbed a hint, an intimation.

The Kotzker wished men to be capable of Heavenly thinking. The approach, the style, and the way of conceiving issues pertaining to the Divine had to be absolutely different from the manner in which worldly matters were understood. How could one speak of God based on human models and clichés? Only a fool would do so.

God as the Antecedent

Theologians usually start their speculation with a concept of God's essence and then proceed to prove or simply discuss His existence. Yet the belief in God does not come through anthropocentric speculation, but in overwhelming moments of the awareness of His existence. These lead to an understanding of His essence.

The reality of God is antecedent to all ideas and values comprehended by man. It is a mistake to start with a human model and then seek to accommodate God to it.

Martin Buber's declaration "Nothing can make me believe in

a God who punishes Saul because he did not murder his enemy" must be contrasted with the Kotzker's statement "A God whom any Tom, Dick, and Harry could comprehend, I would not believe in."

"You shall make for yourself no molten God" (Exodus 34:17), no God fashioned in human images. You could think of Him only in a Heavenly way. Moses's call "Hear, O Heaven" (Deuteronomy 32:1) was interpreted as an injunction by Reb Mendl: "Hear in a Heavenly manner."

The Biblical writers approached the problem free of emotional predispositions and without rationalist dogmas, in fear and trembling and full of wonder and love for Him Who is overwhelmingly gracious. They were able to accept His severity in the same spirit in which they appreciated His compassion. "A man must offer a Blessing over evil just as he pronounces a Blessing over good," the rabbis teach us.

This conception does not exclude any understanding by man of God's ways. It merely states that while some of those ways seem absurd from man's perspective, they are nonetheless meaningful in the eyes of God. In other words, the ultimate meaning of God's ways is not invalidated because of man's incapacity to comprehend it; nor is our anguish silenced because of the certainty that somewhere in the recesses of God an answer abides. To understand God, we must pluck thought from a deadly conceptual thralldom and steer it back along the path of ineffable comprehension, returning it to its roots.

Yet if anyone proposed a definitive formulation of the ultimate meaning of the infinite universe, a meaning which our finite mind could fully comprehend, we would reject it as pompous trash. It is beyond man's power to come upon an adequate solution to the great enigma. Every solution reached by our intellect would be an attempt to accommodate within the narrow confines of the human mind the secret of the *En-Sof*, the Infinite One, of God as He is in Himself.

Meaning beyond Absurdity

The opposite of absurdity is not always intelligible. On what basis can we believe that there is a meaning transcending all apparent absurdity?

No one can deny the reality of our anxiety at the absence of meaning in human life. It results from our frustrated expectation that there must be meaning somewhere. This unease and cry are themselves a sign of sense and meaning. To assume that humanity's cry is an isolated wave of sense in an infinite ocean of non-sense would condemn it as presumptuous. Our goal is not to come upon ultimate solutions to all problems but to find ourselves as part of a context of meaning.

"The Lord is a man of war; the Lord is His name" (Exodus 15:3). God is fighting for meaning. There is a state of war between God and chaos.

We do not need to drink the whole ocean to know what kind of water it contains. One drop yields its salty flavor. Our very existence exposes us to the challenge of wonder and radical amazement at the universe despite the absurdities we encounter. It is possible on the basis of personal experience to arrive at the conclusion that the human situation as far as one can see is absurd. However, to stand face to face with the infinite world of stars and galaxies and to declare all of this absurd would be idiotic.

We are not the final arbiter of meaning. What looks absurd within the limit of time may be luminous within the scope of eternity.

The Kotzker taught that faith did not derive from rational evidence. Man had to live by faith despite his agony, despite his perennial subjection to disputing its validity. "Be in a hell of a mess and survive on faith," he taught.

To be overwhelmed by the transrational majesty of God one has to accept the risk of not understanding Him. The incompatibility of God's ways with human understanding was, according to the Kotzker, the very essence of our being. To rebel against this inadequacy would be like complaining that man was not created Divine. God is God, and man is man, and the twain rarely meet. "For My thoughts are not your thoughts, and your ways are not My ways . . . For as the Heavens are higher than earth, so are My ways higher than your ways, and My thoughts than your thoughts" (Isaiah 55:8f.).

If we maintain that God's ways and man's ways are mutually exclusive, that man is incapable of understanding God, then the impossibility of our comprehending His ways *a priori* excludes the possibility of finding an answer to the ultimate question. And if this is the case, of what avail are man's arguments or reproaches?

Man's inability to understand the ways and acts of God is obviously due to an inherent inadequacy or privation in his nature, to the banishment of Truth from his life. So it is precisely the incapacity of man to share God's Truth that is both the source and the object of his pain.

The wonder is that, while our meaningful efforts sometimes lead to absurdities, we are also given infinite opportunities to carry out acts rich in meaning. At the beginning there was chaos, until the Lord said, "Let there be light!" and the chaos was partly overcome, but partly it stayed on. Lamentably, we take the light for granted and voice our misgivings because of the continuing darkness enveloping us.

The concealment of Truth, in upsetting the equation of existence and meaning and depriving man of clear knowing and right living, was an invitation to falsehood, which rules abusively, oppressively, tyrannously. Falsehood, exceedingly fertile, gives birth to a multitude of shams and delusions, as well as guile and deceit. It is raging like a volcano, and to offer answers would be like pouring buckets full of water to quench it.

And yet if Truth were manifest and strong, man would lose his major task, his destiny: to search for it. He would live without a reason for being. Is it not in the essence of freedom to grope, to choose, to work out rather than to be given Truth? As Lessing wrote:

If God should hold enclosed in his right hand all truth, and in his left hand only the ever-active impulse after truth, although with the condition that I must always and forever err, I would with humility turn to his left hand and say, "Father, give me this: pure truth is for Thee alone." [1]

[1] G. E. Lessing, *Anti-Goeze,* a series of letters published by Lessing in 1778 in reply to Pastor Goeze's inquiry as to what Lessing meant by Christianity.

Thus, concealing the Truth was necessary in order to make possible man's greatest adventure: to live in search. If Truth had not been concealed, there would be no need to choose, to search.

If Truth had been permitted to prevail, Divinity would have overpowered the world and humanity would not have been possible.

If it were possible to demonstrate the existence of God, conclusively—*ecce signum*—putting an end to all debate, then there would also be an end to the humanity of man, the essence of which is to choose and to search.

Man's Responsibility for God

We usually formulate Job's dilemma as a contradiction between God's justice and the presence of evil in human life. A careful examination of the Biblical view of history uncovers man's attempts to oust the Lord from his world and His gradual withdrawal.

A major problem, then, is how to reconcile God's omnipotence with man's effort to defeat Him.

The central ideas in the Bible are the covenant between God and man and the effect of man's conduct upon God's relationship to him. Providence is not a divine ivory tower or a recess beyond the reach of all that human beings think, say, and do.

In a world where God is denied, where His will is defied, Truth flouted, compassion sloughed, violence applauded; in a world where God is left without allies—is it meaningful for man to court-martial Him? The growing awareness of history's tragic predicament gives birth to an intuition that man was responsible for God as God was responsible for man.

In the light of God's mysterious dependence upon man, the problem of anthropodicy and theodicy cannot be separated. The cardinal issue, Why does the God of justice and compassion permit evil to persist? is bound up with the problem of how man should aid God so that His justice and compassion prevail.

Many portions of the Hebrew Bible are implicitly related to the outcry of Job. Some of Israel's Prophets wrestled to reconcile God's silence in the face of evil with their certainty of His goodness. Their ongoing pain over violence and corruption echoes the tacit queries: "Where is God?" "Why does He keep silent?" "Why does he permit iniquity to flourish?"

God's response to Job related to the desire to understand the *why* of evil. His answer to the Prophets related to the issue of *how* to abolish evil. There is no human solution to God's problem, and God's only answer is the promise of messianic redemption.

The Kotzker's concern was not theological, an intelligible answer to the problem of theodicy, but messianic, the defeat of falsehood. As I pointed out earlier, his concern with Truth was existential—how to live Truth—not theoretical—how to know it. His primary demand was not for an explanation of why, at the creation of man, there had been no alternative to burying the Truth. What he craved was an end to falsehood, the resurrection of Truth.

Indeed, the question tormenting us is: will there be no end to agony, to falsehood? Going beyond all speculation as how to reconcile the belief in Divine Providence with the immense torrents of madness and atrocities, our concern is not to find an apology for God but, rather, to put an end to evil, an end to the epilepsy of God's presence.

While Job asked *why* the innocent should suffer, the Prophets addressed themselves to the question of *when* suffering would cease. Our present order is but tentative; at the end of days, in the messianic era, there will be an end to mendacity and violence, as also to death.

Messianic redemption is a marvelous promise. The present chaos will not last forever. But fulfillment did not come during the Kotzker's lifetime, nor in the many years since. All he had, as we have today, is a promise and the expectation. The waiting goes on.

However, mere waiting may be a moratorium, a way of marking time, postponing our response to the challenge. The task is never to forget that by each sacred deed we commit, by each word we hallow, by each thought we chant, we render our modest part in reducing distress and advancing redemption.

Rabbi Jose relates:

Once I was traveling on the road, and entered into one of the ruins of Jerusalem to pray. And there appeared Elijah . . . and waited for me at the entrance until I finished my prayer . . . He said to me, "My son, what sound did you hear in this ruin?"

I answered him, "I heard a divine voice moaning like a dove and saying: 'Woe is me, that I have destroyed my house, and burnt my sanctuary, and exiled my children among the nations!'"

And he said to me, "My son . . . Not only in this hour does it so exclaim, but each day it thus calls out three times! And . . . when the people of Israel go into their houses of prayer and study and respond 'May His great name be blessed!' the Holy One nods His head and says, 'Happy is the King who is thus praised in His house!'"

All pain is shared anguish. Theodicy is a problem for God, not only for man. Why is it that the king's barrels are full of holes?

Medieval Jewish philosophers, motivated by the necessity of eradicating widely spread crude anthropomorphic notions of God fostered by vestiges of apocalyptic phantasmas, advanced a theology of radical transcendence. The profound doctrine of the immanence of God emphatically taught by Rabbi Akiba and his disciples in the classical Talmudic era, the doctrine of the *Shekhinah,* found no echo in Saadia, Ibn Daud, Maimonides, or Gersonides, for example.

It would be a mistake to assume that the purpose of the wrestling that the Kotzker and other Hasidic masters engaged in was to come upon an intelligible answer to a malignant enigma. What would be achieved by such an answer? Can any explanation obviate the terrible agony the world is writhing in?

Deep in meditation about the ultimate mystery, we are suddenly overcome by shame and trembling. How can we reproach the Lord? Does He not bring reproach upon Himself? God Himself is the quintessential Job. "In all their affliction He was afflicted" (Isaiah 63:9). When man is in distress, there is a cry of anguish in Heaven. God needs not only sympathy and comfort but partners, silent warriors.

The perplexity must endure. Saints turn from acquiescence to defiance when adversity seems to contradict the certainty of God's justice. Perhaps it is God's will that man give Him no rest . . . that he cooperate in seeking a way out of the tragic entanglements.

Life in our time has been a nightmare for many of us, tranquillity an interlude, happiness a fake. Who could breathe at a time when man was engaged in murdering the holy witness to God six million times?

And yet God does not need those who praise Him when in a state of euphoria. He needs those who are in love with Him when in distress, both He and ourselves. This is the task: in the darkest night to be certain of the dawn, certain of the power to turn a curse into a blessing, agony into a song. To know the monster's rage and, in spite of it, proclaim to its face (even a monster will be transfigured into an angel); to go through Hell and to continue to trust in the goodness of God—this the challenge and the way.

God writes straight in crooked lines, and man cannot evaluate them as he lives on one level and can see from only one perspective. We are not the final arbiter of meaning. What looks absurd within the limits of time may be luminous within the scope of eternity.

The shattering queries continue to come in such overwhelming cascade, the agonies pile up so dreadfully, that they rinse away the power to speak.

Farewell comfort, farewell tranquillity. Faith is the beginning of compassion, of compassion for God. It is when bursting with God's sighs that we are touched by the awareness that *beyond all absurdity* there is meaning, Truth, and love.

The agony of our problem foments like a volcano, and it is foolish to seek finite answers to infinite agony. Buckets of water will not quench its fury. The pain is strong as death, cruel as the grave. But perhaps it will be in the grave, the dwelling place of Truth, that our own death will somewhat hasten its resurrection.

At times we must believe in Him in spite of Him, to continue being a witness despite His hiding Himself. What experience fails to convey, prayer brings about. Prayer prevails over despair.

Faith comes about in a collision of an unending passion for Truth and the failure to attain it by one's own means.

A friend of mine, Mr. Sh. Z. Shragai, went to Poland as a representative of the Jewish Agency in the late 1940's, when Poland still entertained good relations with the state of Israel. His visit was an official mission concerning the emigration of Jewish survivors of Nazi extermination camps. After finishing his work in Warsaw, he left for Paris and, as a very important person, was given a whole compartment on the train. It was crowded with passengers.

Outside he noticed an emaciated, poorly clad Jew who could not find a seat on the train. He invited him to join him in his compartment. It was comfortable, clean, pleasant, and the poor fellow came in with his bundle, put it on the rack over the seat, and sat down.

My friend tried to engage him in conversation, but he would not talk. When evening came, my friend, an observing Jew, recited the evening prayer (*maariv*), while the other fellow did not say a word of prayer. The following morning my friend took out his prayer shawl and phylacteries (*Talit* and *Tefillin*) and said his prayer; the other fellow, who looked so wretched and somber, would not say a word and did not pray.

Finally, when the day was almost over, they started a conversation. The fellow said, "I am never going to pray any more because of what happened to us in Auschwitz . . . How could I pray? That is why I did not pray all day."

The following morning—it was a long trip from Warsaw to

Paris—my friend noticed that the fellow suddenly opened his bundle, took out his *Talit* and *Tefillin* and started to pray. He asked him afterward, "What made you change your mind?"

The fellow said, "It suddenly dawned upon me to think how lonely God must be; look with whom He is left. I felt sorry for Him."

PART X

❖❰❖❰❖❰

The Kotzker Today

THE KOTZKER, a soul living in dissent, was all protest against the trivialization and externalization of Judaism. Rejecting half-truths, mediocrity, compromise, he challenged even the Lord. Distrustful of whatever the popular eye perceived, he did not seek to make his stand plausible among men of common sense. So he remains marvelous and strange, and individuals who agonize over our world's insanity will respond to him.

His very existence was an embarrassment to all who were devout and smug. Yet he was not the first to call attention to spiritual leprosy. The Prophets of ancient Israel had preceded him.

> Hear the word of the Lord, O people of Israel
> For the Lord has a controversy with the inhabitants
> of the land,
> There is no truth or kindness and no knowledge of
> God in the land.
>
> Hosea 4:1

"Everyone deals falsely" (Jeremiah 8:10). "Every man lies" (Psalms 116:11)—and betrays—even his best friend. Even my own son betrays me, says David.

Yet for the Kotzker the malady had a broader scope. Its danger was more acute. Falsehood, self-deception in particular, was a universal and perhaps fatal disease.

What Kierkegaard called his "terrible introversion" applies with equal validity to the life of the Kotzker. The either/or position taken by both men, which states that every man's pursuit had either God or the ego as its focus and goal—this dilemma is based upon the assumption that God and the ego are mutually exclusive.

But according to the Bible, the satisfaction of man's legitimate needs is a blessing. There is no reason to maintain, then, that in all circumstances disregarding the self should be the norm. The Divine and the human are not by nature conceived to be at odds or in constant tension. Man is capable of acting in accord with God; he is able to be His partner in redemption, to imitate Him in acts of love and compassion.

In his ruthless candor, in his loathing of acquisitiveness and greed, in his disgust with those to whom religion was a career, in his rejection of rampant emotionalism, in his relentless search for living Truth through self-inquiry, and in his encompassing sense of dread, the Kotzker anticipated some of the agitations of contemporary man. A review of his thoughts reveals a modernity that superseded specific concerns.

During periods of comparative calm, of settled convictions and traditions, the normal order of living is easily accepted. In an age when man has been disenfranchised of faith and disabused of the optimism inherent in technological advances, he is avid above all for some intimation of meaning. The Kotzker could be a companion as we search in the labyrinth of belief.

The Kotzker was "a troubler of Israel." Like Elijah, he confronted the people with an either/or choice: "How long will you go limping with two different views? If the Lord is God, follow Him; but if Baal, then follow him" (I Kings 18:21). The Kotzker acted as though he were a reincarnation of the ancient Prophet as depicted in the Bible: stern, defiant, uncompromising, and jealous for God. Like Elijah, he was not concerned with the multitude, but with the few, the spiritual elite, with "all the knees that have not bowed to Baal and every mouth that has not kissed him" (I Kings 19:18).

Significantly, the Kotzker's goal was to have a score of disciples stand with him on the rooftop and exclaim, "The Lord, He is God! The Lord, He is God!" (I Kings 18:39)—the words the people uttered when inspired by Elijah's marvelous deed.

Does man's nature have to be hurt for God's will to be done? Are dread and trembling the only gateways to faith? Cannot mere gratitude for being alive cleanse the soul? As one studies the Hebrew Bible, one arrives at the conviction that God meant man to delight in living.

To this the Kotzker would respond: how is it possible to be comfortably happy in the face of so much mendacity and cruelty? For him the ugliness of the world quenched all joy. Although some of his thoughts deviate from Biblical views on humanity and reality, his words echo the Prophets' voices calling on men to reject falsehood, sham, and pretense, to search their hearts and lives, lest they die for the sake of lies, for the sake of idols.

Following the Bible, Jewish tradition has had respect for the claims of normal living. It has not exacted perpetual heroism, the life of a volcano, but quiet conformity to a pattern of piety. Only in exceptional cases, to avoid being forced to commit grave sins, is the Jew expected to become a martyr. In ordinary times he is to be guided by the awareness that he ought "to live by" the Torah, not die for it.

Reb Mendl's demands for self-sacrifice that condemns self-seeking, for total honesty that tolerates no pretensions, for excellence that rules out mediocrity or compromise were merciless. They were compatible neither with what we commonly consider to be human nor with the divine attributes of love and compassion.

310 A Passion for Truth

On the other hand, we should keep in mind that harsh and bitter words may act as shock treatment in the cure of a fatal disease. The ancient Prophets of Israel were neither mild nor gentle when they chastised their people. Severity may be necessary when gentleness fails.

The soul is a realm of confusion. Some intentions are meant for God, others for the ego, and they are nearly always intermingled. The Kotzker sought to make things clear, to simplify the soul.

Judaism demands all of men, the whole man. But what the Kotzker observed around him was fractional piety, bits and pieces of ritual floating in the vortex of disordered lives. He was a man at war with himself and society. Rigorous and intemperate, he would not yield. Having discovered that the world was dominated by the powers of falsehood, he demanded that religious existence at least should not give in to them.

Antisocial, shocking, an enemy to all established convention and propriety, the Kotzker continually and relentlessly attacked the soft spots in man's self-image, pointing up the difference between candor and pretense, authenticity and sham. What grieved him was the thin borderline between piety and opportunism, people's readiness to adapt their religious views and acts to further their vanity.

What did the Kotzker want? To flood souls with dissent, to shatter hypocrisy? To penetrate a world that was infected with death? To set up a graveyard where lies should be buried?

Neither Kierkegaard nor the Kotzker was a reformer in the sense that he criticized the doctrines of his traditions or introduced new tenets. Each drew attention to a new perspective and saw his role as corrective only. The gist of the Kotzker's thoughts did not originate in his own mind. He only stretched to extremes what his predecessors had carried halfway. At one time he regarded his work as a climax in the history of Hasidism. Once he listed the six great Hasidic masters who preceded him, adding, "And I am the seventh. I am Sabbath!"

Inherent in Jewish history is an eagerness to preserve, to uphold views and customs of the past, even when some of these have become irrelevant. As a result, the observance of trivia may even interfere with actions of supreme importance.

Like Kierkegaard, the Kotzker was exasperating, attacking the moral and spiritual equilibrium which people enjoy when their favorite assumptions or those of the tradition are not challenged. The average devotee of a religion seeks to worship and practice the rituals which he has inherited and is content to follow without thought. Reb Mendl rejected the principle that age sanctified a custom, that novelty in religion was an act of desecration. He insisted, on the contrary, that God loved "news." A religious act ought never to become stale, repetitious, graceless. It must be vibrant, alive, always a surprise in the soul.

Thus the Kotzker sought to jolt minds out of their complacency. His utterances jarred people who were accustomed to sermons in praise of piety. He unleashed pangs of anguish. It seemed that his concern was to unsettle, to question accepted habits of thought.

The Kotzker refused to live in the past and felt no commitment to revere his ancestors because they were dead. Nor did he feel respect for many of his enterprising contemporaries, whom he believed to be dead, though they themselves did not know it.

Such a message was most unlikely to win acclaim. Had Reb Mendl preached love, compassion, rapture, and joy, people would have applauded him. But here was a man to whom shock or dismay was the norm. Shutting out as foolish all the sweet consolations of the world, he concentrated on imperatives that save.

The Kotzker was the kind of man who would say today that Hiroshima and Nagasaki continue to agonize. After so many years? people would wonder. Is not the Holocaust, too, a matter of the past? Is it not time to let it slip into oblivion? Why let memories that conjure up atrocities affect our moral imperatives? What good will come out of it?

The Kotzker dared to look hypocrisy in the face and to blast out what most of us conceal or allow to abash us. He called the monster by name and sought to quell it. He will forever endure as an enemy of pretentious mediocrity, complacency, and compromise.

Other thinkers considered love or obedience the normative aim of religious existence. The outstanding contribution of the Kotzker was to teach that mediocrity was the fundamental religious concern. This realization led to religious radicalism, for Truth shunned all moderation. To be moderately loving might be virtuous, but to be comparatively truthful was foul. There lay behind us a long horrible history of the decay of Truth. Compared with the task of fostering its recovery, all other religious issues were trivial. Truth, said the Kotzker, was attained only by the High Priest during that brief moment once a year when he entered the Holy of Holies. This statement illustrated the insuperable difficulty.

Is it at all possible to be honest, to disregard self-regard? Did not the Kotzker expect the leopard to change its spots? Do not his visions remind us of Don Quixotism? Are not honesty and life in society, veracity and interpersonal relations essentially incompatible?

The Kotzker sought to square the circle! people might say. But if this objection is valid, maybe we are all demented. For can one call our species sane when we remain unruffled in the face of mass murder, the fruit of mendacity, man-made agony without end?

Of what avail is an individual's effort to stop a tornado? The Kotzker would probably have responded that an individual's effort was part of an infinite process of approximation. At each stage its results are inadequate; to be unaware of this inadequacy is to be unaware of the finiteness of man and to run the risk of being presumptuous.

Accomplishment should not be measured by one human life, as it is but an infinitely small part of history. But what is impossible for a single man may be possible in terms of history in its entirety. A striking feature of the Kotzker's thinking is the fact that, while he strongly emphasized the importance of the individual's spiritual striving, he was averse to his concentrating on his own salvation, for this would constitute surrender to self-centeredness.

Without being explicit, the Kotzker projected the image of a new man, one who, according to a contemporary revolutionary theory, must learn "the spirit of absolute selflessness." Perhaps he was the man whom Truth named its friend. He set his chisel to work on the hardest stone. It is comparatively easy to preach joy and fervor, but to demand Truth is like shaping marble without tools. And so he went looking for a few surging people and called loudly upon their souls to bend their conceit and see the Truth beneath the soil.

Some did see, and they learned to overcome the deception found above ground. Truth's friend spoke his dissonant song: meaning is not in answers but in the question itself. There may be no pearl within the shell, but cleansing and refining the shell is more precious than all the pearls put together.

This was not a philosophical inquiry into the nature of Truth but a scrutiny of men's lives in relation to Truth. Religion, the Kotzker maintained, was not simply an act of adopting a system of beliefs and certain modes of conduct; test and trial were needed, and one had to ascertain through introspection whether one's beliefs were genuine or not, and whether one acted out Truth or lived a life of pretense. Permanent Truth was not within our grasp. Sporadic flashes of enlightenment came to us. Only they could redeem us. Truth endured under the ground, and flowers blossomed in that earth, waiting to greet the coming of the dawn.

Reb Mendl had scorn for things symbolic, for ceremonious feasts, for faith become ostentatious. He loved the hidden and the sudden; all else was second-best. Turn away, he counseled, from those whose voices outshouted their hearts.

Maimonides in his *Guide of the Perplexed* established the ceiling to which the mind's loftiest conceptions of God could reach. The Kotzker's concern was how an individual could in good conscience live in the presence of God and not die of embarrassment. Where was the prophetic voice to call for renewed authenticity? Other rebbes were preoccupied with the correction of minor flaws or adding luster to Jewish existence.

The Kotzker felt a vast dissatisfaction with every aspect of Jewish piety as carried out by many people. Judaism had been weakened from within; its insights had become clichés, its loyalties stale. He was appalled by the discovery that even virtue could be a disgrace and sought to call attention to the crisis by unveiling the overlapping of Truth and falsehood in the hearts of men.

Reb Mendl's denunciations were strong enough to disarray an order that it had taken centuries to establish. Yet soon his impact waned. When he died in 1859, the mantle of leadership fell on his loyal friend Reb Yitzhak Meir of Ger, a great and noble spirit, who decided to steer the movement of Kotzk onto a straighter path, avoiding dangerous or dizzy leaps. Thus, he softened the master's radicalism.

Independence and audacity were the minimal qualities the Kotzker expected of his disciples. One could not be a beggar, expecting charity from God. He presupposed heroic possibilities. He might have said that the opposite of the believer was not the heretic but the coward. Be brave or perish!

The Kotzker was a threat to those who hugged the path of simple piety. He spurned the despotism of habit and routine as he despised intellectual stereotypes, spiritual complacency, or quietism. He realized that ennui could lead to petrification. Religion ought never to become dreary; it exacted a strong life, life *in extremis*.

He loathed dead formulas, domesticated ideals. He was nauseated by pretensions, claims to respectability, and diluted conceptions of God's mysteries. He sought to disabuse his disciples of some of the pious decoctions to which Jewish thought and behavior were boiled down. Thought is born out of concern and should remain linked to it; when the umbilical cord between them is cut, thought forfeits authenticity. Man would have to shed many pretensions and clichés before he could present his soul to his own mind.

Religion as understood by Kierkegaard and the Kotzker is radical, pertaining to the roots of belief and motivation. Its demands are thoroughgoing, favoring drastic changes in the makeup of man. It tolerates no pretense, compromise, or camouflage.

But is pure religion possible at all in a world innately ambivalent, in which human beings are afflicted with ambiguities and spiritual halfheartedness? The Kotzker's diagnosis of the human situation goes beyond the scope of the strictly religious and extends to the realm of the social and political. Understanding can begin only when man undeceives himself, for he cannot survive in deceit. For instance, can peace be secured among the nations by a politics that is laden with deception? Will a statesman whose decisions are determined exclusively by the desire for personal benefit deserve the confidence of his people and promote their welfare?

It is ironic that the natural sciences have long since abandoned the assumption that man is the center of nature and ultimate end of the evolutionary process, but that we still regard it as unnatural, even inconceivable, for man not to act primarily in his own interests in human relations. Having left scientific anthropocentricity behind, we cling to egocentricity in religion and morality. One of the failures of Western man is due to the equation of religion and self-interest, whether it is the survival of the people within the Jewish context or the personal salvation that is the center of concern in Christianity. With our ears attuned to the mystery of living, and our eyes beholding the marvel of being, our hearts open to the anguish of humanity which surpasses our capacity for compassion, we must surely feel ashamed of a life lived within the confines of mere self-regard.

Achieving self-transcendence is an exceedingly difficult task. Man must constantly work at it. Yet autotherapy is not sufficient; divine assistance is required. As Kierkegaard realized, "It is necessary to assume an assistance of God in order to amend oneself." [1] For Reb Mendl contentment of achievement could not

---

[1] Journal entry, June 6, 1836, quoted in Lowrie, *Kierkegaard,* p. 144.

be the measure of existence; surging forward and upward was called for, leaping over hurdles. An easy life was not worth living.

The Kotzker's demand to discard "the world" was spiritually extravagant, almost untenable. Yet the insight that may have motivated the demand was far from absurd. It was the need to shatter complacency, immoral presumptuousness, satisfaction with the *status quo*. He enjoins us not to accept a humanity indifferent to atrocity, a world permeated with falsehood and corruption. To cherish the established order makes us accomplices in an ongoing accommodation to evil. Implicitly, this repudiates the validity of waiting for the Messiah.

Those who are ready to accept the world as it is, reconciled to the *status quo*, to mendacity as a social necessity, will belittle the Kotzker's demands as unrealistic. Others will examine the tacit assumptions held by many people that Truth may be a menace to survival.

Is it not possible that some of the convictions we live by are products of insanity? Those who are mad fall victim to a distorted imagination, while those who are vile are victims of dishonesty. Are the vile less mad than the mad?

Much of what the Kotzker taught sounds unbearable. Yet even those who cannot appropriate all his injunctions as norms will accept many of them as correctives. For ideas that are not acceptable as categorical imperatives may yet help us attain higher goals.

Kierkegaard made it his task "to reintroduce Christianity into Christendom." The Kotzker sought to reintroduce authenticity to Jewish life. Kierkegaard's posthumous impact has been powerful. But has the Kotzker affected Jewish self-understanding?

It may seem as if the Kotzker's work has been in vain. Jewry today continues to be satisfied with banal and bloodless customs and ceremonies. Books written about Judaism show few signs of his impact. Nevertheless, his legacy must necessarily influence if Judaism is to survive as more than a mere commonplace.

If Kierkegaard and the Kotzker had been asked why religion had failed to prevent humanity from sinking into the quagmire, their views would have been similar: religion as it was taught and lived was counterfeit. The Kotzker denounced complacent scholarship, respectable devoutness, automatic obedience, the combination of ecstatic piety and material acquisitiveness. He felt that the rabbis canonized religious mediocrity. They did not listen to his warnings, and eventually Jews fell from observance in droves.

Was the Kotzker capable of bringing about a renaissance in Judaism? Neither by temperament nor by inclination was he qualified to be leader of a movement. He was polemical, he was sarcastic. In addition, since his thinking was seminal rather than conclusive, he waged battles instead of accepting a *modus vivendi*. Some of his repudiations are hardly defensible, and some of his omissions are grave.

The Kotzker is still waiting for his disciples, for individuals who will make explicit in concrete language what he hinted at by subtle suggestion. They will be willing to stake their existence on the worth of spreading his ideas from person to person through the generations, guarding them from trivialization or desecration.

Reb Mendl's life is a parable of man in agony. We are only now aware of the inner conflicts he faced: how to live Judaism as Truth, not merely in behavior but in the understanding of man, his passions and ambiguities, his deficiencies and perplexities. Preconceived notions are best laid aside if wisdom is to be born, according to the Kotzker.

The people and their institutions have hardly been affected by the Kotzker's attacks. But anyone who ever falls under his spell will never again feel at ease with conventional religious conceptions or his habitual way of worshipping. For involvement with the Kotzker tolls the end of spiritual nonchalance. No student whose conscience is open to the problems the Kotzker wrestled with, who empathizes with his readiness to stake his entire life on Truth as the only road, and who has a measure of appreciation for his tremendous intellectual power and moral courage—no such student would want to evaluate his theories in terms of his own standards, for in judging him, he is judged by him. Though he did offer us an ideology, he confronted us with a challenge, which we either face or evade.

Why are the Kotzker's insights important today? Because in their light many popular and glittering expositions of Judaism are easily unmasked as façade, lacking in substance. To mistake the front for the interior is an affront to Truth.

Many interpreters have sought to accommodate Judaism to preconceived points of view; for the Kotzker Judaism was *the* point of view. Other thinkers have sought to improve the image of the Divine. God has been conceived as a caretaker of the people, a custodian of prosperity and security, specializing in loving kindness, as if He looked at the entire cosmos exclusively from the perspective of love and easy forgiveness.

In the past Jewish philosophers have tried to be detached observers of skeptics and nonbelievers. New generations will engage in the struggle of believing. They will not assume that compliance with a rule always takes precedence in the eyes of God over the prevention of human agony.

Religious truth must be lived. A law unrelated to life is both futile and fatal to faith. Rigidity and love of life cannot always be reconciled. If, as rabbinic authorities have declared, the aim of fulfilling the Law is in the ennoblement of the person, Jewish jurisdiction should take this into account.

If he were alive today, the Kotzker would look aghast at the replacement of spirituality by aesthetics, spontaneity by decorum. Like Kierkegaard, he would vehemently condemn an aesthetic concept of Judaism acted out in customs, ceremonies, sentimental celebrations, and polished oratory, as well as in decorative representations of God in terms of grandiose temples. He would also reject the reduction of Judaism to an outward compliance with ritual laws, strict observance mingled with dishonesty, the pedantic performance of rituals as a form of opportunism.

The Kotzker would call upon us to be uneasy about our situation, to feel ashamed of our peace of mind, of our spiritual stagnation. One's integrity must constantly be examined. In his view, self-assurance, smug certainty of one's honesty was as objectionable as brazen dishonesty. A moderately clean heart was like a moderately foul egg. Lukewarm Judaism would be as effective in purging our character as a lukewarm furnace in melting steel.

Gone for our time is the sweetness of faith. It has ceased to come to us as a gift. It requires "blood, sweat, and tears." We are frightened by a world that God may be ready to abandon. What a nightmare to live in a cosmic lie, in an absurdity that makes pretensions to beauty.

The predicament of contemporary man is grave. We seem to be destined either for a new mutation or for destruction. Some of the Kotzker's and Kierkegaard's insights may help us tap sources for a renewal of faith.

It seems as if Reb Mendl's unfettered soul anticipated ineluctable disasters that sheer mendacity was to incite and to abet. To the gloom that this realization cast upon him was added the knowledge that people refused to listen to a message of dismay. He faced defection, misinterpretations. Indeed, the disciple in whom he had placed the greatest confidence, from whom he had expected the most, and to whom he entrusted the spiritual training of the novices who came to Kotzk, defected, left his master, and established a school of his own, in sharp opposition to his mentor.

The Kotzker could not anticipate the disaster that befell his people during the Holocaust. He did not deal with the political situation of the Jews or with the phenomenon of anti-Semitism. Nevertheless, he seems to have had a haunting awareness of the terrible danger of human cruelty. He may not have analyzed the dynamic nature of persecution, yet he was profoundly aware that in a world of lies the demonic had a free reign. Had he been alive in the 1940's the Holocaust would not have come as a surprise to his soul.

Indeed, when human beings establish a *modus vivendi* on the basis of mendacity, the world can turn into a nightmare. This may explain the obsessive preoccupation with falsehood in the Kotzker's thinking. For the Holocaust did not take place suddenly. It was in the making for several generations. It had its origin in a lie: that the Jew was responsible for all social ills, for all personal frustrations. Decimate the Jews and all problems would be solved.

The Holocaust was initiated by demonic thoughts, savage words. What is the state of mankind today? Has the mind been purged, have the words been cleansed of corrupt deceit? How shall we prevent genocide in the years to come? Has mankind become less cruel, less callous?

To understand the Kotzker or Kierkegaard, we must learn to abandon the view that religion is simply morality tinged with emotion. It is above all a world of its own, a private, secret realm of relationships between God and man. The supreme rule in this world is not that beauty should reign supreme but Truth: a precarious virtue, indeed; yet only in Truth can exaltation come to pass, an exaltation that raises the whole man to the level of the Divine.

Kierkegaard taught that the religious stage rose beyond the ethical and that the two stages were sometimes irreconcilable. As a classical example, he cited the story of Abraham's readiness to offer Isaac as a sacrifice.[2] The Kotzker came close to this view. Although he maintained that religious existence could not be fully realized without ritual and ethical content, the demands he made on his disciples implied a clear disregard of their moral obligations toward their families.

Kierkegaard wrote in his journal, "My life will cry out after my death." Decades later the Western world began to hear his cry. Similarly, the Kotzker's cry of alarm may now begin to be heard.

If all agony were kept alive in memory, if all turmoil were told, who could endure tranquillity? Reb Mendl was one of those who stressed the speciousness of tranquillity. He chased away all comfort, all calm.

In a world that contains so much sham, the Kotzker continues to stand before us as a soul aflame with passion for God, determined to let nothing stand between him and his Maker. In the

2 See *Fear and Trembling*, 1843, translated by Walter Lowrie (Princeton, N.J., 1941).

nineteenth century he was a towering figure, in solitary misery as in grandeur. Yet his spirit, his accent are those of the post-Auschwitz era.

We recall him still, Reb Mendl of Kotzk. He has not fled from us by dying. Somehow his lightning persists. His words throw flames whenever they come into our orbit. They burn. Who can bear them? Yet many of us shall thereby shed our masks, our pretensions and jealousies, our distorted notions, and then messianic redemption may approach its beginning.

What did the Kotzker leave behind? He published no books, left no records; what he wrote he burned. Yet he taught us never to say farewell to Truth; for God laughs at those who think that falseness is inevitable. He also enabled us to face wretchedness and survive. For Truth is alive, dwelling somewhere, never weary. And all of mankind is needed to liberate it.

Index

Thing, 242n; radicalism of, 149–167; *Repetition: An Essay in Experimental Psychology,* 203n; self-deception, 126–9; *The Sickness unto Death,* 214n, 253; *Stages on Life's Way,* 54–5, 140n, 204n, 217n; on suffering, 250–1; *Three Discourses in Various Spirits,* 163; *Training in Christianity,* 104n, 105n, 130n, 144n, 151n, 164n, 166n, 202n, 217n, 225n; transcendence of God, 31; will and, 120–2, 184; *Works of Love,* 111n, 113n

king, parable on election of, 5

Kinyan, 188

Kitev (Kuty), Poland, 28

Korah (Biblical), 270

Kotzk, Poland, xii, 8, 13, 14, 15, 36, 40, 41, 46, 58, 69, 71, 78, 185, 222, 239, 321

Kotzker, the, *see* Menahem Mendl of Kotzk

Krailsheimer, A. J., *Studies in Self-Interest,* 100n

La Rochefoucauld, 99, 100, 101

Laban (Biblical), 61

Leah (Biblical), 279

Lessing, G. E., 186; *Anti-Goeze,* 296n

Levi Yitzhak of Berditshev, *Kedushat Levi,* 17

Lishensk, Galicia, 65

Loew of Prague, Rabbi Judah ("the Maharal"), 58, 59, 78; *Tiferet Israel (The Splendor of Israel),* 58

love, 45–6; of God, 47–51; of Is-

rael, 65–9; power of, xiii; self-love, 98–104, 113, 128–9

Lowrie, Walter, *Kierkegaard,* 110n, 149n, 150n, 203n, 204n, 209n, 217n, 220n

Lublin, Poland, 10, 239

Luria, Rabbi Isaac (Yitzhak), 5, 6, 78, 214

Luther, Martin, 152, 246, 252n, 255, 260

Maariv, 302

MacLeish, Archibald, *J.B.,* 258n

Maggid of Kozhenitz (Kozienice), 68, 176

Maggidim (itinerant preachers), 28

"Maharal, the," *see* Loew of Prague

Maimon, Solomon, *An Autobiography,* 136n

Maimonides, 5, 64n, 194, 215, 222, 300; *Code of Maimonides,* 61; *Commentary on Makkot,* 135n; *The Guide of the Perplexed,* 137, 222n, 314; *Introduction to the Mishnah,* 244

man, nature of, 252–7; and relationship to the Divine, 263–303, 308

Marmorstein, A., *The Doctrine of Merits in Old Rabbinic Literature,* 255n

marriage, Kierkegaad and the Kotzker on, 216–22

Martenson, Prof., 111, 149

Maskil, 198

Mehel of Zlothshov, Reb, 98

melancholia, 206–7

Melville, Herman, 201

Menahem Mendl of Kotzk ("the

Index of References

About
JEWISH LIGHTS Publishing

P eople of all faiths and backgrounds yearn for books
that attract, engage, educate and spiritually inspire.

Our principal goal is to stimulate thought and help all
people learn about who the Jewish People are, where
they come from, and what the future can be made to
hold. While people of our diverse Jewish heritage are
the primary audience, our books speak to people in the
Christian world as well and will broaden their understanding of Judaism and the roots of their own faith.

We bring to you authors who are at the forefront of
spiritual thought and experience. While each has
something different to say, they all say it in a voice that
you can hear.

Our books are designed to welcome you and then to
engage, stimulate and inspire. We judge our success
not only by whether or not our books are beautiful and
commercially successful, but by whether or not they
make a difference in your life.

We at Jewish Lights take great care to produce beautiful
books that present meaningful spiritual content in a
form that reflects the art of making high quality books.

Spiritual Inspiration for Family Life

MOURNING & MITZVAH
A Guided Journal for Walking the Mourner's Path Through Grief to Healing

by *Anne Brener, L.C.S.W.* • WITH OVER 60 GUIDED EXERCISES •

"Fully engaging in mourning means you will be a different person than before you began."

For those who mourn a death, for those who would help them, for those who face a loss of any kind, Anne Brener teaches us the power and strength available to us in the fully experienced mourning process. Guided writing exercises help stimulate the processes of both conscious and unconscious healing.

"A stunning book! It offers an exploration in depth of the place where psychology and religious ritual intersect, and the name of that place is Truth."
—Rabbi Harold Kushner, author of *When Bad Things Happen to Good People*

"This book is marvelous. It is a work that I wish I had written. It is the best book on this subject that I have ever seen." —Rabbi Levi Meier, Ph.D., Chaplain, Cedars Sinai Medical Center, Los Angeles, Orthodox Rabbi, Clinical Psychologist

7 1/2" x 9", 288 pp. Quality Paperback Original, ISBN 1-879045-23-0 **$19.95**

LIFECYCLES, Vol. 1
Jewish Women on Life Passages & Personal Milestones

Edited and with introductions by *Rabbi Debra Orenstein*

In self-aware, passionate, and insightful voices, 50 leading thinkers come together to explore tradition and innovation in personal ritual and spirituality. Speaking to women of all backgrounds, it covers the entire spectrum of life's passages, from ceremonies around childbirth to new perspectives on aging. Other topics include marriage, singlehood, conversion, coming out, parenting, divorce, and midlife.

"An invaluable resource for women who want to connect Jewish feminism to the actual occasions of their lives." —Judith Plaskow, author of *Standing Again at Sinai: Judaism from a Feminist Perspective*

6" x 9", 480 pp. Hardcover, ISBN 1-879045-14-1 **$24.95**

HEALING OF SOUL, HEALING OF BODY
Spiritual Leaders Unfold the Strength and Solace in Psalms

Ed. *Rabbi Simkha Y. Weintraub, CSW* for the Jewish Healing Center

A source of solace for those who are facing illness, as well as those who care for them. The ten Psalms which form the core of this healing resource were originally selected 200 years ago by Rabbi Nachman of Breslov as a "complete remedy." Today, for anyone coping with illness, they continue to provide a wellspring of strength.

Each Psalm is newly translated, making it clear and accessible, and each is introduced by an eminent rabbi, men and women reflecting different movements and backgrounds. To all who are living with the pain and uncertainty of illness, this spiritual resource offers an anchor of spiritual comfort.

"An inspiration and guide to those who want to rejoice in their affliction, and bring healing and salvation to themselves and those around them."
—Dr. Bernie Siegel, author of *Love, Medicine and Miracles*

6" x 9", 128 pp. illus., 2-color text. Quality Paperback Original, ISBN 1-879045-31-1 **$13.95**

Bring Spirituality into Your Daily Life

BEING GOD'S PARTNER
NEW!
How to Find the Hidden Link
Between Spirituality and Your Work
by *Jeffrey K. Salkin*
Introduction by *Norman Lear*

A book that will challenge people of every denomination to reconcile the cares of work and soul. A groundbreaking book about spirituality and the work world, from a Jewish perspective. Helps the reader find God in the ethical striving and search for meaning in the professions and in business. Critiques our modern culture of workaholism and careerism, and offers practical suggestions for balancing your professional life and spiritual self.

Being God's Partner will inspire people of all faiths and no faith to find greater meaning in their work, and see themselves doing God's work in the world.

"His is an eloquent voice, bearing an important and concrete message of authentic Jewish religion. The book is engaging, easy to read and hard to put down — and it will make a difference and change people." —Jacob Neusner, Distinguished Research Professor of Religious Studies, University of South Florida, author of *The Doubleday Anchor Reference Library Introduction to Rabbinic Literature*

6" x 9", 192 pp. Hardcover, ISBN 1-879045-37-0 **$19.95**

NEW!

SELF, STRUGGLE & CHANGE
Family Conflict Stories in Genesis
and Their Healing Insights for Our Lives
by *Norman J. Cohen*

How do I find greater wholeness in my life and in my family's life?

The stress of late-20th-century living only brings new variations to timeless personal struggles. The people described by the biblical writers of Genesis were in situations and relationships very much like our own. We identify with them. Their stories still speak to us because they are about the same problems we deal with every day.

A modern master of biblical interpretation brings us greater understanding of the ancient text and of ourselves in this intriguing re-telling of conflict between husband and wife, father and son, brothers, and sisters.

"In this very human book, Rabbi Cohen renews our spirit, guiding us through our own struggle with faith as we confront the lives of each biblical character."
— Dr. Kerry Olitzky, author of *Sparks Beneath the Surface: A Spiritual Commentary on the Torah*

6" x 9", 224 pp. Hardcover, ISBN 1-879045-19-2 **$21.95**

SO THAT YOUR VALUES LIVE ON
Ethical Wills & How To Prepare Them
Edited by *Rabbi Jack Riemer* & *Professor Nathaniel Stampfer*

A cherished Jewish tradition, ethical wills—parents writing to children or grandparents to grandchildren—sum up what people have learned and express what they want most for, and from, their loved ones. Includes an intensive guide, **"How to Write Your Own Ethical Will,"** and a topical index. A marvelous treasury of wills: Herzl, Sholom Aleichem, Israelis, Holocaust victims, contemporary American Jews.

"This remarkable volume will enrich all those who will read it and meditate upon its infinite wisdom." — Elie Wiesel

6"x 9", 272 pp. Quality Paperback, ISBN 1-879045-34-6 **$16.95** HC, ISBN -07-9 **$23.95**

Add Greater Understanding To Your Life

Add Greater Meaning to Your Life

FAITH AFTER THE HOLOCAUST?

Spiritual Inspiration for Daily Living . . .

THE BOOK OF WORDS
Talking Spiritual Life, Living Spiritual Talk
by *Lawrence Kushner*

In the incomparable manner of his extraordinary *The Book of Letters: A Mystical Hebrew Alphabet*, Kushner now lifts up and shakes the dust off primary religious words we use to describe the spiritual dimension of life. *The Words* take on renewed spiritual significance, adding power and focus to the lives we live every day.

For each word Kushner offers us a startling, moving and insightful explication, and pointed readings from classical Jewish sources that further illuminate the concept. He concludes with a short exercise that helps unite the spirit of the word with our actions in the world.

6"x 9", 152 pp. Hardcover, beautiful two-color text ISBN 1-879045-35-4 **$21.95**

"It is wonderful! A surprise at every page. His translations and elaborations provoke and stimulate the religious imagination." —*Rabbi Neil Gillman, Chair, Dept. of Jewish Philosophy, Jewish Theological Seminary*

"Breathes new life into a vocabulary that many may have thought to be irrelevant or outdated. Kushner is one of the great spiritual teachers of our time. He once again succeeds in offering us wisdom and inspiration."

—*Ellen Umansky, co-editor,* Four Centuries of Jewish Women's Spirituality: A Sourcebook

Sample pages from *The Book of Words*

The Kushner Series

otivation & Inspiration for Recovery

TWELVE JEWISH STEPS TO RECOVERY
A Personal Guide To Turning From Alcoholism & Other Addictions...Drugs, Food, Gambling, Sex

by *Rabbi Kerry M. Olitzky* & *Stuart A. Copans, M.D.*
Preface by Abraham J. Twerski, M.D.
Introduction by Rabbi Sheldon Zimmerman
Illustrations by Maty Grünberg
"Getting Help" by JACS Foundation

A Jewish perspective on the Twelve Steps of addiction recovery programs with consolation, inspiration and motivation for recovery. It draws from traditional sources, and quotes from what recovering Jewish people say about their experiences with addictions of all kinds. Inspiring illustrations of the twelve gates of the Old City of Jerusalem.

6" x 9", 136 pp. Quality Paperback, ISBN 1-879045-09-5 **$12.95**   HC, ISBN -08-7 **$19.95**

RENEWED EACH DAY
Daily Twelve Step Recovery Meditations Based on the Bible
by *Rabbi Kerry M. Olitzky* & *Aaron Z.*

VOLUME I: Genesis & Exodus
VOLUME II: Leviticus, Numbers & Deuteronomy

Using a seven day/weekly guide format, a recovering person and a spiritual leader who is reaching out to addicted people reflect on the traditional weekly Bible reading.

Beautiful Two-Volume Slipcased Set

6"x 9", V. I, 224 pp. / V. II, 280 pp., Quality Paperback Original, ISBN 1-879045-21-4 **$27.90**

ONE HUNDRED BLESSINGS EVERY DAY
Daily Twelve Step Recovery Affirmations, Exercises for Personal Growth & Renewal Reflecting Seasons of the Jewish Year
by *Dr. Kerry M. Olitzky*

4¹/₂" x 6¹/₂", Quality Paperback Original, 432 pp. ISBN 1-879045-30-3 **$14.95**

RECOVERY FROM CODEPENDENCE
A Jewish Twelve Steps Guide to Healing Your Soul
by *Rabbi Kerry M. Olitzky*
Foreword by *Marc Galanter, M.D., Director,*
Division of Alcoholism & Drug Abuse, NYU Medical Center
Afterword by *Harriet Rossetto, Director, Gateways Beit T'shuvah*

For the estimated 90% of America struggling with the addiction of a family member or loved one, or involved in a dysfunctional family or relationship. A follow-up to the groundbreaking *Twelve Jewish Steps to Recovery.*

"The disease of chemical dependency is also a family illness. Rabbi Olitzky offers spiritual hope and support."
—*Jerry Spicer, President, Hazelden*

"Another major step forward in finding the sources and resources of healing, both physical and spiritual, in our tradition."   —*Rabbi Sheldon Zimmerman, Temple Emanu-El, Dallas, TX*

6" x 9", 160 pp. Quality Paperback Original, ISBN 1-879045-32-X **$13.95** HC, ISBN -27-3 **$21.95**

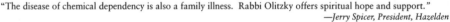

al Inspiration for Family Life

BUT GOD REMEMBERED NEW!
Stories of Women from Creation to the Promised Land

by *Sandy Eisenberg Sasso*
Full color illustrations by *Bethanne Andersen*

But God Remembered
Stories of Women
from Creation
to the
Promised Land

by Sandy Eisenberg Sasso

A fascinating co̲n̲c̲e̲r̲n̲ our different stories of women only briefly mentioned in biblical tradition and religious texts, but never before explored. Award-winning author Sasso brings to life the intriguing stories of Lilith, Serach, Bityah, and the Daughters of Z, courageous and strong women from ancient tradition. All teach important values through their faith and actions.

9" x 12", 32 pp. Hardcover, Full color illus., ISBN 1-879045-43-5 **$16.95**

NEW! IN GOD'S NAME For children K-5

by *Sandy Eisenberg Sasso*
Full color illustrations by *Phoebe Stone*

Like an ancient myth in its poetic text and vibrant illustrations, this modern fable about the search for God's name celebrates the diversity and, at the same time, the unity of all the people of the world. Each seeker claims he or she alone knows the answer. Finally, they come together and learn what God's name really is, sharing the ultimate harmony of belief in one God by people of all faiths, all backgrounds.

"I got goosebumps when I read *In God's Name*, its language and illustrations are that moving. This is a book children will love and the whole family will cherish for its beauty and power."
—Francine Klagsbrun, author of *Mixed Feelings: Love, Hate, Rivalry, and Reconciliation among Brothers and Sisters*

9" x 12", 32 pp. Hardcover, Full color illus., ISBN 1-879045-26-5 **$16.95**

For children K-4 GOD'S PAINTBRUSH

by *Sandy Eisenberg Sasso*
Full color illustrations by *Annette Compton*

MULTICULTURAL, NON-SECTARIAN, NON-DENOMINATIONAL. Invites children of all faiths and backgrounds to encounter God openly in their own lives. Wonderfully interactive, provides questions adult and child can explore together at the end of each episode.

"An excellent way to honor the imaginative breadth and depth of the spiritual life of the young." —Dr. Robert Coles, Harvard University

• AWARD WINNER •

11"x 8$^{1}/_{2}$", 32 pp. Hardcover, Full color illustrations, ISBN 1-879045-22-2 **$15.95**

NEW!

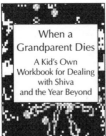

When a
Grandparent Dies
A Kid's Own
Workbook for Dealing
with Shiva
and the Year Beyond

WHEN A GRANDPARENT DIES
A Kid's Own Workbook for Dealing with Shiva and the Year Beyond

by *Nechama Liss-Levinson, Ph.D.*

The death of a grandparent is often a child's first encounter with grief. Drawing insights from both psychology and Jewish tradition, this workbook helps children participate in the process of mourning, offering guided exercises, rituals, and places to write, draw, list, create, and express their feelings.

9" x 12", 40 pp. Hardcover, illus., ISBN 1-879045-44-3 **$14.95**

Spiritual Inspiration for Family Life

THE *NEW* JEWISH BABY BOOK
Names, Ceremonies, Customs — A Guide for Today's Families
by *Anita Diamant*
Foreword by *Rabbi Norman J. Cohen, Dean, HUC–JIR, NYC*
Introduction by *Rabbi Amy Eilberg*

A complete guide to the customs and rituals for welcoming a new child to the world and into the Jewish community, and for commemorating this joyous event in family life–whatever your family constellation. Updated, revised and expanded edition of he highly acclaimed *The Jewish Baby Book*. Includes new ceremonies for girls, celebrations in inter-aith families. Also contains a unique directory of names that reflects the rich diversity of the Jewish xperience.

"A book that all Jewish parents—no matter how religious—will find fascinating as well as useful. It is a perfect hower or new baby gift." — Pamela Abrams, Exec. Editor, *Parents Magazine*

6"x 9", 328 pp. Quality Paperback Original, ISBN 1-879045-28-1 **$15.95**

PUTTING GOD ON THE GUEST LIST
AWARD WINNER

"Best Religion Book of the Year"

How to Reclaim the Spiritual Meaning of Your Child's Bar or Bat Mitzvah
by *Rabbi Jeffrey K. Salkin*
Foreword by *Rabbi Sandy Eisenberg Sasso*
Introduction by *Rabbi William H. Lebeau, Vice Chancellor, JTS*

Joining explanation, instruction and inspiration, helps par-nt and child truly *be there* when the moment of Sinai is recreated in their lives. Asks nd answers such fundamental questions as how did Bar and Bat Mitzvah originate? What is the lasting significance of the event? How to make the event more spiritually meaningful?

"Shows the way to restore spirituality and depth to every young Jew's most important rite of passage." — Rabbi Joseph Telushkin, author of *Jewish Literacy*

"I hope every family planning a Bar Mitzvah celebration reads Rabbi Salkin's book."
— Rabbi Harold S. Kushner, author of *When Bad Things Happen to Good People*

6"x 9", 184 pp. Quality Paperback, ISBN 1-879045-10-9 **$14.95** HC, ISBN -20-6 **$21.95**

Classics on Spiritual Life

NEW! THE EARTH IS THE LORD'S
The Inner World of the Jew in Eastern Europe
by *Abraham Joshua Heschel*

JEWISH LIGHTS Classic Reprints

Powerfully and beautifully portrays a bygone Jewish culture.

"Re-creates the mind and character of a whole people and of an entire era. Not only Jews, but all who regard the culture of the inner life as important will find this book moving and meaningful."
—Virginia Kirkus

5.5"x 8", 128 pp. Quality Paperback, ISBN 1-879045-42-7 **$12.95**

NEW! A PASSION FOR TRUTH
by *Abraham Joshua Heschel*

n his final book, completed a few weeks before his death, one of the most eloved religious leaders of our time gives us a personal exploration of the tension etween despair and hope in Hasidism and of how great religious teachers of radition affect and shape our own personal spirituality.

5.5"x 8", 352 pp. Quality Paperback, ISBN 1-879045-41-9 **$18.95**

Order Information

_____	Aspects of Rabbinic Theology (pb), $18.95	_____
_____	Being God's Partner (hc), $19.95	_____
_____	But God Remembered (hc), $16.95	_____
_____	The Earth Is the Lord's (pb), $12.95	_____
_____	The Empty Chair (hc), $ 9.95	_____
_____	God's Paintbrush (hc), $15.95	_____
_____	Healing of Soul, Healing of Body (pb), $13.95	_____
_____	In God's Name (hc), $16.95	_____
_____	The Last Trial (pb), $17.95	_____
_____	Lifecycles, Volume One (hc), $24.95	_____
_____	Mourning & Mitzvah (pb), $19.95	_____
_____	The NEW Jewish Baby Book (pb), $15.95	_____
_____	A Passion for Truth (pb), $18.95	_____
_____	Putting God on the Guest List (hc), $21.95; (pb), $14.95	_____
_____	Seeking the Path to Life (hc), $19.95	_____
_____	Self, Struggle & Change (hc), $21.95	_____
_____	So That Your Values Live On (hc), $23.95; (pb), $16.95	_____
_____	Spirit of Renewal (hc), $22.95; (pb), $16.95	_____
_____	Tormented Master (pb), $17.95	_____
_____	When a Grandparent Dies (hc), $14.95	_____
_____	Your Word Is Fire (pb), $14.95	_____

• *The Kushner Series* •

The Book of Letters

_____	– Popular Hardcover Edition (hc), $24.95*	_____
_____	– Deluxe Presentation Edition (hc), $79.95, *plus* $5.95 s/h	_____
_____	– Collector's Limited Edition, $349.00, *plus* $12.95 s/h	_____
_____	The Book of Words (hc), $21.95*	_____
_____	God Was in This Place... (pb) $16.95*	_____
_____	Honey from the Rock (pb), $14.95*	_____
_____	River of Light (pb) $14.95*	_____
_____	THE KUSHNER SERIES — 5 books *marked with asterisk above*, $93.75	_____

• *Motivation* & *Inspiration for Recovery* •

_____	One Hundred Blessings Every Day, (pb) $14.95 *	_____
_____	Recovery From Codependence, (hc) $21.95; (pb) $13.95*	_____
_____	Renewed Each Day, 2-Volume Set, (pb) $27.90*	_____
_____	Twelve Jewish Steps To Recovery, (hc) $19.95; (pb) $12.95*	_____
_____	**THE COMPLETE RECOVERY SET – 20% SAVINGS** 5 Books *marked with asterisk above* + **Print Portfolio** — $99.75	_____

For s/h, add $3.50 for the first book, $2.00 each additional book $ _____

All set prices include shipping/handling	Total $ _____

Check enclosed for $_____ *payable to:* JEWISH LIGHTS Publishing
Charge my credit card: ☐ MasterCard   ☐ Visa   ☐ AMEX
Credit Card # _____ Expires _____
Name on card _____
Signature _____ Phone (_____) _____
Name _____
Street _____
City / State / Zip _____

Phone, fax, or mail to: JEWISH LIGHTS Publishing
Box 237, Sunset Farm Offices, Route 4, Woodstock, Vermont 05091
Tel (802) **457-4000**   *Fax* (802) **457-4004**
Credit card orders (800) **962-4544** (9AM–5PM ET Monday–Friday)
Generous discounts on quantity orders. SATISFACTION GUARANTEED. Prices subject to change.
AVAILABLE FROM BETTER BOOKSTORES. TRY YOUR BOOKSTORE FIRST.